CHAOS

and

CATHARSIS

-

15 Years of Politics, Philosophy, and Passions

-

ALEX KNEPPER

ACKNOWLEDGMENTS

THANK YOU: Jenna Line, Zack Desotelle, Emily Myers, Anthony Ward, Cinzia Croce, Tim Hulsey, Bruce Bawer, Kavon Nikrad, Sean Trende, Josiah Schmidt, Susannah Fleetwood, Michael Tracey, Jon Rowe, Josh Price, Peter Prosol, Aron Goldman, Charlie Szold, Graham Vyse, Will Bower, Josh Jacobs, Will Fisher, Mark Pietryzk, Niklas Blanchard, John Althouse Cohen, Dan Clements, Prof. Thomas Merrill, William Braithwaite, and everyone else who has ever given me a writing position, agreed to give me a recommendation in politics, written with or for me, mentored me, or just been there for me — and of course, to my wonderful family, especially Mom.

ALEX KNEPPER

Contents

Political Theory, Philosophy, and Religion

Introduction | 06.28.18

I've always wanted to publish a book like this.

When I was growing up, I was always so impressed by the voluminous output of the political journalists I liked. How gratifying must it be, I thought, to be able to look back on 10, 15 years of writing, and see it all in one place.

It occurred to me this year that I finally had enough worthy material to publish such a collection. As I dug deep into my personal archives (and Google), I was pleased to discover that it was no longer a question of whether I had enough material, but a question of what really ought to be included.

I organized the material so that it becomes progressively more complex, starting with articles about myself and personalities who fascinate me, then moving on to gay issues, campus issues, foreign policy, Islam, political theory, and ending with a few pieces on religion and philosophy. I have chosen to include the good, the bad, and the ugly, in an attempt to provide a panorama view of my thinking over the last 15 years. I have added very little commentary, choosing to let my work speak for itself.

All in all, I have drawn from about fifteen sources, from my current website the New American Perspective to the American University *Eagle*, from the *Huffington Post* to the *Daily Caller*, from my Facebook and personal website to syndicated articles for UWIRE, blog posts for Race 4 2012 and Frum Forum, and more. Thankfully, copyright was almost never an issue; when it is an issue, I have provided representative excerpts.

Thanks to everyone who helped out, especially Jenna for the lovely cover art; Peter, Josh, and Mom for financial help, and Josh Price for first making me believe this was really worth doing.

Me

My breakthrough in my perception of myself as truly being able to pursue political opinion journalism came when I was just a freshman in high school, when I was featured on the front page of my hometown's paper, the *Herald Mail*. To open the book, I have selected representative excerpts from that article.

Teen Takes On the Left, In Book, Online, In Person

Andrew Schotz, Herald Mail | 09.30.04

"Self-published political author Alex Knepper is so intent on seeing John Kerry's presidential candidacy thwarted, he seems eager to debate the senator himself tonight.

While politics is old hat for Kerry, 60, though, it's a new phenomenon for Alex, 14, who lives in Hagerstown.

It wasn't until early this year, as Democrats jockeyed to be the party's presidential nominee, that Alex first paid attention.

He listened closely to his stepfather, Kurt Britner, and learned. He read and researched.

Then, he set out on a path of Republican punditry.

He likes President Bush - although not entirely - and he likes to debate with whomever will argue back, on the Internet or in person.

'Throw me a Democratic talking point and I'll rebut it,' he said.

While the No Child Left Behind Act is intrusive and heavy-handed and illegal immigrants shouldn't get special rights, Bush has done a commendable job fighting terrorism, Alex said.

In a two-week period this summer, Alex dashed off his first book, which is titled 'Carnival: The Sideshow Act Liberals Have Become Through the Eyes of a Teenage Conservative' and had it published through a Web site called Lulu.

In his book, he lights into Hillary Clinton, Michael Moore and affirmative action ...

The paper then talks about my failed run for class president, and then continues with commentary from my mother and stepfather:

"I think he'd like a spot on (the TV show) The O'Reilly Factor, but I don't know if he'll get there ....," said Alex's mother, Amy Britner, a North Hagerstown High School special education teacher. "He has to be in a career where he can express his viewpoints."

She said Alex's peers rarely can back up opinions about the election, if they have them, with the knowledge he has.

Alex can't get enough of conservative commentators Ann Coulter and Michael Savage. At the same time, he'll read everything liberals Al Franken and Michael Moore write, so he knows what they're up to.

Kurt Britner said he might have indoctrinated Alex in conservatism, but Alex still must establish his own thoughts, to make his ideology and his books meaningful.

"I can see him doing it as long as he runs the course of experience that's necessary to become interesting, to give himself depth, so his opinions are his own, his experiences are his own, his thoughts are his own," Kurt Britner said, "and I think he's on his way."

Race 4 2008, the *Eagle,* and the UWIRE 100 | 04.27.2009

My breakthrough in political writing came from Kavon W. Nikrad of Race 4 2008, who offered me front-page posting privileges on his site. As the youngest and most socially liberal member of the team and an avid Rudy Giuliani supporter, I attracted a lot of controversy. That controversy came to a peak when I attended the Republican National Convention that year but spoke out against Palin to whoever I could find — including governors, senators, and pundits. This would normally be very cool, but it angered my benefactors, and I was stranded in my hotel with my press pass revoked for the latter half of the convention. Around the same time, I was accepted as one of six out of over 100 applicants to be an opinion columnist for the American University *Eagle*, and my audacity in speaking out against Palin impressed former Bush speechwriter David Frum, who called me a "brave and brainy writer of real promise" and said yes when I asked to be a part of his new group blog.

In April 2009, as a freshman, I was named by UWIRE which functioned in its time like an Associated Press of college papers, as one of the top student journalists in the country, and was selected by them to write for their website and have my columns syndicated to national outlets like CBS News. With the rise of the internet, the service shut down, but proof of my award remains:

The Eagle ✔ @TheEa... · Apr 27, 2009 ⌄
Congratulations to Eagle columnist Alex Knepper, a UWIRE 100 journalist! http://tr.im/jQ8I Read his latest column! (http://tr.im/jQ8D)

The 'Date Rape Column' Controversy | March-April 2010

In the second semester of my freshman year at American University, I penned an inflammatory column denouncing campus feminists' concept of date rape. By this time, I had already gained notoriety on campus as one who tried to push buttons — I remain convinced that Milo Yiannopolous stole my campus act — but this time I had gone too far in the eyes of the activists, who rounded up every paper on campus and trashed them in front of the office of the office of the *Eagle*. Of course I would choose my words differently today, but the controversy is a major moment in my life; the story was covered by national outlets, including ABC, CBS, the *Washington Post*, NPR, and has been cited in more than one academic paper. I choose to let my words speak for themselves here, first with the column itself and then with articles about the controversy and excerpts from interviews.

Dealing With AU's Anti-Sex Brigade

American University Eagle | 03.28.10

Jeremiah Headen likely lost the vice presidency of the Student Government over a hyperbolic Facebook note. Its contents — a blast of old-school masculinity — slammed men for not realizing that being manly had nothing to do with what is between one's legs, but rather is about values, stoic resolve and hard work. It ended with a silly, all-caps call to raid booty and women from neighboring villages.

The comments on The Eagle's Web site, mostly by Gay Party activists and feminists, condemned Headen for being an "anti-queer misogynist" and for undermining American University's commitment to being "safe space" for the "gay community." He was also rebuked for using the term "hermaphrodite" instead of "intersex."

What a sniveling bunch of emotional cripples! I have never encountered a more insular, solipsistic view of human sexuality than at this college. The rigidity of Pat Robertson has nothing on feminism.

Feminist religious dogma, long ago disposed of by neuroscientists

4

and psychologists, states that men are essentially born as eunuchs, only to have wicked masculinity imposed on them by an evil society. This is usually presented as "social construction theory."

Like the other great religions of the world, though, the goal of contemporary feminism and Gay Party activism is not to explain sex, but to abolish its passion. The yin and yang of masculinity and femininity is what makes sexual exploration exciting. Sex isn't about contract-signing. It's about spontaneity, raw energy and control (or its counterpart, surrender). Feminism envisions a bedroom scene in which two amorphous, gender-neutral blobs ask each other "Is this OK with you?" before daring to move their lips any lower on the other's body. Worse yet: a gender-neutral sexuality can have no conception of the inherently gendered thrills of fetishism, sadomasochism, kink or cross-dressing. How blasé! For my pro-sex views, I am variously called a misogynist, a rape apologist and — my personal favorite — a "pro-date rape   protofascist."

Let's get this straight: any woman who heads to an EI party as an anonymous onlooker, drinks five cups of the jungle juice, and walks back to a boy's room with him is indicating that she wants sex, OK? To cry "date rape" after you sober up the next morning and regret the incident is the equivalent of pulling a gun to someone's head and then later claiming that you didn't ever actually intend to pull the trigger.

"Date rape" is an incoherent concept. There's rape and there's not-rape, and we need a line of demarcation. It's not clear enough to merely speak of consent, because the lines of consent in sex — especially anonymous sex — can become very blurry. If that bothers you, then stick with Pat Robertson and his brigade of anti-sex cavemen! Don't jump into the sexual arena if you can't handle the volatility of its practice!

Feminists don't understand history, psychology, biology or sexuality. To repair this desperate situation, I have altruistically prepared a list of five favored books about sex and gender: "The Myth of Male Power" by Warren Farrell, "The Sexual Spectrum" by Olive Skene Johnson, "Vamps and Tramps" by Camille Paglia, "Philosophy In the Bedroom" by the divine Marquis de Sade, and "Who Stole Feminism?" by Christina Hoff Sommers. Put down the Andrea Dworkin and embrace the fires of sexuality!

CBS Early Show | 04.02.10

Maggie Rodriguez first asked me if I meant what I said:

"Yes...and I used the word indicating very deliberately. Men cannot know what women don't tell them. And if she heads back to that room, at any time, she may say 'No', and that point it constitutes rape. Absolutely. That's not in dispute. What I am in dispute of is that she can wake up the next morning regretting drunken sex and accuse the man of being a rapist. There are so many men out there whose lives have been devastated by false claims of rape. Everyone remembers the Duke Lacrosse case. There are thousands of such cases that don't get talked about in the media."

After a student opposing my view spoke and said that women should not have to "live in fear" of rape, I replied:

"No, and let me reply to the point that no one should have to live in fear. In a perfect world, no one would have to live in fear. But in the real world, there are risks, there are dangers, and as adults, we have to be responsible for the situations that we put ourselves in. Let me try to bring this down to Earth. I'm a gay man. In a perfect world, I would be able to walk down a rural Mississippi neighborhood holding a guy's hand. In the world that we live in, I know that this is risky behavior. As an adult, those are things that I need to understand before I partake in that behavior."

Another progressive student leader described me to ABC:

American University Erupts Over Date Rape

ABC | 04.01.10

"Knepper, an openly gay political science major and a two-year columnist with the Eagle, is known as a provocateur, according to CASJC member Drew Franklin."
'It's not typical of what you see at American, a very liberal school,

but it is typical of Alex,' he said."

I described my experience at Frum Forum:

Knepper: I'm Not Backing Down

Frum Forum | 04.03.10

Over the past week, I've been thrust into a media storm over a column I penned for the American University *Eagle* attacking our ever-broadening concepts of what constitutes rape. As has been pointed out countless times by now, it is a provocative argument — and one that hasn't really been touched since Camille Paglia and Katie Roiphe were in the spotlight in the 90's. But it's proven that the uncomfortable questions that feminists thought were dead and buried actually still have life. Outside of the establishment's bubble, personal responsibility still retains some of its popularity.

The outpouring of support that I have received from Middle America has been heartening and reassuring. The essence of my argument — don't engage in volatile, risky situations unless you're prepared to deal with the consequences of your actions — is a common sense, mainstream argument among everyday Americans. Indeed, the backlash seems mainly to be coming from pampered, upper class white people from the coasts who don't want to admit that ours is a world filled with risk and imperfections. The media discourse surrounding this event has mainly revolved around the latter's interpretation of the world. Is it any wonder that the mainstream media is losing the trust of Americans?

The ABC News coverage of my column, for instance, was nothing less than a hit piece. The original title of the article, penned by Susan Donaldson James, was "American University Erupts Over Date Rape: Girls Who Drink and Go to Frat Parties Deserve Date Rape, Says Student Newspaper Columnist." Deserve. The same word was also included in the first paragraph, as well as a discourse-poisoning remark that this month is Sexual Abuse Awareness Month and a description of my piece as a "diatribe." After an angry e-mail exchange with the reporter, she changed the two instances of 'deserved' to 'invite' and 'responsible for' — neither of which are particularly accurate descriptors of my point, either, but are certainly a step up from the outright libel of "deserving to be date-raped."

The CBS News experience, which occurred 24 hours after the ABC piece hit the web, was designed to intimidate. The producer assigned to my story went out of her way to put me ill-at-ease, barking orders at me ("Come on — get in the car!") and sarcastically snipping "I'll bet your mom is going to enjoy this," in the sort of tone that asked "Don't you just hate women, you misogynist bastard?" (My mother, in fact, has been extremely supportive of me and is most responsible for my embrace of adult responsibility.) Originally, I was to appear live from the American University campus, but our reception — notoriously spotty — failed us and we hurried to the CBS bureau in a mad rush, racing up stairs and through the studio with two minutes until airtime. My throat was dry by the time I sat down in my seat, barely giving me time to get a cup of water.

If one has never appeared on national television, it's difficult to imagine how strange the situation is: it's designed to be intimidating. You don't look at a screen and respond to your opponent: instead, you stare into a big black box that operates as the camera while listening to mid-quality audio coming from a microphone connected to your ear. It's all very impersonal, and it almost seems surreal as it's going on.

Maggie Rodriguez's questions were somewhat patronizing, both of them asking me, in essence, if I "really believed it" or "wanted to take something back." (I felt like Ann Coulter or something; another television interview ran the headline: "Did He Go Too Far?") Colleagues have told me that they suspect that these interviews, in part, occurred because they expected me to issue mealy-mouthed apologies, giving the news organizations an opportunity to look like Good Guys who put the college douche in his place.

All of the television interviewers — all of whom have been hostile to or at least uncomfortable with my column — have conspicuously omitted the fact of my homosexuality. The lingering assumption that they want people to take away is that I'm a privileged frat boy trying to justify his bad behavior — and many comments on national websites prove as much. It's maddeningly dumb that this should actually make a difference, of course, but with the narrative being as it is, it softens the blow of the argument. It truly seems that the media has so embraced the feminist date-rape propaganda that the only people who can even vaguely "get away" with telling straight men's side of the narrative are women — such as Paglia and Roiphe — and gay men.

The radio format has given me insight as to why conservatives have fled to that venue, though: only when I appeared on the radio did I feel completely confident that I'd fully have a chance to flesh out my ideas, explain myself in context, and not have to worry about being subject to a hit piece. The mainstream media deals in soundbites; radio actually deals in discussion of the issues. I have appeared on radio shows all over the country now, and every one of the hosts, whether on my side or not, has given me a chance to engage in a vigorous debate.

Sometimes, we end up being surprised by the lessons that we learn from events. Entering the belly of the media beast has given me a new-found appreciation for Middle America's ability to move beyond soundbites and embrace common-sense dialogue. That the media keeps spitting on their values is testament to the fact that it has willingly embraced suicide.

Pulitzer Prize-nominated conservative columnist Gregory Kane sang my praises in the *San Francisco Examiner:*

A Young Prodigy of Political Incorrectness

Gregory Kane, San Francisco Examiner | 04.08.10

"Knepper writes an op-ed column for The Eagle, the campus student newspaper. His writing is articulate, eloquent, brash and refreshingly free of politically correct dogma."

One of my last media appearances during this controversy was a spot on NPR. My words are excerpted below:

Date Rape Article In Student Newspaper Stokes Anger

NPR, 'Wait, Wait...Tell Me More' | 04.14.10

MARTIN: Alex, I want to start with you. I just wanted to ask what sparked the column as briefly as you can. What was on your mind?

Mr. KNEPPER: In the past couple of weeks before the column was written, there was a student government candidate for the vice presidency who had arguably lost the position because of a Facebook note that he had written that was an over-the-top tongue-in-cheek rant about old school masculinity. He approved of it and the campus feminists and the gay party activists, it's a nickname I use to distinguish from mainstream gay people like myself, were up in arms about this. And so I thought it would be a good jumping point to get back to basics and start lobbing more missiles at (unintelligible) follies.

MARTIN: So, are you telling me you're gay?

Mr. KNEPPER: Yes.

MARTIN: Okay. And I don't know if that's relevant, I just want to be sure that that's what you were disclosing to us. Can I just ask, though, were you intending to be tongue-in-cheek or do you really feel that if women have had enough to drink, or a lot to drink and they are alone with a young man, that they are in fact inviting sex?

Mr. KNEPPER: I'm saying that when you inject yourself into that kind of arena when you're dealing with alcohol, when you're dealing with anonymous sex, that the rules change. That there are certain signals that you're sending out that the man can reasonably interpret as an invitation to sex. You're not going back to his room to rhapsodize philosophical about Plato. You're not going to discuss homework tips. These are the rules of the arena. And the point that the column makes in the later paragraphs is that if you're uncomfortable with this, then you shouldn't be having anonymous sex. Of course, if she says no at any time, then that implicit consent has been revoked and at that point it would constitute rape.

MARTIN: Okay. And the reaction was what?

Mr. KNEPPER: The reaction to the piece on campus was fairly universally negative and the people that spoke out, the people who were on my side kept contacting me and telling me that they were afraid of people calling them rape apologists. Most people don't want their names Googled and having that behind them.

After this, the interviewer turned to the other guest, a fellow student who was also a member of the male feminist group Men Can Stop Rape, who rattled off a number of questionable statistics about rape on campus and claimed that my article should not have been published in the first place because it was unconstructive and needlessly harmed survivors of sexual assault. I replied:

Mr. KNEPPER: Obviously no one is saying that sex without consent is acceptable. What I'm saying is that the lines can become very blurry when anonymous sex and alcohol are involved. And the laws currently hold a double standard against men that infantilize women. I say that when you drink five cups of the jungle juice, that's an act that you partake in of your own free will and that you should be held responsible for that, whether you're male or female. If a male is drunk, he doesn't say, oh, well, I didn't know what I was doing when I was drunk. You can't hold me responsible under the law. I'm saying that we should hold a woman to the same standard in saying that if she gives consent while drunk, that's legitimate.

MARTIN: That's not really true, though, is it?...And our own reporting suggests that men are very rarely severely disciplined for acts of date rape precisely because there is as much ambiguity around it.

Mr. KNEPPER: No, I'm saying they should if there is sufficient evidence there. However, a lot of these cases just turn into he said, she said kind of incidents, which is why it's imperative to be responsible.

...I'm saying you can't punish someone without sufficient evidence. And this is why it's so important that if you do inject yourself into the arena, you need to know the risks and responsibilities beforehand. Accept the risks, accept the dangers, but understand that when you do put yourself into that arena, that bad things might happen. You might end up doing something you regret. You might end up having something happen to you that you wouldn't have wanted to happen.

She asked me if the same rules apply to men:

Mr. KNEPPER: Of course. But men have already accepted this. There aren't the equivalent of feminist groups on the men's side saying that people shouldn't be held responsible for what they do while intoxicated. I'm saying that a drunken yes is a legitimate yes because it was her choice to drink. And that a regret is not a rape.

Finally, is it a problem that I'm judging this issue while being gay and therefore not being able to understand the dynamics of this situation on a firsthand basis?

Mr. KNEPPER: No, and this is one of the ridiculous aspects of this postmodern society that somehow if you don't have the ability to give testimony about an incident, you're not allowed to judge it. Part of being an adult is judging situations, looking at different scenarios, looking at the moral aspects involved and trying to come to a rational conclusion.

The Lives of Otters: An Interview With Alex Knepper

Andrew F., The New Gay | 04.05.10

"In the two years we've shared as undergrads at American University, this will be the first time I've crossed paths with Alex Knepper. The self-described "renegade conservative" writes a column for The *Eagle*, AU's independent student newspaper, and in that capacity has been involved in more than his fair share of controversy. His most recent piece, "Dealing with AU's Anti-Sex Brigade", has drawn heavy criticism from students who understood it to be trivializing date rape – criticism which quickly escalated from angry letters to the editor to organized protests, acts of vandalism, and threats of bodily harm.

I sit down with Knepper late Sunday afternoon. He seems remarkably well-composed for a college sophomore who's been at the center of a heated debate on free speech and sexuality that has by now extended beyond campus to local and national media coverage, not to mention the flurry of blog attention from sources as diverse as the *Huffington Post* and David Horowitz's News Real, to which Knepper regularly contributes. After chatting briefly about how lousy Randians are in the sack (Knepper begs to differ) and his recent encounter with Christopher Hitchens at a house party hosted by David Frum, I finally figure out how to work my audio recorder and get down to business with the young man who might well be, for the moment, the most notorious homosexual in the District of Columbia. —

TNG's Andrew F: I notice your body guard isn't with you today.

Alex Knepper: Jesus is my body guard, and he is risen today.

TNG: So how has the past week been? You're twenty years old, studying political science at American University, and you find yourself quite unexpectedly cast into the middle of what you've termed a national media firestorm.

AK: I have the feminists to thank for all of this. If they hadn't trashed the papers, none of this would have happened. I've written columns in the past that have been controversial, usually they receive about 50-60 comments at a time. I figured this would be like anything else, but I underestimated the fury with which feminists would disallow a discussion about rape.

TNG: I think this is important to build some background for our readers: you've described yourself elsewhere as a gay intellectual conservative. In a climate in which any two of those terms might seem to be mutually exclusive, what's it like to live your life?

AK: I don't so much like the term "conservative" on its own. I describe myself variously as "renegade conservative" or a "classical liberal." My beliefs in ten seconds are: laissez-faire capitalism, a robust foreign policy, social tolerance, anti-religion, pro-sex, and anti-psychiatry. I think there's a niche out there for a contrarian in the media that needs to be filled. As far as what's it like, I think it's done me more good than harm, reaching out to people, because there is a dearth of voices that are speaking in the same ideological fashion that I am.

TNG: The fact of your homosexuality –which you've never concealed — you described yourself on the CBS morning show as an openly gay man – has been conspicuously absent in a lot of the media coverage. The Huffington Post story and ABC News interview come to mind. I'm wondering what you think of this resistance, willful or not, to factor your sexual orientation into the dynamics of the controversy?

AK: The subtext of all of the interviews has been that I'm a douchey fratboy trying to justify his way with women. Half of the interviews that I walk in to, I get the feeling that the media are trying to perform a community service in being the capital-G "Good Guy" and putting this douchey college fratboy in his place. Mentioning my sexual orientation flips the script. It's a shame we can't have a dialogue about this detached from identity, and when women like Camille Paglia or Katie Roiphe or gay men like myself can even halfway get away with talking about this. But that's the state of identity politics and victim politics right now.

TNG: You've talked about, sort of, the Duke Lacrosse phenomenon, situations where it doesn't so much matter who people are or what they've actually done, so much as where they fit in a politically convenient script...

AK: It seems like there are two crimes in this country in which people are considered guilty until proven innocent, and those are rape and child molestation. You see this in the media coverage of any rape case in which the accuser is referred to as "the victim." It's an inversion of how the justice system is supposed to operate, and we can't even talk about this rationally because it's Judeo-Christian morality that's locked in sexual behavior as the pinnacle of what constitutes morality.

TNG: Speaking of child molestation and Judeo-Christian morality, happy Easter. AK: Arrest the pope.

TNG: In your piece on the Frum Forum you write about what you've characterized as an "outpouring of support from Middle America," and that most of the backlash as you've experienced it so far has come from a "pampered, middle class, white demographic from the coasts." I'm wondering what form that's taken.

AK: It's kind of knocked some of the elitism out of me. Almost unanimously from racial minorities I've received support. Racial minorities are used to living in a world with risks. They're more used to reading signals when partaking in risky behaviors. These wealthy, upper-class white suburbanites have never had any problems in their lives and have never bothered to read any philosophy, literature, history, or psychology, and so they don't even have the intellectual background to understand it. So I guess I'm not really surprised in hindsight. But in Middle America, this is still a common sense view. If you're going to inject yourself into risky behaviors, you need to understand what you're getting in to before the fact.

TNG: Of course I have to ask, because this is for a gay blog, and both of us like cocks...

AK: I like cocks.

TNG: ... because you've established this dichotomy of common-sensical Middle America on the one hand and a sort of out-of-touch elite on the other – have any of those supportive Middle Americans engaged the matter of your sexuality and if so, how?

AK: No, most of them don't care. And this has been something that's continually irritated me about the left and even some of the elites on the right , their continual conflation of the religious right with the Republican party and Middle America. The religious right is a loud, well-heard minority of the Republican party. Everyone else is completely open and willing to dialogue, and I would even say that most of the religious right, in my experience, is. I have never received as much hatred from the religious right as I have from the gay left.

TNG: On a related note – and by the way, if you keep talking so reasonably about these things, you run the risk of convincing me, so this could be dangerous...

AK:(chuckles)

TNG: You've talked about what you've termed, on campus, the "AU anti-sex brigade" and the two groups at its helm: "feminists" and the people you refer to as the "gay party." These are terms that mean a lot of things to a lot of different people. What do you mean when you use them?

AK: Victim groups. Self-styled "victims." People who need

mommy government or mommy administration of American University to step in and make them empowered. Truly self-empowered individuals derive that strength from philosophy and from values. This is how it's been in the entire Western tradition. But they're ignorant of the Western tradition and so they have no basis on which to judge whether this is an accurate means of empowering one's self or not. Anyone who's ever read Marcus Aurelius or Epictetus can attest to the fact that self-empowerment does come from values. But these people don't even know who Marcus Aurelius is. They know who Jacques Derrida is, they know who Andrea Dworkin is, but they have no idea who the great classical writers are.

TNG: I find it interesting, this sort of intellectual question, if you will. There were something like fifteen words that set off the tinderbox of sexual politics on campus , and then the national conversation, and the other 95 percent of your piece has been neglected by everyone but Amanda Hess at the *City Paper.* If we could just sort of bracket the "rape question" altogether – let the record show that I'm using quote fingers right now, so as not to seem presumptuous...

AK: (chuckles)

TNG: This is what interested me the most: the claim that, in order to have any fulfilling or meaningful kind of sexual relation there has to be a certain dynamic of submission and domination, of hierarchy and asymmetry. I'm wondering if you could talk about that now, maybe in a way that you couldn't in the space that the *Eagle* allots you.

AK: I'm saying that what makes sexual exploration exciting is that exchange of energies, and, as I explained it to Amanda Hess, femininity in sex is not literally about being female. It's about assuming a role of surrender or submission, and that simply relates to the metaphysical nature of "the female." And that's extrapolated from there. If somebody asks me, is it bland to be gay in light of this, well, absolutely not. There's a lot more wisdom in the old question "which one of you is the girl?" than it gets credit for. Well, which one of you is playing the female role in sex? Who's taking the dick? That's the person playing the female role. This isn't homophobic. This isn't insulting. It's hot.

TNG: So there is that element, right, and I think it plays out in the sexual ecosystem of Washington, DC. But I can't help but think of another perspective, and first I'll address this question theoretically: What if we worked with a picture of sexuality that involved, rather than, as you've put it "two amorphous, genderless blobs, asking if they can place their lips below each other's nipples" – what if we moved from that toward a robustly homoerotic, egalitarian, and democratic picture of sexuality we get from someone like, for instance, Walt Whitman, who writes in stunningly poetic language about gay sex that is thoroughly and beautifully non-hierarchical, thoroughly and beautifully egalitarian?

AK: … so you're asking me about a model of sex based on egalitarianism?

TNG: Right, and I think there are important moral and political consequences to be discussed here…

AK: I think we can separate romantic sex from pure sexual exploration, and especially in the context of the column I was talking specifically about anonymous sex. Romantic sex is more emotional, sexual exploration is primarily erotic and physical. I think you have to be able to separate the two. The hotter element is definitely the latter. No, I don't think you can separate gender from pure eroticism, it's impossible. As long as you have a receiver and a giver, you're dealing with the twin powers of masculinity and femininity. I speak also in the column of fetishism, kinks, masochism, an erotic cross-dressing. These are inherently gendered, because of that. So, when we're dealing with cross-dressing, for instance, you can't cross something if it isn't said to exist. If we take radical feminism to its logical conclusion, there can't be cross-dressing, and it completely loses its erotic element.

TNG: To begin wrapping up – I appreciate your honesty on these questions of sexuality, and I think that if more Republicans were as in tune with and transparent about their kinks as you are, we'd have a more interesting kind of national political conversation…

AK: I don't see any Democrats being up front with their kinks…

TNG: .. Snorkeling? Nancy Pelosi's heels? Really?

AK: This is the hilarious thing about what the left-wing narrative about gay rights and the place of gay culture within American culture. The Democrats are as bad as the Republicans. Honestly, it's because they're beholden to the cultural interests of racial minorities which are overwhelmingly anti-gay. That's the elephant in the room that nobody wants to talk about. Black people voted against proposition eight 85 to 15. No one wants to talk about this. The Democrats can't make a move on this because they're going to piss off a third of their constituency. It's terrible, the Democrats really can't make moves on anything because they have such heterogeneous constituencies, all with clashing interests and linked together only by their sense of victimhood. If they lose that connection, they lose the entire coalition. And that's why nothing ever gets done, not only for blacks or Hispanics but for gays.

TNG: Speaking of coalitions, the conventional wisdom on the left is that there is, or should be, an alliance between all the people represented by the letters in "LGBTQ" and people who identify as feminists. I'll hazard a guess that you don't agree.

AK: No, because it's all rooted in victimhood. You can't live a fulfilling life as a gay person *qua* gay person or just as a human being living in constant victimhood. We can't have a nation of infants, a nation of whiners, we have to have people that say, "Fuck the government, I don't need the federal government to validate my existence." All these people making these marches on Washington and equality pride marches – these are people whose self-esteem is at risk. If the government isn't validating their marriages or their existences – I support same-sex marriage because I think the federal government shouldn't be hoarding benefits for heterosexual couples. If it were up to me, the federal government would get out of the marriage question altogether and leave it to the market, or perhaps civil unions for all. I don't think that the Human Rights Campaign would be satisfied with that.

TNG: You mentioned in your column– and we'll end here, I promise – the set of intellectuals who have come to inform your views on sexuality. People like Camille Paglia, Christina Hoff Summers, and the man you describe as the "divine" Marquis de Sade. In the spirit of unflinching self-analysis that these thinkers represent, and to have something interesting and inflammatory to tack on to the end of the column, would you describe the most intense sexual fantasy you've ever had?

AK: (long pause) To preserve my mother's sanity I'll omit this.

TNG: Those don't sound like the words of a "truly self-empowered individual."

AK: (chuckles) I love my mom.

Why I'm Leaving the *Eagle*

American University Eagle | 04.18.10

I've been writing for The *Eagle* for two years, longer than any other columnist. I applied at the beginning of my freshman year and was hired by Charlie Szold, now The Eagle's editor in chief. Since that time, through the tenures of Graham Vyse and current Editorial Page Editor Joe Wenner, there has been a fairly laissez-faire policy toward columnists' submissions. Save for grammatical errors and statements whose truth was dubious, columns were typically printed as is.

I think that this has been good policy. The job of a columnist is to say what's on his mind, and editors should ideally act only as referees, correcting for obvious fouls. This has served my own tendencies well: I write because I enjoy writing. I love the world that I live in, and I enjoy contributing my ideas to it. My writing is not a gift to the community. That is: I am not an altruist. I am, however, a proud moral absolutist: if at any time I cease to enjoy writing for a publication, I'm not one to stay on board for the sake of "loyalty," or for resume-padding.

The *Eagle*'s revised editorial policies are to include a ban on columnists commenting online, in addition to a stricter filter for columns that are "inflammatory" (that is: the only ones worth reading — and writing, for that matter). In other words: my columns are to be neutered, and I will no longer be allowed to engage with my readers. Because of these changes — which the editors ludicrously assert are long overdue — I am not willing to write for The *Eagle* any longer. If I cannot write what's on my mind without the need to self-censor, why should I write? If I cannot engage my readers, what's the point?

The *Eagle*'s new policies reflect a moral failing. We now have unequivocal proof that if a pressure group on campus makes enough noise, it will be granted a veto stamp over the rest of the campus' behavior. Moral fortitude demands that bullies be resisted, not appeased. But what we have here is the latter. I cannot morally sanction this; therefore, I must leave.

My resignation has nothing to do with any of the following fantasies: a secret deal cut with the editors, internal politics, second thoughts about my previous column, buckling under media pressure, or an admission that I truly do not reflect "community standards." If The *Eagle*'s policies were not changing, I would be attempting, as with every previous semester, to remain on board. But they are, and I'm not.

My advice to incoming columnists is this: know your audience. Nobody read anything I wrote until I started writing about campus issues. Nobody cares one whit about what a 20 year old in the *Eagle* thinks about the president's nuclear policies. But there's only one place where people can read about AU's campus culture, and that's *The Eagle.* If you want to rant about President Barack Obama, do it on a blog about national politics. That's what I do: fans (and detractors) can continue to follow my writings at David Frum's FrumForum.com and David Horowitz's NewsRealBlog. It's fantastic to be engaged in national policies. But in The Eagle, for God's sake, please write about something relevant to campus issues. And with that, I bid thee farewell!

I expressed some regret at my life path in 2013, when I left the Republican Party. However, I was also busy writing articles for LibertyNews.com, the *Huffington Post,* and a group called the Republican Reason Caucus, started by former Race 4 2012 writer Josiah Schmidt. I also wrote again for Race 4 2012 after Mitt Romney tapped Paul Ryan for VP and I got on board with the ticket. In 2013, I began my master's program at St. John's College – Annapolis. Here is what I wrote around that time:

On Entering Politics Early

Facebook 10.13.13

A fairly significant life regret of mine is that I became involved in politics at far too young an age. I first became interested when I was only 13 years old. I was drawn to Fox News and right-wing pundits because they were entertaining and passionate, while offering superficially plausible arguments that I figured I could trust, because — hey, why would a professional political writer make shit up? By age 14 I had already read books by Hannity, O'Reilly, Coulter, Savage, and others, and watched Fox News for several hours a day. I volunteered for the Republican Party in 2004 and even self-published a little collection of small essays and rants that got me on the front page of the local newspaper. At that age, I determined to become a political commentator.

At age 17, I became significantly more libertarian and went through a major Ayn Rand phase that lasted for a couple of years, but I still retained an affinity for right-wing media, due mostly to the fact that I had spent several years of my adolescence developing an emotional attachment to it: it was part of my identity. (Hell, at age 15, I even went through a phase where I tried to convince myself to be a Christian, since it was the more properly conservative thing to do.) As I started to find success in the right-wing media, I tried to 'square the circle' by positioning myself as a contrarian libertarian voice, but it was never a comfortable fit — not philosophically, not culturally, and not temperamentally — and in hindsight I realize that it was never, ever actually going to work. It is manifestly obvious to me now that I never actually fit in with the right-wing activist crowd. I wonder if, had my first real exposure to politics been at age 16 or 17 instead of 13, I might have realized that and not ever been sucked into the black hole of right-wing media in the first place.

In 2016 I founded my first truly independent project, the New American Perspective, with Cinzia Croce. This is where my thinking stands today, in 2018:

A Small Statement of Purpose

New American Perspective | 4.19.18

I feel so much better. Like my mind can juggle more ideas at once, like fragmentary parts are coming together. I feel like my politics has matured now: I like to combine the compassion of progressivism with the clear-eyed test-of-time driven assumptions of conservatism and the idiosyncratic individualism of libertarianism, coupled with a belief that liberalism, while highly imperfect, is the best we've got going for us, so it ought to be nurtured and supported — given tough love, yes, but not despised and mocked. Progressives must resist writing conservatives into history as the 'bad guys' of the American story, and they must resist becoming Puritan-like and sanctimonious. Conservatives have to resist the impulse to be in full-time troll mode and remember to separate opposition to progressive sanctimony and bad progressive policy from loathing toward progressives as people, and the groups progressives try to help. The groups progressives try to help should remember not to glamorize their oppression or act like it grants them special moral status. They are victims, not heroes — and being a victim of something means asking for understanding, not seeking revenge. And instead of 'checking their privilege,' 'privileged' people should start counting their blessings instead, and using their advantages to help uplift others instead of cash in and gain notoriety. Our society, our Constitution was built on compromise. We find ourselves in a strange new world of unipolar status and global communications — we have no more major external enemies, and many new opportunities. Right now we need to do to the hard work of confronting the enemy within: our fallen state as human beings — to put more love and understanding and listening back in our politics, culture, and society, so we can do the hard work of becoming a truly great country.

Personalities

I love presidential politics. My preferred candidates have lost the last three elections, so my support seems to be a curse, but I still love to chronicle their quests for power and glory. The only presidential candidate since Rudy Giuliani in 2008 I passionately supported was Hillary Clinton, in 2016. Therefore, the first part of this section will be about her. After that, there are sections on the two personality cult leaders who defeated her, and some choice articles about various right-of-center figures, one of which also details my prescience in predicting Donald Trump as the 2016 Republican nominee.

Hillary Clinton

This Time, Hillary Is Inevitable

Personal Website | 03.26.15

The pundits can't keep Elizabeth Warren's name off their lips. Not since the swift rise of Barack Obama has a senator skyrocketed to such prestige within the Democratic Party in such a short period of time — and, for a second time in a row, this talented senator seems to have arrived at just the right moment to keep a nascent Hillary Clinton presidential campaign from becoming little more than a coronation. Clinton's 'inevitability' may be an illusion, once again.

But a careful examination of the facts of the 2008 primary campaign demonstrates that the circumstances of the 2016 race are already radically different from last time — and in a way that benefits Hillary to such an extent that she is almost certainly better-positioned to win her party's presidential nomination than any non-incumbent since Dwight Eisenhower.

In November 2006, then-Sen. Clinton could scarcely reach 40% in public polls of registered Democrats. A USA Today-Gallup poll from Nov. 9-12, 2006, showed Clinton with only 31% support, with Barack Obama at a respectable 19% — a gap of only 12%. No 2006 poll ever showed Clinton with more than a 22% lead. Her largest lead at any point in the cycle was 34% — in September 2007. But a recent ABC-Washington Post poll of registered Democrats shows Hillary Clinton with a colossal 53% advantage over Elizabeth Warren — 64% to 11%, with Vice President Joe Biden taking 13% of the vote. She not only has more than double the support she had at this point in the 2008 cycle, but an almost 20% greater lead than she had at any point in 2008. Even Vice President Al Gore, perhaps the best example of an 'inevitable' presidential nominee in modern history, was up by just 26% in the autumn of 1998.

This matters significantly because Clinton only barely lost the nomination last time, after having begun from a far weaker starting point — and, for all of her gifts, Sen. Warren is not the phenom President Obama was: not only does she lack his oratory skill, but if she were to run, she would be extremely unlikely to capture the near-unanimous support of the black community that President Obama gained shortly after his win in the Iowa caucuses — support that was absolutely vital to his success. If it were not for the unity of the black community, Barack Obama would not be president today. Warren will not be able to recapture that history-making energy. Moreover, President Obama's 2008 victory was heavily dependent on his ability to catch Clinton asleep at the wheel in caucus states, where she totally failed to organize — a mistake she most certainly will not make twice.

Clinton's old Achilles' heel — her support for the Iraq War — has lost much of its potency, too, as the vote to go to war recedes further and further into the public's memory. Nearly a decade's time has elapsed between her first presidential announcement and now — and her foreign policy knowledge after a largely successful run as Secretary of State is unquestioned. She remains somewhat to the right of the foreign policy center-of-gravity among primary voters — but she is still thoroughly within the Democratic mainstream.

Finally, parties are always more cautious about their choice of nominee when they sense they are in a position of weakness. In large part because of President George W. Bush's failures, the political climate of 2008 was as favorable to progressives as it had been in at least a generation: the Democratic Party was fresh off of a sweeping victory in the 2006 midterms, and the country was utterly fatigued of Bush. It is not surprising that Democrats felt more comfortable with selecting a bolder nominee than Clinton in 2008. But in this cycle, the circumstances are reversed. Like Republicans in 2008, Democrats will almost certainly prioritize 'electability,' and Clinton remains the party's best chance at holding the White House.

She may not have been inevitable in 2008, but in 2016, the nomination is hers. Democrats who are not yet Ready for Hillary had better make their peace.

The Case for Hillary Clinton

Personal Website | 04.13.15

The first question in politics is always what is at stake. The presidency is not awarded by cosmic fiat to the man or woman most fit for the job, but is chosen by the people from among those who choose to present themselves as candidates. Accordingly there can be a number of legitimate criticisms leveled against a candidate without rendering her unworthy of support. If someone were tasked with scouting the nation in pursuit of the most qualified citizen for the presidency, it is unlikely that he would decide that Hillary Clinton is the best person for the job. But the question at hand is not whether Hillary Clinton is the best person for the job, but whether Hillary Clinton is a better person for the job than the other viable candidates — probably Jeb Bush, Scott Walker, and Marco Rubio. What is at stake, therefore, is whether we will be governed by the best among these candidates or by the worst. Excellence in anyone is rare, perhaps no less so among politicians. That there are no absolutely good candidates does not excuse us from the duty of deciding which among them is most suited for the presidency. I will not attempt here to extensively compare Hillary with her rivals, but to explain why she is worthy of support. I will leave the reader to decide whether it is a strong enough case to prefer her to her opponents.

Like most celebrities, Hillary Clinton considers herself

misunderstood. The press delights in portraying her as a contemporary Richard Nixon: cold, secretive, and calculating. Perhaps. Her critics assert that since she exhibits these traits, she therefore lacks the character for the job. Of course most of these critics would vote against her even if they did admire her personally. It is certainly the case that character is of paramount importance when selecting a president — but it is difficult enough to communicate our true character even to our closest friends. Surely we cannot judge what sort of president she would be by considering her missteps and gaffes in isolation, or from only observing her on the campaign trail. It may be the case that she is simply less shrewd than most politicians at disguising her contempt for 'the game.' Her weaknesses as a 'retail saleswoman' are certainly all the more striking when juxtaposed with her husband's unaffected, boyish charisma. But it seems unlikely that a person's character radically changes from their early years. It is imperative to examine Hillary's life in its totality, and to look at the principles that have consistently governed her conduct — how they began, how they matured, and how she wants to apply them to her presidency.

Hillary's political awakening began as an adolescent, when one of her high school teachers recommended Barry Goldwater's Conscience of a Conservative. Upon entering Wellesley, she quickly became active in the College Republicans, where she served as president. But she soon found herself at odds with the Republican Party on social issues and the Vietnam War. In the midst of her transformation from Young Republican to committed Democrat, she told her youth minister that she considered herself "a mind conservative and a heart liberal."

Soon after graduating from Wellesley, she began law school at Yale, where she met Bill Clinton. After graduation, the two of them moved to Arkansas, where she became the first female partner at the highly prestigious Rose Law Firm, served on the board of Wal-Mart, and briefly taught law. She repeatedly turned down Bill's marriage proposals, fearful of losing her distinct professional identity. It is not out of the question that she decided to marry Bill when she did primarily for political reasons; she only very reluctantly adopted the roles traditionally assigned to women. This was most evident in Bill's 1992 presidential campaign, during which Hillary (in)famously offended socially conservative voters by declaring that she "could have stayed home and baked cookies" rather than pursuing a career, and that she was not a "little woman standing by her man like Tammy Wynette." She quickly developed a reputation as a famously "polarizing" and distinctly modern first lady.

Early in Bill's first term, Hillary suffered her most embarrassing professional setback. Her utter mismanagement of her husband's attempts at health care reform resigned her to a more traditional role for the rest of his presidency, and helped pave the way for a sweeping Republican takeover of Congress in 1994. She prudently recast her image as a champion of women's rights. Perhaps the most admirable of her actions as First Lady was her 1995 speech about women's rights at a UN conference in Beijing. She dispensed with the diplomatic formalities of not directly criticizing foreign leaders on their soil and all but explicitly challenged the social policies of the autocratic Chinese regime on Chinese soil.

Her 2000 Senate campaign was unremarkable, and she triumphed against a rather unremarkable opponent — but she quickly was embraced by a resounding majority of New Yorkers, to such an extent that no serious challenger emerged in her 2006 race for re-election. Her concrete accomplishments as senator are few, but she served for long enough, and in consequential enough times, that we can discern a general sense of her ideology: domestically center-left, and a 'liberal hawk' on foreign policy. She certainly never proposed or supported anything patently unreasonable. Perhaps her worst moment was her opposition to the surge in Iraq, which was instrumental in securing the stability we abandoned in 2011. In general, she was a competent but seldom — if ever — exceptional senator.

Some say that Hillary never risks anything when communicating with voters; that she won't exhibit the 'courage of her convictions.' But this is patently and obviously false: if she had recanted her vote for the Iraq War, loudly and repeatedly, early in her 2008 presidential campaign, it would have mitigated the not-insignificant damage it caused her against Barack Obama, who had opposed the war from the beginning. To the very last primary, she would not disavow her vote. Some might say she was simply trying not to appear weak or indecisive — but if that is the case, she decided she would rather project strength than secure more primary votes against a candidate who was deftly able to make her vote for war an issue. Moreover, she rejected Barack Obama's populist pandering by arguing against a raise in the capital gains tax. Even today, reporters wonder whether she will hold onto this position, which is unquestionably rejected by her party's base. Is that a woman who will say anything for a vote? I imagine that progressives will read this and wince — when she sticks to her guns, it seems to more often than not stem from conservative impulses. But the truth about Hillary's convictions is right in front of our eyes.

As Secretary of State, she of course operated under the direction of President Obama. When judging her accomplishments, or lack thereof, we must remember what was her sphere of influence and what was not. There is no 'Hillary Doctrine,' but we know what policies she pressed for, behind the scenes. We know that the humiliating parade of errors that was President Obama's response to Syria's use of chemical weapons would not happen in a Hillary Clinton administration. We know that she rejects the notion that America should merely respond to events as they happen. We know she believes that a foreign policy that seeks nothing but stability is insufficient and morally base. We know that she does not hold delusional, romantic views about the Israeli-Palestinian conflict, and we know that she does not think Benjamin Netanyahu is the reason why there is no Palestinian state. In a word, we know that her sense of moral clarity is vastly superior to President Obama's. A Hillary Clinton administration would be good for the Democratic Party on this count, and would therefore be good for the country as a whole, since this would see both political parties more sharply focused on what is at stake on the world stage. Her frequently-cited extensive travel — one of her favorite points to make to reporters — is not a policy accomplishment, but it is a practical advantage against someone like Jeb Bush when it comes to making judgments about foreign policy. If a new crisis breaks out in the Middle East, or Eastern Europe, or North Africa in 2017, nobody will doubt that she is familiar with the key players or the details of the issues at hand.

Taking the whole of her life into account, we see a woman who avoids extremes, accepts the reality of the persistence of power politics in both domestic and foreign affairs, and is animated by a sense of purpose — the sort of purpose that we can anticipate will grant her the confidence to advocate as president for American greatness in word and deed. She embraces liberal principles without sliding into progressive dogma; she is no European-style social democrat. She is without a doubt a flawed politician, and perhaps is even more flawed as a campaigner —

and there is of course no guarantee that her presidency will be successful — especially considering that Republicans will still own a commanding majority in the House, if not also the Senate. But from among the available options, Clinton seems best-prepared for the duties of the job, and I am happy to support her.

Hillary Clinton for President

New American Perspective | 01.31.16

Hillary Clinton is an American icon. She has rebounded from uncertainty time and again to confound her critics and build one of the most impressive resumes in American politics. But 'familiarity breeds contempt,' and many in our country have grown tired or uninspired with Secretary Clinton. Her presence in national public life began just a year after I was born. Hillary has always 'been there' for as long as I can remember. When I was introduced to politics in 8th grade and brainwashed myself into believing right-wing dogma, I learned quickly that Hillary Clinton was Enemy No. 1. In 2008, I supported Rudy Giuliani in part because I believed he was the candidate most likely to defeat Clinton in a general election. I voted for Mitt Romney in 2012 and do not regret it. Now, in 2016, I am an enthusiastic and unapologetic supporter of Hillary Clinton's presidential bid, and have believed strongly in her inevitable nomination this year. Many of my ex-allies in conservative politics have been mystified — not to mention many family members. How could I have come to support Hillary Clinton?

The very best reason to support Hillary Clinton is for her foreign policy perspective and expertise. Let us not play games: Clinton is a dyed-in-the-wool Cold War liberal. She is more like Joe Lieberman than Chuck Hagel. She believes strongly and sincerely in American global leadership, and views the United States as having a special role to play in world history. Her approach to Iran? "Distrust but verify" — "Iran is not a partner in the deal, it is the subject of the deal." Her moral clarity concerning the Israeli-Arab conflict is sharp, and she is not blind to Hamas' propaganda. She advocated early and often to President Obama for increased U.S. engagement in Syria, which may have enabled us to gain a real foothold in the conflict before Russia changed the game.

There certainly would have been none of the humiliation surrounding President Obama's astonishing decision to back down from his 'red line' threats to Assad, had Secretary Clinton been president instead. She has declared, in a shot at President Obama: "'Don't do stupid stuff' is not an organizing principle." In 1995, as First Lady, she courageously defied diplomatic custom to rebuke the Chinese government on Chinese soil for its treatment of women. And she's not shy about her hatred for tyrants: she is steely-eyed and as awake to the realities of power as a commander-in-chief must be: witness her cheering over the death of a hated enemy, Moammar Gaddafi. Robert Gates even reports that she privately supported the 2007 'surge' in Iraq — in addition to, as we know, supporting the 2009 surge in Afghanistan. Against Vice President Biden, she advocated for going forward with the raid on Osama bin Laden. One wonders whether she would have unilaterally withdrawn from Iraq in 2011. She is also deeply learned and widely traveled: if there is a sudden crisis somewhere in the world, she will not have to be given a crash-course about the stakes and the players. She will likely already know about them — or even know them first-hand.

Bernie Sanders has served as the ideal foil to Hillary: he is so utterly indifferent to foreign policy that he appears to not have any regular advisers on the matter. She has not had to move one iota to the left, and in office, she will be able to serve both as a corrective to President Obama's incoherent foreign policy while also serving to help reshape the Democratic Party on these issues.

On domestic issues, Hillary is a conventional liberal, would appoint Ruth Bader Ginsberg-style justices to the Supreme Court, speak out loudly on women's and children's issues, push for additional gun control, immigration reform, more reform of regulations in the banking and financial sectors, a minimum wage hike, and — most promisingly, since the House GOP might actually agree to something on this count — criminal justice reform. There is a strong chance she could truly govern to the left of Obama. What is crucial is that she is moderate by temperament, open to negotiation, and seldom patently unreasonable in her proposals. She is someone the House GOP under Speaker Paul Ryan should be able to work with on certain issues. And she has a mastery of policy detail few of her rivals in either party can match.   Republicans already have strong majorities in both the House and Senate, in addition to controlling a majority of governorships and state legislatures — and a relatively friendly Supreme Court. The balance of power in this country is in danger of shifting too far to the right, and the GOP is in dire need of being corralled back to more moderate discourse and ambitions. If a Democrat is not in control of the presidency, our country will be subject to one-party rule by a fractured and undisciplined party, possibly led by a man with a volatile temperament. The GOP is a radicalized party in disarray. Frontrunners Donald Trump and Ted Cruz manifestly lack the temperament to be commander-in-chief and head of state, and Marco Rubio is too unseasoned. For the sake of balance and order, the Republicans ought to be denied the presidency.

Of course, Hillary Clinton is far from an ideal candidate: she finds it difficult to inspire people anymore, and 25 years in public life have made her guarded and cautious. There are a handful of examples of Hillary walking into ethical and legal 'grey areas.' But there is absolutely no evidence she has committed any crime, and no evidence she has ever done anything to harm the country.| When we examine the potential alternatives, there is no comparison. The Republicans seem intent on nominating a candidate that will lead them to a Barry Goldwater-style wipe-out, and Clinton's opponent specializes in offering false promises to people who deserve practical solutions. For her foreign policy acumen, unrivaled range and depth of experience, reasonable and cerebral temperament, and her ability to prevent our country from falling into one-party rule, the best choice for the presidency, despite her imperfections, is Secretary Hillary Rodham Clinton. If she lives up to her potential, she could become America's Iron Lady.

Hillary Clinton for President: There Is No Alternative

New American Perspective | 06.07.16

Although Hillary Clinton's historic primary victory has turned out to be decisive, there is undoubtedly a streak of joylessness to it. Her major victories were concentrated in the three 'Super Tuesdays' of the calendar, while losing constantly in the caucus-heavy lull periods, making the path to the nomination feel like a bit of a long slog at times. Between this, her seeming inability to escape the constant drip-drip-drip of harmful new information about her use of a private server while

Secretary of State, and an unusually ideological and tenacious opponent, being a Clinton supporter has often felt like — how to put this? — less a reason to be excited than a responsibility.

Before we proceed, let us not forget that the final outcome of this race has been clear for some time; at least since the first Super Tuesday, in which Clinton swept the South — and that any candidate but Bernie, who, unusually, owes nothing to the Democratic Party and has hated it for decades, would be out by now. Ultimately, Clinton will have won over 55% of the popular vote, command a pledged-delegate lead in the 300-400 range, and hold the near-entirety of the Mid-Atlantic, Southwest, and Deep South, as well as most of the country's major states, including NY, FL, TX, IL, PA, VA, and even MA. Her victory would have been even more decisive had it not been for Bernie's string of non-representative caucus victories. Consider that Bernie won Washington state by 50 points but that Clinton actually won the state's non-binding primary. Hillary also won Nebraska's non-binding primary, despite losing the caucus and hence losing in the state's delegate count. Who is really the candidate with the silent majority?

Clinton's most excellent foreign-policy-centered speech last week, which of course was aimed at taking down Donald Trump, was a potent reminder of why I expressed support for her when she entered the race and again right before the voting began. She coolly lobbed bombs with a wink and a nod while hitting Trump where he bruises most: his ego. She made fun of his feuding, mocked the notion that he even has policy ideas, and got under his "very thin skin": Trump flinched in his response, lashing out impotently that she is a "phony" who ought to be in jail and whining at her for reading from a script. After a year of witnessing Clinton treating Sanders with kid-gloves, it is timely to remember that she can cuttingly take down a Republican foe. Maybe it's time to whip out the old Hillary nutcracker novelties.

Clinton is always at her best when she's got a great Republican foil. She and her husband can always count on Republicans to overreach. It's like an art: they bring out the worst in their opponents for all to see, from Newt Gingrich's stunningly hypocritical marital behavior during the Lewinsky affair to the hyper-politicized insanity of the endless Benghazi circus. No doubt Trump will add some new entries to the canon.

Contrary to my colleague Cinzia's recent criticisms, Clinton in fact did lay out a coherent foreign policy agenda, and demonstrated again why she is the only responsible choice in this race. First, she demonstrated that she understood the stakes:

"And if America doesn't lead, we leave a vacuum – and that will either cause chaos, or other countries will rush in to fill the void. Then they'll be the ones making the decisions about your lives and jobs and safety – and trust me, the choices they make will not be to our benefit."

In an important sense, this is simply the triumph of the reality principle. If we don't act when we can, where it counts, then Russia, China, Iran, or some other unfavorable ambitious entity will help determine the fate of world affairs instead. This is where liberal internationalists and so-called 'neoconservatives' meet: Samantha Power or Robert Kagan could have penned this line. We may fail sometimes, but we are not autocrats or authoritarians, and preventing regimes molded in that nature from spreading their influence is an inescapable dimension of our national interest.

Sounding more like Truman or Reagan than like Obama, she spoke of her vision for American foreign policy in big-picture, action-oriented terms:

"I believe in strong alliances; clarity in dealing with our rivals; and a rock-solid commitment to the values that have always made America great. And I believe with all my heart that America is an exceptional country – that we're still, in Lincoln's words, the last, best hope of earth. We are not a country that cowers behind walls. We lead with purpose, and we prevail."

Clinton's aim is twofold: reject the excesses of both the Bush and Obama years — and seek a synthesis of what they got right. In a repudiation of George W. Bush, Clinton insists we must honor our alliances and wield our power in a manner that elicits respect rather than fear or resignation — but in a repudiation of Barack Obama, she insists on treating our enemies unequivocally like enemies. She has explicitly accused Putin of tyranny, has vigorously condemned Hamas before progressive audiences, and laughed at the death of Moammar Qaddafi. This is the woman who insisted in 2008 that Obama was naive for thinking we could reason with theocratic radicals, the woman who famously insisted that 'don't do stupid stuff' is "not an organizing principle." Indeed, the speech was her most unapologetic defense of her view of America as the 'indispensable nation' since her 2014 Atlantic interviewwith Jeffrey Goldberg, still a must-read for understanding how Clinton 'ticks.' What is a proper organizing principle, though? She wants our foreign policy to be informed by morality, not simply by raw calculations of material interests:

"In particular, Israel's security is non-negotiable. They're our closest ally in the region, and we have a moral obligation to defend them."

A moral obligation — we are loyal to the Israelis not because we cannot exist without them but because abandoning them would mean abandoning our values. Donald Trump wants us to be neutral in potential new rounds of peace negotiations; President Obama has a famously tense relationship with Benjamin Netanyahu. Clinton has promised to invite him to the White House in the first month of her administration and to "take our relationship to the next level." Whatever our differences, she says, our true bottom line — one that is more important than economics or national identity, is this: we stand united against tyranny.

Besides treating Hamas and Israel as moral equals, Donald Trump's foreign policy ideas include bombing the oilfields of Iraq — after looting what we can by making a big ring around them while letting our companies go to work there — handing over Syria to Vladimir Putin, shrugging our shoulders at the possible first domino in the disintegration of the European Union, slapping a 40% tariff on Chinese goods, and attempting to force Mexico to pay for a wall along our southern border. It is still a little surreal that we are even discussing this — and yet, this is the alternative the Republican Party has given us. Over 40% of the people want to elevate the man boosting those 'ideas' to the office of the presidency. Trump's outrageous character ensures this election will be first of all about whether a man like him represents this nation.

Ultimately, I believe Clinton is worth electing on her policy merits, and that her key foreign policy interviews and speeches demonstrate this — but those who have been reluctant to demonstrate even tepid support must consider the last available alternative and ask whether it wouldn't be an indictment against our republic to elevate such a man to the presidency. Even if her tenure turns out to be a crushing disappointment, the nation is guaranteed to survive relatively unscathed after four years of Clinton, who, on the domestic front, represents little beyond a continuation of the status quo under President Obama — which, we ought to remember, is broadly popular relative to the Republican agenda. But America — and the office of the presidency — would never be the same after a President Trump, whose campaign has seemingly-impossibly degenerated even further, this week into outright racist attacks — and the ugly decline in our civic culture he would represent would accelerate the splitting of our social fabric from a slow tearing to a piercing rip.

An Open Letter to Hillary Clinton From a Supporter

New American Perspective | 09.12.16

I want very badly for you to win this election. Politicians say during every election cycle that it is the most important election of their lifetime — but this time, at least for this 26-year-old's short lifetime, it's probably true. I also want you to know that I've taken a lot of heat for you: after a decade of exclusively — and very publicly — supporting Republicans, I chose this time to throw my support to you, a candidate passionately hated by many people I regard as friends and colleagues. I suspect I may have even closed certain professional doors by publicly supporting you. I've written three different op-eds supporting you for president and have defended you time and again on issues regarding the Clinton Foundation, Benghazi, and even your private server. At this point, I am not a fair-weather supporter.

So, understand the urgency in my voice when I say that, while I want very badly for you to win this election, I also want very badly for you to know that you screwed up very badly this time. You have once again failed to plan for a worst-case scenario, and once again it is because you decided to put your personal preference for privacy first. Personally, I don't give much of a damn about most of the stuff people — especially reporters — drone on about regarding 'transparency.' I can't stand how self-righteous they are about it. They sound overly pious, and their motives are usually questionable. I think most people would make wiser political decisions if they didn't know as much about how the sausage is made — we both know that being 30% informed is worse than being 5% informed, and we both know very few people take the time and energy to get to 80% informed so they can understand the 30% in that broader context. And I know you think the press trumps up a whole lot of trash and whips the mob into a frenzy over nothing — and you're totally right about that, too! They do that all the time. But for a lot of people, especially reporters, this kind of thing matters a lot — and — I'm being honest with you, right? — being open about current health ailments is far from unreasonable.

Here's the thing: a reasonable degree of openness and public-mindedness not just in policy but also in personality is one of the demands of public life in a democracy. So it's not that you're being a liar, as your critics say. I really don't think you are hiding something disqualifying. No — the problem you have is that you're being selfish, because when you aren't being open about this, your supporters end up having to waste all their time defending you over stupid bullshit, again and again, instead of talking about the future and the stark differences between what your presidency would look like and what Donald Trump's would look like. Coming down with pneumonia right now is incredibly inconvenient and unfair, given the malicious rumors, and you've probably gotten away with hiding illnesses before. But this is a critical moment — and you have got to trust that enough voters will understand how to contextualize a president being sick. A certain degree of transparency is in your self-interest — it's not just to throw bones to the press. You're not going to be applauded for it, no — but you do it anyway, so you avoid incidents like this, which unsettle even your staunchest supporters and has them speculating unnecessarily.

The country doesn't want Donald Trump. You are on the verge of winning the presidency practically by default. Now is the time when you have to use all the discipline you've cultivated over the last 68 years and put it to work to tame this tragic flaw. You can do this — you must do this. The stakes are simply too high.

Love,

Alex

The View From the Settled Dust

New American Perspective | 12.12.16

I waited for a month to write anything here. I wanted to give myself time to absorb what happened. At the same time, I have not emerged from the blog-wilderness with any special insights. What is most important for me as a writer and analyst is simply to figure out what my blind spots were, and try to make adjustments. I will not attempt to falsify history: my election prediction, like just about everyone else's, was quite bad. I missed the popular vote margin by 3% and gave Clinton an electoral lead of over 100, taking Wisconsin, Michigan, and Pennsylvania totally for granted. I do not believe it is because I neglected the concerns of the white working-class or ignored the existence of my Big Fat Elite Coastal Bubble — I was berating my ex-party about these concerns during the primary season, and I forecast that primary quite precisely. So I will perform a merciful act today by sparing my readers any new 'think-pieces' about these already-exhausted topics.

I always knew that Hillary was a bad candidate, and I had a few mischievous moments during which I marveled that this crazy saga was actually going to work out for this most flawed and fascinating of candidates. In September, I wrote that Hillary was about to win the presidency by default. I half-jokingly remarked in the summer that I was convinced God wanted her to be president.

Clinton's loss was so narrow that any one factor could be said to have made the difference for her — so it is misleading to blame it on this-or-that particular. If she has a 'tragic flaw' at the bottom of it all, it is probably, as Colin Powell remarked, hubris, which is also the general character flaw for which Washington is being punished. The post-election focus on the white working class, stemming from Trump's surprise victories in the Rust Belt, is misleading. One could marginally tweak the results in just Michigan and Florida and produce a Clinton victory with a totally different narrative: one about how changing demographics did just enough in Virginia, Colorado, and Nevada to save her from what was otherwise a Republican wave.

The Trump victory represents an important turning point for the republic. It is too soon to speak too much about what it all might mean, but it should serve first of all as a reminder that there is no intrinsic law of history dictating that America is destined to resolve its problems — such as angry, bitter political polarization — in a satisfactory manner. There is also no law stating that the advance of progressivism is guaranteed. I became a bit sanguine about this, and resigned myself to a lot of progressive social ills to try to protect an international arrangement I continue to believe is worth preserving. I underestimated the resilience of the right and failed to anticipate the strength of the rebellion against their being written into the history books as the bad guys of the American story. (That is a pretty good reason to be angry, by the way.) And as Clinton, whom I like as an individual, fades from view, I am reminded why I voted twice for Republicans against President Obama and for various Republicans in 2010 and 2014, and why the Democratic Party — with which I am stubbornly remaining registered, for now — is so unappealing as an alternative to the Republican circus.

There is no way around it: Trump is really bad. But I refuse to spend the next four years in perpetual disappointment, embarrassment, and outrage over what is likely to be a long series of unfortunate events. I will cheer Trump when he succeeds, and I hope he defies expectations in the best way. But I cannot pretend that I see my country the same way I did two months ago: Clinton was right, at least, that we are even more divided than we thought. Our nation is deeply confused about its moral purpose and its place in the world in a post-Cold War, post-Iraq, post-financial crisis era, and we cannot count on History to deliver us a Lincoln. The future of liberalism is up for grabs in a way it has not been in decades. The boundaries of what is politically imaginable today are opening up for the first time since the collapse of the USSR.

I have tried to use this website as my small example of how people who disagree strongly can still try to understand each other, work together, and debate the issues forcefully but honestly, frequently finding common ground. As the Trump era dawns, these are some of the ideals we need most. Take heart, Trump opponents: the republic will endure, and maybe, if God is in a good mood, we will even get to learn something from all this.

Why Won't People Stop Lying About Hillary and the DNC?

New American Perspective | 11.21.17

It's the lie that won't die: the Democratic National Committee 'coronated' Hillary Clinton, so that St. Bernie Sanders, the disruptive outsider with a heart of gold and a record of purity, couldn't crash their insider party.

Damon Linker of the *Week*, who is obviously very pleased that his content-cow Clinton hasn't yet retreated from the public spotlight, makes the latest case (emphasis mine):

"Hillary Clinton was a deeply flawed candidate who ran an atrocious campaign and should never have been anointed as the presumptive nominee by the Democratic National Committee in the first place. If Clinton wanted to run for president while under investigation by the FBI, that was her business. But why on Earth would the DNC and the party's "superdelegates" *decide so far in advance that a candidate running with that kind of baggage should be considered the inevitable victor?* Aside from the obstacles it placed in the way of her one serious challenger (Bernie Sanders), it helped to discourage many others (including Joe Biden and Elizabeth Warren) from jumping into the race. Why bother when you know the party is standing against you?

That decision on the part of the DNC had fateful consequences..."

This is an utterly bizarre rewrite of history — one which has gained currency because it is unfathomable to people like Linker that anyone could actually like the Worst Woman In the History of the Planet, or actually think she would have made a good president. In their minds, St. Bernie was so obviously a superior candidate — and superior person — that only manipulation from on-high could explain her nomination, and that her voters must have been brainwashed, or the victims of Donna Brazile-engineered propaganda — or maybe voting with their vaginas or something. It would be too much to suggest that any of this can be interpreted as white men and college kids lashing out at the fact that women and non-whites had the decisive role in determining the outcome of the primary. But it certainly is an astounding case of bad memory.

It is easy enough to forget now, after the more-competitive-than-expected primary season, but Hillary entered 2015 with a 30-50-point lead in the polls. The reason that every other Democrat with a marquee name declined to run against her is not because the Democratic National Committee was coronating her, but because she was crushing the competition democratically. The field wasn't cleared for her. She cleared the field herself — because she came in a very close 2nd place in the 2008 contest against President Barack Obama and went on to serve under him for four years, during which time she routinely registered approval ratings in the 50s and 60s. It would not be too much to say that Hillary Clinton, detached as she was from the major political battles of the day, was the most popular politician in the country during most of Obama's second term.

Of course, Clinton knew that when she became a political figure again, her numbers would fall back down to Earth. Everyone knew that. But nobody knew when they would fall, or how far they would fall. Traditional presidential campaigns require many long months of planning and organizing to get off of the ground — and by the time the likes of Warren and Biden realized there really was an opening to defeat Clinton, it was too late: on Warren's part, because by summer 2015, Sanders had already captured the energy that was waiting for her — and by autumn 2015, there was simply not enough time for Biden to mount a viable run — to say nothing of the obstacle called grief.

It is — again, bizarre is the only word I can use — to see people like Linker, who have been involved in politics for a long time, pretend to believe that they think the Democratic National Committee is some kind of omnipotent central body that determines the presidential nominee. The anti-Clinton propagandists get away with this lie because, quite frankly, nobody is in much of a mood to defend Debbie Wasserman-Schultz, Donna Brazile, or any of the other party hacks who, to be sure, personally favored Clinton over Sanders. The propagandists count on confused or half-informed readers to conflate the personal loathsomeness of these women with actual legal or ethical malfeasance — even though the only tangible example they can come up with is Brazile stupidly telling Clinton about a CNN debate question, which we are apparently supposed to believe transformed the state of the race.

The Democratic National Committee organizes the primary calendar and apportions delegates to each state (well in advance of the vote) based on its population and importance to the party. It also helps arrange the debate schedule, which in 2016 included as many debates as took place in every contest prior to 2008. The DNC is not responsible for any of the following: managing voter rolls, setting voter registration deadlines, determining whether independents can vote in a state's primary, or overseeing precinct activity on Election Day. The 'superdelegates' exist — aside from their role as a vanity title for self-absorbed insiders — as a backstop against the nomination of an obvious loser like George McGovern. They are there 'just in case'; never in the history of the party has the winner of the majority of pledged delegates not gone on to receive the support of superdelegates — in 2008, they flipped from Clinton to Obama, and, indeed, in 2016, many superdelegates indicated that they would switch to Bernie if he was truly the people's choice.

But he was not the people's choice. The Worst Woman In the History of the Planet was. St. Bernie was the choice of a loud and angry slice of Democratic primary voters — a group of people who felt totally entitled to win by virtue of the purity and holiness of their candidate and the horribleness of the opposing candidate. But it was the Worst Woman In the History of the Planet, not St. Bernie, who won the popular vote by double-digits nationwide. It was the Worst Woman In the History of the Planet, not St. Bernie, who won the pledged delegate count by about 350. It was the Worst Woman In the History of the Planet, not St. Bernie, who decisively won primaries in Florida, Ohio, Pennsylvania, Virginia, North Carolina, Arizona, and Georgia, and more closely in Nevada and Iowa. She won these primaries on the back of the support of registered Democrats, women, non-whites, and older voters. The only swing states Bernie Sanders won against Clinton that she failed to win in the general were Wisconsin and Michigan, both of which were won by Sanders only very narrowly. On top of this, Clinton also won every major Democratic stronghold, including California, New York, Maryland, Illinois, and Massachusetts.

But there's more, still: it was actually Bernie Sanders, not Hillary Clinton, who benefited from the Democratic National Committee's contest rules: it was Sanders' heavily-young, heavily-white, heavily-male demographic that was peculiarly well-suited for winning caucuses. Witness the final set of contests, which happened to include both North Dakota and South Dakota. South Dakota held a primary and Hillary Clinton won by 2%. North Dakota held a caucus and Bernie Sanders won by 40%. Yet somehow we never hear about this insane disparity between primary and caucus results.

Linker and St. Bernie's legions of fans are free to believe that the Worst Woman In the History of the Planet was a bad candidate — I've said it myself on many occasions. They are not free to lie about the way the contest unfolded, or about the role of the Democratic National Committee. Honest debate is necessary — but the staggering degree of dishonesty contained in this DNC-centric arguments must go.

A Clinton Compendium

Carnival: The Sideshow Act Liberals Have Become | 2004

"Mrs. Hillary Clinton! Let's give the reader a little background on you, Hillary: you were named after Sir Edmund Hillary (who just so happened to have climbed Mt. Everest after you were born, a very minor technicality), you're an earnest wife (who stays with a cheating husband for political gain) and you're a superb senator (who voted to spend more money than any other junior senator in history and has made myriad slip-ups!). Yes, Hillary's got her share of problems. She even says that she 'puts on her political hat' on occasion and will 'say things that she doesn't mean.' She says that the people who tried to convict Bill need to 'see the light.' But she wants to become president in 2008. The same lady who 'says things she doesn't mean.'"

"She said once that she 'doesn't want to put the war in a political context.' I'd say she's having a field day bashing the administration over a 'fake war'...The Bush Administration had the same damned intelligence Clinton saw. Yet Clinton says the intelligence was faulty and can veer away from liberals, but when Bush supporters present the same argument — well, let's just ask Michael Moore what happens then, shall we?"

"You know, one thing I've never understood about Mrs. Clinton is why she still remains with Bill. He, in front of the world, lied and cheated her, lied about it, again, to the world, and was exposed for what he was — a fraud. Hillary, instead of being a strong-minded, independent woman, stayed with Bill...I believe it's for political gain...This sends a resounding message to women everywhere to stay with their lying men...C'mon Hillary, even you're better than that."

"Hillary Clinton is quite a darling among the liberals, isn't she? I think the conclusion we can come to is that you do not come first in Hillary Clinton's eyes. She may talk a good game in some of her speeches, she may act like she's got you first on her webpage, 'dear friend,' but one person comes before anyone else in any Hillary Clinton campaign, and that's Hillary Clinton."

"Why would I waste my time writing about Bill Clinton?"

10 Things I Dislike About the Clintons

Facebook | 10.28.16

1. The way they selfishly drag their supporters and associates into having to deal with so much stupid, petty, distracting bullshit — none of which is ever a deal-breaker but which is nearly always frustrating

2. The way they keep deluding themselves into thinking they can 'get away' with things they can't actually get away with (the fact that they keep trying to indicates that they do get away with a lot, too)

3. Their unsavory *nouveau-riche* attitude — they seem to feel like they have something to prove to the power elite they always so desperately wanted to join; their presence among those who come from families that are already rich and powerful seems unnatural at times

4. Their loyalty to their allies and associates, like George W. Bush's, often extends to the point of madness

5. Her inability or unwillingness to articulate a powerful defense of her political vision — seemingly driven by fear that it will turn off too many people she needs to win; she prefers to try to split the difference — rendering herself acceptable to many but exciting to few.

6. Their inability or unwillingness to balance their transparently 'Machiavellian' tendencies with conspicuous acts of high statesmanship

7. The way they count on right-wing radicalism to win and retain power — they are always at their best when they have a Republican foil — and when voters feel like there is no serious alternative to them

8. Her unwillingness to take any major risks — which demonstrates a lack of passionate resolve — which is not to say she is 'calculating' — though she sometimes is — but rather to say that she has lost a certain 'fire' that motivates people to enter politics in the first place

9. Their mediocre judgment in deciding who to use their power to elevate — I am sure I do not need to provide any names

10. Her domestic policies are mediocre and often misguided — e.g., her dogmatic belief in the non-existent 'pay gap,' her support for 'campaign finance reform,' her quixotic fixation on doomed gun control measures, the way she is beholden to teacher's unions, her assent to identity politics, etc.

Ayn Rand

Coming to Grips with My Ayn Rand Phase

Frum Forum | 08.09.10

As for so many alienated sixteen-year-olds, the works of Ayn Rand granted me solace. She heralded the primacy of ideas in a culture that seemed impervious to them; she dared to tell me that my accomplishments were valuable when the world seemed to be telling me that everything I did should be in the name of self-sacrifice; she promised me that truth and rationality were achievable. And, best of all: she told me that I didn't need an omnipotent government or a god to do this.

Throughout my teenage years, I delved deeply into her writings. Most people who encounter Rand read Atlas Shrugged or The Fountainhead, find their concepts intriguing, and move on. For a small minority of Rand's readers, including me, her works penetrated at a much deeper level. I came to devour every syllable the woman ever uttered: the books *Ayn Rand Answers* and *The Ayn Rand Lexicon* sit on my bookshelf, for instance.

Rand's points are easily misunderstood, which was often her own fault. She wrote in a harsh style that was accessible usually only to those already predisposed to agree with her. She was also, at her core, a radical, and often fiercely anti-prudential. She condemned Ronald Reagan for being pro-life and preposterously said that she hoped to die before he became president (alas, she did not live to see him carry us to victory in the Cold War). She said that Milton Friedman and Friedrich Hayek were ultimately useless since they refused to mount a truly philosophical argument for capitalism. (She contended, in essence, that if socialism were discovered to be more efficient, the Friedmans of the world would jump ship and join the socialists.)

Still, Rand had a way of getting to the bottom of things. She wielded her pen like a razor and stripped away the layers of public-relations nonsense to get to the philosophical premises of her opponents. She cared deeply about language and demanded specificity in semantics. Because of this, she was able to tear apart the agents of class warfare like few others. Her denunciations of the left's cultural pretensions are breathtaking. Opining on those who suggest raising taxes on millionaires at every turn, she wrote: "They don't want to be rich, they want you to be poor. They don't want to succeed, they want you to fail... our culture tells you to be successful — but God help you if you are! Be happy — but don't show it!" Of the 1960s' Democrats' proposal for a so-called second Bill of Rights, including the right to healthcare, recreation, and a job, Rand demolished the whole thing by noting one simple aspect: They list everything desirable under the sun without ever bothering to answer — who exactly is to provide all of these things, and what is to happen to them if they prefer not to spend their lives laboring for strangers?

Rand's followers are more at home on the right than most libertarians because of her uncompromising moral absolutism. Rand and her disciples were strongly anti-Communist, deeply pro-Israel, and, today, usually find themselves allied with neoconservatives on the foreign policy front. Rand's contemporary followers mostly supported the wars in Iraq and Afghanistan, and they all want America to use its platform to stick up for Israel and speak against Islam (not terrorism — Islam). If any one politician on Earth is using his platform to crusade for Randian ideals, it's not Ron Paul — it's probably Geert Wilders. Many media commentators used Rand Paul's name to make jokes about how Ayn Rand would have loved to see him triumph, but Ayn Rand would have absolutely despised Rand Paul, mostly for his belief that America has little business taking the fight to America's Islamist enemies.

Yes, then, she was a cogent writer. Her arguments are arresting and her style is hypnotic: the arid prose of Friedrich Hayek is nothing like Rand's philosophical essays, which are infused with the novelist's flair. Her broader philosophy appealed to me, as to so many other alienated teenagers. But as I felt liberated to have encountered her, I felt equally liberated to have thrown her restrictions off.

The real danger in embracing Rand's works too tightly is that hers is a system without room for skepticism or doubt. She would be aghast at the comparison, but there's something of a religious component to Objectivism (itself, like 'psychoanalysis,' an inappropriate name; no system devised by a single person should be named after anything other than its founder). Rand proudly claimed to have become privy to the Absolute Truth. Deviations from her philosophy thus become not disagreements over substantive points in the great conversation of Western civilization, but objective errors in understanding. Disagreement with Rand's opinions becomes a character flaw, rather than a philosophical dispute. It is simply impossible to embrace her works for any period of time and not internalize this fact. Thus when, at nineteen, I became intrigued by the arguments of thinkers like Hobbes, Burke, and Wittgenstein, I quite frankly felt a bit dirty for it. Rand was the woman who gave me confidence at a time when I felt isolated, alienated, and generally miserable. And now I dare betray her?

Rand's inability to engage other systems of thought on a serious level is the fatal conceit of Objectivism. She did not see herself as part of a great Western tradition of inquiry, but as a revolutionary renegade who was shaking the West's assumptions to its core. Indeed, she claimed to owe no philosophical debts to any thinker except Aristotle (even though her own bookshelf reveals that the works of Friedrich Nietzsche, Max Stirner, and Herbert Spencer influenced her). The fact that she was never taken seriously by professional philosophers cannot simply be dismissed as a postmodern/analytic joint conspiracy against system-builders and capitalists. Robert Nozick was taken entirely seriously in his libertarian years. The problem with Rand was her hit-and-run style of argument; her total lack of respect for people she disagreed with. She abhorred the philosophy of Immanuel Kant, for instance, but was more keen on calling him a "monster" out to "destroy man's mind" than to address his arguments substantively. Rand is the type of person who would literally cast people out from her inner circle if they dared to suggest that, for instance, David Hume might have had a point about the nature of knowledge.

She was no less contemptuous of people who should have been her intellectual allies. She bizarrely dismissed Adam Smith and John Stuart Mill's arguments for the free market and minimalist state out of hand for not defending her conclusions from the same angle as her. Smith, for instance, defended capitalism on what are admittedly collectivist grounds: it strengthens society and helps others by channeling man's naturally self-serving instincts into something mutually beneficial. Rand despised this line of argument, preferring instead to point out how capitalism allows men to act as free agents, rather than as masters and servants, as a command economy insists upon. Now, I unequivocally agree with Rand that it is not a duty to devote one's life to helping the poor — but there's something wrong with a system of thought that makes its adherents feel guilty about using that argument in favor of capitalism. The ability of the free market to lift up the poor from their misery is one of its most beautiful aspects. It really ought to go without saying that one doesn't need to be a bleeding-heart leftist to think that this is a highly compelling argument for capitalism. And yet, in the thousands of pages of Rand's writings that I digested, I don't think that I ever came across more than a couple of paragraphs celebrating it.

I know many people, young and old, who claim to have entered and exited "Ayn Rand phases" in their youth. It is interesting that one rarely encounters a person who says that he went through a "Burke phase" or a "Plato phase." If one becomes less enamored of Plato's arguments, he simply says that there is much merit in Plato but that he has been persuaded that his arguments are ultimately incomplete.

This is, I think, a mature way of transitioning out of a 'Rand phase.' To cast off Rand forever and spit on her insights — which really were often quite brilliant and which she often stood nearly alone on the right in making — is to engage in the same kind of all-or-nothing mentality that one erred in by embracing her unquestioningly. Her condemnations of left-wing cultural pretensions, her glorification of productive work and achievement, and her love of this Earth are breathtakingly inspiring. There is no other figure embraced by the right who arouses the same emotions in defense of liberty that Rand does. Ultimately, she is too radical, too anti-pragmatic, and does not understand well enough the limitations of human action to be embraced wholesale — but what thinker can be embraced wholesale? On balance, I am comfortable saying that there can be little doubt about the fact that Rand is an asset — flaws and all.

Sarah Palin, Mark Levin, and the Tea Party

2010 Voters: Anti-Moderate Not Anti-Incumbent

Frum Forum | 09.17.10

In their quest to impose a narrative onto the primary season, pundits and newscasters have latched onto the idea that we're witnessing a wave of anti-incumbent anger directed against all of Congress. This is simply not backed up by any evidence: while it is true that, in contested races, anti-establishment candidates have tended to prevail, most races have not been contested at all. Over four hundred and fifty Congressmen and Senators up for re-election have either been re-nominated or have witnessed their establishment successor win the nomination.

Republican or Democrat, win or lose, however, the party-favored nominees who have faced legitimate challenges have invariably been more moderate than those they were opposed by. The left presented Blanche Lincoln and Michael Bennet with serious opponents, while Arlen Specter was successfully toppled. Thanks to the Tea Party, the right's challenges have been more fruitful, knocking off Bob Bennett and Lisa Murkowski, denying nominations to Mike Castle and Charlie Crist, and giving John McCain a scare. None of these people's challenges have had anything to do with ethical reasons, or because they were unpopular with the state at large: they were all punished for not adhering to ideological orthodoxy.

A new Public Policy Polling survey shows that two-thirds of Republican primary voters want to ditch Olympia Snowe in 2012 for a more conservative candidate. In an environment like this, what can Snowe, popular amongst Maine voters as a whole, do? If she switches parties, she may well face the same fate Arlen Specter did. Ben Nelson, also up for re-election in 2012, faces similar questions.

Is there any room for moderates in national politics? One may point to the Blue Dogs, but they comprise an astonishingly high proportion of the Democrats likely to lose their House seats this November. We are witnessing an incredible polarization of the parties. But politicians like Ben Nelson, Mike Castle, and Olympia Snowe — with American Conservative Union ratings of roughly 50 — have to go somewhere. There is no obvious party for such people; it comes down to a matter of priorities. Are today's political activists ready to deny all of them seats at the table?

At the bottom of things, the problem may rest with the closed-primary system. Americans are not nearly as polarized as the parties are. New Hampshire's open system may be worth emulating: Republicans vote in their primary, Democrats vote in theirs — but independents may select either ballot. If Delaware had such a system, the state could never have produced a Christine O'Donnell. It will weaken the power of state parties, of course, which is why such policies aren't as common as they should be. But the results it produces are undeniably sane.

How to Throw Away a Senate Seat

Frum Forum | 09.14.10

Jim DeMint, Mark Levin, and the Tea Party Express have declared war on America.

The Republican Party is being hijacked by those who care more about inflating their egos than stopping the destructive Obama agenda. If we agree as Republicans — and I think we can — that failed stimulus packages, phony healthcare "reform," and subdued attitudes abroad are bad for the United States, then we must conclude, as a matter of basic logic, that an axis of egotists worked against American interests last night.

If there were any evidence that Mark Levin and Jim DeMint cared about promoting conservative principles, I might retain a modicum of respect for them. But what we witnessed in Delaware last night was not the elevation of Christine O'Donnell: it was the purging of Mike Castle. Christine O'Donnell is a quixotic, fraudulent, gold-digging liar with no job and no accomplishments. DeMint and Levin would endorse Mahmoud Ahmadinejad if he promised to purge the party of RINOs.

It is true that Mike Castle supports cap-and-trade. So does Chris Coons, who, thanks to the Tea Party, is about to coast to what will probably be a cushy, lifetime job in the Senate. Castle, however, unlike Coons-style liberal Democrats, voted against Obamacare, against the stimulus package, and in favor of Republicans to fill the all-important House leadership positions. Chris Coons will be one more vote in favor of Harry Reid for majority leader (I would have written Chuck Schumer, but thanks to the DeMints and Levins of the world, that too is in doubt). Spare me any nonsense about Christine O'Donnell's ability to win: she can't win, and she doesn't deserve to. The only Republican in Delaware who could win that seat is Mike Castle, and his career came to a shocking and humiliating conclusion last night.

Republicans from deeply-red states like South Carolina and Alaska are utterly ignorant of what it actually means to sacrifice moderates on the altar of purity. Hailing from states where people like Christine O'Donnell and Joe Miller regularly win statewide elections, DeMint and Palin are completely unable to comprehend the real-world consequences of their actions. Republicans in left-leaning states like Delaware and neighboring Maryland — my own home state — quickly learn to compromise with moderate and center-right candidates like Mike Castle and the victorious Bob Ehrlich. When we blue-state Republicans nominate unelectable candidates, we actually have to live out the consequences: here in Maryland, we have put up with years of the tax-raising, government-expanding leadership of Martin O'Malley, and few

Republicans here are interested in going through another four of them in the name of "purity." We in the blue states are the ones who suffer the greatest consequences of out-of-state propaganda from the likes of DeMint.

Stopping the Obama agenda is not on the minds of Jim DeMint, Mark Levin, Sarah Palin, and the Tea Party Express. The only agendas this band of narcissistic posers care about are personal ones: how they can inflate their egos and fatten their wallets — even if it means flushing a Senate seat down the toilet.

What the Angry Right Has Lost

Frum Forum | 07.13.10

It's perhaps inevitable that when a philosophy transforms into a mass-movement, its subtler points will be lost. It's difficult, after all, to rally around abstractions that aren't absolute in nature. There has to be an exciting common denominator; something that is not only new, but bold. Still, the atmosphere that surrounds the Tea Party — just like the atmosphere that surrounded the anti-war protesters of the George W. Bush era — strikes me as particularly intellectually noxious.

I probably agree with Glenn Beck on at least two out of three policy points. He does a lot of good when he gets tens of thousands of people to finally pick up a copy of Friedrich Hayek's Road to Serfdom. And yet, when I listen to him — or other popular icons of the activist right, such as Sarah Palin or Mark Levin — there's a dissonant undercurrent that makes it impossible for me to embrace them. It runs deeper than policy disagreements: I'm not a "moderate Republican" and I don't ally myself with the Olympia Snowes of the world. It's something more fundamental. Conservatism proper is a disposition. It's a tradition that runs through Socrates, Thomas Hobbes, Adam Smith, Edmund Burke, Friedrich Hayek, Russell Kirk, Michael Oakeshott, and Thomas Sowell. These men disagree on as much as they agree on, but there's a common current that runs through their thought: it is skeptical, wary of claims to alter or improve the human condition, and — as David Frum brilliantly describes Kirk's thought — offers us a vision, not a program.

Sarah Palin, Mark Levin, and their allies offer us a program. Levin's manifesto Liberty and Tyranny, for instance, begins with a bullet-point agenda of what constitutes conservatism in the year 2010, complete with demands concerning taxes, immigration, and the welfare state. It's incredible that anyone could miss the point so utterly. How did conservatism, which positioned itself as an anti-ideological strain of thought, transform into a bullet-point ideology ready to cast out anyone who isn't a True Believer?   Russell Kirk aptly described ideology as a drug. Meditate on that. Ideology, in the classical conservative worldview, is something that provides a person with a comfortable, affixed set of dogma that serves itself, rather than the interests of the individual and his community. Traditional conservatives, skeptical that anyone can really remake society from on high, want to pierce through these absolute claims, not come up with their own. Those who want to examine their beliefs ought to act as Socrates did, asking questions even about those beliefs that are taken as axiomatic.

Edmund Burke lambasted Thomas Paine's incredible pretensions that we can "start the world anew." We can't make the world anew. We can't remake society from on high. We can't fix the troubles of the human condition with a bullet-point agenda.

Enough With Levin's My Way Or the Highway Conservatism

Frum Forum | 07.14.10

Mark Levin's *Liberty and Tyranny* is too "deep" and "sophisticated" for me. Or, at least, that's what Levin says, in his reply to my criticisms of where he is guiding the conservative movement:

The book is much more sophisticated than Knepper's ability to comprehend. Or maybe he just didn't read it, which is more damning. Apparently he finds it un-conservative to explore conservatism on a philosophical and principled level and then apply conservatism to a political agenda in current times. Moronic.

In an astounding attempt to be as literal as possible, he says that I'm wrong that he begins his self-proclaimed classic book with a bullet-point agenda. I would simply ask him to turn to page seven.

But wait, says Levin: that's not the beginning-beginning! Before the agenda begins, he notes that conservatism cannot be deduced by a scientific or mathematical formula, after all. Fine. But his half-hearted disclaimer can't mask the fact that there actually is a bullet-point agenda that begins on page seven and ends on page thirteen. I'm not going to ignore the entire remainder of the book because of some maxim uttered on page six. I actually don't have anything against bullet-point agendas in themselves — it's the insistence upon his own as the One True Path that's so jarring to me. Levin doesn't say that his agenda is one that he personally recommends, or that it's what his prudence has led him to, or that we can argue around the edges. No, to the contrary: this agenda is something that "the Conservative will have to do if the nation is to improve." The Conservative, with a capital-c, has to enact what Levin recommends, or else the nation will degenerate.

So, it would appear that Levin thinks that he has stumbled upon, at least to some degree, a workable formula — one that actually produces some very radical measures, such as eliminating lifetime tenure for judges. Am I less of a conservative for thinking that efforts to democratize our courts are as dangerous as lifetime tenure? Levin also lambastes secularism — a cardinal principle of our own Constitution — as a destroyer of civil society and insists that only faith can justify our moral order. Now, according to Paul Johnson's History of the American People, many religious leaders at the time of its writing decried the Constitution as an irreligious document. It never mentions the Bible, God, or Jesus, and it mentions religion only once: to note that the federal government should not be sponsoring it. Levin's insistence on pure faith in preserving our republic is, I think, disturbing: it seems to be saying that there is no rational, evidence-based justification that can be given for our style of government.

Levin notes that dispositions must inevitably be applied to policy, as if I were actually implying that conservatives should simply sit around like Epicurus in his garden and ignore the world around us. My point, of course, is that reasonable conservatives should be able to disagree on policy prescriptions without the fear of being accused of "hating the Constitution," as Levin has yelled at dissenting callers to his shows. Might one, for instance, advocate a pathway to citizenship as the most prudent measure in dealing with illegal immigrants? Can we at least consider this in good faith? The answer is No: that'll earn you the nickname "Juan McCain" — which totally isn't race-baiting — or "Lindsey Grahamnesty." They are RINOs and must be purged.

Finally, the melodramatic shrieking about "tyranny" has got to go. Liberals aren't tyrants. Saddam Hussein was a tyrant. Pol Pot was a tyrant. President Obama and Speaker Pelosi are misguided politicians. Edmund Burke, in his Reflections On the Revolution In France, counseled us to remember that it's inevitable that governments will misbehave: it's simply in the nature of man to do so. Instead of being quick to anger about it, Burke recommends that we nurse its wounds like a child would to a father. In this respect, at least, Levin and the Tea Party movement are channeling Tom Paine's overreaching *Rights of Man* far more so than Burke's *Reflections*. Anyone who accuses intellectual critics of "hating the Constitution" definitely ain't a conservative in my book.

Why Do Feminists Hate Palin?

Frum Forum | 06.01.10

Mytheos Holt doesn't know the half of Jessica Valenti. Having identified her merely as a "Washington Post writer'" Mr. Holt proceeds to take apart Ms. Valenti's attack on Sarah Palin's "conservative feminism." But there's more to it than that. Valenti, the author of multiple books on Generation Y Feminism, is a fairly radical feminist, still clinging to shopworn bromides about patriarchy, institutional sexism, and the ever-looming threat of misogyny. She's wrong about the history of feminism. And she couldn't be more off-base when it comes to Sarah Palin.

When I criticized feminist date-rape propaganda two months ago, I was criticized by the feminist blog world — including one of Valenti's own blogs, "Yes Means Yes" — for not realizing that there were "feminisms," and not merely "feminism." Since Valenti claims that Palin opposes "real feminism," whatever that is, can we finally dispose of this meaningless line? To borrow a line from Simone de Beauvoir on psychoanalysis: when one criticizes the letter of the doctrine, it's insisted that one must actually just embrace the spirit of the argument, but once one embraces the spirit of the argument, they just want to bind you to the letter of the doctrine! (Of course, Valenti speaks out of both sides of her mouth, since later she claims that there is no true feminism and that it's actually a highly intellectually diverse movement. So I'm not sure what to argue with.)

I can't say that I'm a fan of Sarah Palin, but if she doesn't embody everything that feminism ought to stand for, then what we have on our hands is a manipulative language game. She "has it all": a college degree, a family, a high-profile career, and a history of taking on powerful, entrenched men in established institutions — and winning. The presidential race of 2008 exposed feminist ideology for the charade that it is. What a riot that Hillary Clinton, who rose to power on her cheating husband's coattails, was hailed as a feminist hero — while Sarah Palin, a self-made woman, was spat upon!

Of course, feminism originated as a classical liberal movement. Despite an organized effort by radical feminists to bury the true legacy of Mary Wollstonecraft, Elizabeth Cady Stanton, and Susan B. Anthony, these women had far more in common with Sarah Palin than with, say, Gloria Steinem — or Jessica Valenti, for that matter. Wollstonecraft and Stanton, especially, were adamant about the primacy of Enlightenment values. Radical feminists pay these women lip service as forerunners but dismiss their actual arguments as quaint or archaic. Stanton, in the famous Seneca Falls Declaration of 1844, purposely borrowed words from the Declaration of Independence. Like her counterpart Frederick Douglass in the early civil rights movement, Stanton did not dismiss the Founding Fathers as part of a 'hegemonic power discourse' intent on 'subjugating women and people of color.' She believed that America had to move forward because it was not being true to its own standards. The cure for women's ills was in more Enlightenment values, not a revolutionary program against them.

Valenti cites Betty Friedan as a founding mother of the modern feminism that Sarah Palin is somewhat dismissive of, but Friedan has been somewhat dismissive of recent feminism, as well, saying that it's gotten too victim-oriented. Susan Faludi decried her as having sold out to the patriarchy, and Friedan's pro-porn views put her at odds with the now-dominant feminism of Andrea Dworkin and Catherine MacKinnon, whose anti-pornography standpoint has found admirers in conservative women like Tammy Bruce, as well as much of the religious right. Sarah

Palin would probably find a lot to like in Dworkin's *Pornography: Men Possessing Women*.

Sarah Palin is typically feminist insofar as she complains about (generally non-existent) "glass ceilings" and "media sexism." She nauseatingly hails Geraldine Ferraro and Hillary Clinton as people who helped blaze the trail for her. And she has long been a member of Feminists for Life. But she is not drunk on fashionable nonsense such as the kind that came from, say, Kate Millett. She does not believe that feminism must be a "structural analysis of a world that oppresses women, an ideology based on the notion that patriarchy exists and that it needs to end." When you hear Foucault-esque jargon like "structural analysis [of power relations]" you know you're dealing with an airhead.

Valenti's feminism is uncommonly silly, actually. She is the author of a hilariously bad book called He's a Stud, She's a Slut, purporting to expose "double-standards" against women. Among the worst is the contention that while "she's a cougar, he's dating a younger woman." Really? I'm twenty years old and I can't even say that I think that Justin Bieber is cute without being called a pedophile by some people. Since when have men gotten away with being into younger people? Another: "He's an activist, she's a pain in the ass." Most people think they're all pains in the ass, actually. "He's hot and heady, she's brainy or boobilicious." Really? I think that most guys out there can attest to the jock/nerd dichotomy. "He's drunk, she's a victim." Hey! Now there's a real double-standard. That might make for a good article.

Feminism as we once knew it is dead. And, as the classical feminist Valenti criticizes, Christina Hoff Sommers, is apt to point out: that's a good thing. It means that its work is basically done. Now, the focus should shift back to the eternal question facing us all — men and women — the latter no longer merely the 'second sex': what does it mean to be a fulfilled member of one's sex? Sarah Palin's answer is as worthy of debate as Valenti's. Let's have this discussion. It's one well worth having.

The GOP's Real Problem? It's Not Conservative Enough

Huffington Post | 01.28.13

The Republican Party has simply become too conservative. This diagnosis of the right's electoral woes is ubiquitous. Polls show that a majority of Americans now agree.

With the rise of the Tea Party, it is hard to argue against the contention that the GOP has drifted significantly to the right in the Age of Obama. Talk radio, Fox News, and right-wing online news outlets like the Drudge Report have ensnared the party base in a nexus of what David Frum smartly called a "conservative entertainment complex." Red-state politicians like Sen. Rand Paul (R-KY) who toe the ideological line have been rewarded by that complex. But their brand of right-wing populism is as far removed from the true philosophical tenets of conservatism as the liberalism that it loathes.

The guiding principle of philosophical conservatism is prudence, or, applied wisdom. It's not a sexy term, and it doesn't elicit the sort of passionate reactions seen and heard at Tea Party rallies and on talk radio. It bows to circumstance, does not shun compromise, and is in touch with the lived experiences of individuals. It rejects radicalism and abstract ideology in the name of a down-to-earth realism that recognizes that the world's complexity and diversity. This is fundamentally a disposition — not a bullet-point agenda: unlike right-wing populists, real conservatives can disagree amongst themselves without threatening purges and excommunications.

This disposition has its modern roots in the speeches and writings of the 18th-century British statesman and political theorist Edmund Burke. In his most famous work, Reflections On the Revolution In France, he wrote:

> "Circumstances (which with some gentlemen pass for nothing) give in reality to every political principle its distinguishing colour, and discriminating effect. The circumstances are what render every civil and political scheme beneficial or noxious to mankind."

In other words: conservatism is practical. It's not a my-way-or-the-highway, all-or-nothing approach to governance — which is what makes the continuing influence of Tea Party radicals on the GOP so repellent.

Burke is also proof that conservatism proper is not socially reactionary or blind to the experiences of minority groups. He was an early opponent of slavery, spoke out against colonial abuses in India, and even supported the American Revolution. He stood opposed to abuses of power — and to those who treated other people like pawns on a chessboard to be manipulated in the name of a grand ideological vision.

Seen through a Burkean lens, the GOP's radicalized elements are simply not conservative. When Congressmen attempt to hold the country's financial system hostage to make a short-term political point about the national debt, that's not conservative — it's radical. When state legislatures insist on pushing through bills that require drug-testing for welfare recipients in spite of the fact that it wastes money on a problem that exists only the margins, that's not conservative — it's radical. When politicians refuse to admit that it is simply impossible to deport twelve million people to Mexico, that's not conservative — it's radical. The problem is not that right-of-center positions on the national debt or illegal immigration are illegitimate — it's that the approach that the far-right takes to governance on these issues is out-of-touch with its real-world consequences. There is nothing conservative about that.

Philosophical conservatism is not a panacea to our nation's problems — it can be too stuffy, too trusting of tradition, and too attached to visions of a mythical past. But it is a vital component of a healthy political system. If the Republican Party wants to become nationally competitive again, it will have to rediscover its virtues — and marginalize the radicals who deny them.

Ryan Sorba

"Well, I Don't Really Want to Shake Your Hand, You're Intrinsically Evil"
Andrew Sullivan, The Atlantic | 02.21.10

"Alex Knepper, an openly gay conservative, bumped into the young student of "natural law" at CPAC, who gave the entirely meretricious attack on the inclusion of "GOPride" [sic] at CPAC above. It's a revealing exchange. Sorba is quite fixated on the issue of homosexuality, for some reason. But here's the full exchange:

"My recollections are not perfect, of course, but Nate Gunderson should be able to help me fill in the details. The exchange is roughly as follows.

"So, you're the infamous Ryan Sorba," I said.

"Yep!"

"You've made quite a name for yourself."

"Haha, yeah. Where are you from?"

"I go to college around here, American University."

"What are you studying?"

"I was double-majoring in Political Science with a political theory focus and International Relations with an Islamic Studies focus, but I think I'm going to drop the latter. I can't take the relativistic preaching, the whitewashing of the burqa, Sayyid Qutb, the entire religion."

"Yeah, I know what you mean. So what did you think of my little tirade, then?"

"Oh, I thought it was quite evil, actually. I'm gay."

"You mean you think you're gay."

"No, I'm gay. Do you think it's a choice?"

"I think it's the result of a complex process of social and environmental factors, but that it's reversible."

"So, like, why is it that over one hundred animals have been observed engaging in homosexual sex in nature?"

"Well, only 0.2% of animals are known to do that."

" I mean, mammals, obviously, not ants, birds..."

"You know, animals masturbate, your dog humps your leg. Does your dog talk with a lisp?"

"Do I talk with a lisp?!" I yelled. "A little bit." (I later asked a couple of gay friends if I have a small lisp; both of them said I have no lisp whatsoever. Aron, who is straight, has said my voice is sometimes theatrical, but that I don't have a lisp.)

"Rudy Giuliani has a lisp. Is he gay?"

And then he went off on what he affectionately called "his tirade" giving the same mangled pseudo-Aristotelian spiel about how natural rights have to be grounded in natural law, meaning substance, and the final result of the reproductive organ must be a reproductive act, and all of that.

"Yeah, yeah, I get your argument, I understand it, " I tried to interrupt, But he said that I didn't, and he finished.

"But the vast majority of married couples partake in sodomy oral sex, anal sex, fetishes. Hasn't your girlfriend ever given you a blowjob? I think the government should just get out of the whole marriage business!"

Everyone around us agreed with that statement. Sensing some momentum, I went on:

"I'm the one who says that my values shouldn't have anything to do with government. It's you who wants to impose his own biases upon the rest of the world!"

Nate Gunderson pondered why it was such a burning issue for Ryan. "Because conservatives should not be upholding groups who support homosexual marriage and sodomy."
I said something I don't quite recall, and he mentioned something about how he could "take me on" physically if he needed to, to which I mentioned that his quick resort to force and threats said a lot about his political philosophy.
He said at around this point that he needed to go, and put out his hand to say goodbye. I stared at him, refusing to shake his hand, and he said "Well, I don't really want to shake your hand, you're intrinsically evil."
We all started walking away, with him talking to his girlfriend, and

me talking to Nate, blasting Sorba more. Someone who was with him asked Sorba:

"Really, though, he had a point: why do you care about this so much when the economy is in shambles and the debt is growing and spending is out of control?"

"Because it corrupts the youth and the culture," he replied. When we reached the area near the escalator downstairs, he turned on his camera. I put out my arms, striking a mocking pose, but realized he kept holding the camera at me.

"Wait, are you recording or taking a picture?" He was recording.

"Ah! OK…Well, I'd like to say, then, that the person behind the camera is a Hitler Youth waiting for a *fuhrer* to sweep him off his feet into a grand national project so he can sacrifice individuals like stock-fodder to his own biases."

He turned off the camera and approached me. I told him he should get his girlfriend to give him a blowjob so that he could experience the joys of sodomy. He put two of his fingers an inch from my face and said that he'd want to fight me if a girl wasn't around. "Ah, the use of force!" I said again. It essentially ended, there."

Scott Adams

Scott Adams, the Donald Trump of Punditry

New American Perspective | 09.26.16

Anyone who has subjected himself to the stream of brain-droppings of pundits and their peanut galleries on social media has undoubtedly crossed paths with some intrepid soul heralding the Gospel of Scott Adams. Mr. Adams, the creator of the witty comic strip Dilbert, has cultivated a cadre of disciples breathlessly proclaiming that he not only predicted the rise of Trump, but has unlocked the psychological secrets behind Trump's masterly art of persuasion. According to Mr. Adams, Trump is, whether by nature or study, privy to a host of so-subtle-only-a-fellow-master-can-detect-it techniques in rhetoric, body language, and more. He is playing four-dimensional chess while Hillary is playing checkers. More than this: a Trump landslide is likely impending, owing to a reserve of 'shy Trump voters' who are charmed by the man but won't admit it to pollsters — hell, maybe not even to themselves.

One obvious retort to this argument is that it is curious that a master of persuasion would find himself as the least-popular presidential nominee in American history — less popular than a woman Adams regularly suggests is a lying, dying, weak, weird, probably-criminal, uniquely unlikable representation of everything bad about ye olde Status Quo.

Adams' disciples will usually brook no criticism of their guru owing to their false belief that nobody predicted the results of the Republican primary with the same degree of accuracy.

Well, I did:

* Before the voting started, I declared that Trump has put Reaganism on death-watch and that the rank-and-file Republican voter is far less devoted to conservative ideology than the DC-NYC set believes.

* After Marco Rubio's strong third-place showing in Iowa and the betting markets pegged him as the likely nominee, I called him overrated, said the edge is still with Trump…

* After Trump's strong first-place showing in New Hampshire and Rubio's humiliating fifth-place finish, I said that the race was "effectively over," that Rubio blew his opportunity, and that Ted Cruz would meet the same electoral fate as Rick Santorum

* After Rubio's strong second-place showing in South Carolina and Bush's withdrawal, I said Rubio's standing in the race is an illusion… and reiterated that Cruz has no path to the nomination…

* After Super Tuesday, I called Trump's triumph 'staggering' and pointed out that he was building a non-traditional North-South coalition…"

…so let's move on to the dissection of Mr. Adams' work.

I should note that we cannot discount the possibility that Adams is a masterly troll enacting an election-long social experiment to see how many suckers he can reel in by imitating Trump's communication methods. Dilbert itself is a clue to this: it's strange to imagine Adams, who famously skewers corporate culture and capitalist excesses, would see a kindred spirit in Trump. But perhaps the comic is rooted in a sense of cynicism rather than irony; perhaps Adams truly believes the grandiose liars, shameless manipulators, and propagandists really do run the show in America, and wants to show off that knowledge.

At any rate, the essence of his appeal is that he performs the role of elections-analysis guru, projecting extraordinary confidence in his highly general predictions with the flimsiest of evidence: armchair 'psychologizing' is the most common trope in his quiver of pseudo-analysis, but he also employs convoluted marketing propaganda to convince his readers that up is down and black is white. When a birther-related controversy popped up for Trump last year, Mr. Adams argued that his juvenile rebuttals — a series of tweets — were in fact making use of a brilliant marketing technique called 'thinking past the sale,' in which Trump throws so much shit at the wall that something is bound to stick — something is bound to burrow in your mind and subtly move your perceptions of Trump as a possible president one or two tics closer to the zone of acceptability. The fact that this 'opportunity' took place in the context of bizarre incompetence, lies, and genuine racism is apparently irrelevant; all is subordinated to the 'wizard'-like principles of marketing.

Adams virtually never tells Trump supporters anything other than what they want to hear — but with his 'guru' cap on, he intimates not only that what his readers want to hear is the truth about the election (though he cynically hedges his bets by declaring that he's not, strictly speaking, a truth-teller — whatever), but that they are actually special people for hearing that truth. He doesn't state this directly: the seduction has to retain at least a gloss of subtlety for the one being seduced. But it is simply impossible to interact with his fans on social media and not perceive that this is the effect he has on his loyalists. The logical extension is that the guru has the most truth of all, and anyone who was also right about what the guru was right about could have only been right because their reasoning so happened to overlap with that of the guru.

Of course, it could be that what we see is what we get. It could be that Mr. Adams is a true-blue Trumpian charlatan who truly thinks he's an elections-analysis guru. In this case, his work is best read as unconscious autobiography. For instance, when he makes a claim like "Trump is a master persuader," we should instead read this as: "Trump is a master at persuading me, Scott Adams." If he says "There are lots of Shy Trump Voters," all it means is "I, Scott Adams, am a Shy Trump Voter." In this interpretation, Mr. Adams recognizes a fellow charlatan-entrepreneur in Trump and is convinced that being a bullshit artist always pays off when it comes to wealth, prestige, and power. Adams fundamentally agrees with P.T. Barnum and H.L. Mencken that there is a sucker born every minute and that no one has ever gone broke by underestimating the intelligence of the American people. Basically, then, Adams is just rooting for one of his own.   Let us now examine at his piece about the first presidential debate:

"Clinton won on points. She had more command of the details and the cleaner answers. Trump did a lot of interrupting and he was defensive. If this were a college debate competition, Clinton would be declared the winner. I call that victory on the 2D chess board. But voters don't care about facts and debating style. They care about how they feel. So let's talk about that."

Adams strongly implies here that he has special insights into what we could call voter psychology. He provides not a shred of empirical or theoretical evidence for this — just an emphatic tone ("Believe me!"). He also props up a false dichotomy — that the question before us is either about facts and style, or else feeling — rather than being about a mixture of many factors. He takes the dichotomy he made up as obviously accurate and simply moves on.

"For starters, Trump and Clinton both seemed "presidential" enough. That mattered more for Trump. We haven't seen him off the teleprompter lately. So Trump passed that test by being sufficiently serious."

Says who? According to what? Not the opinion polls. But, alas — we cannot interpret the polls without the help of the guru, since the guru knows something special about the polls; therefore, no appeal to evidence to the contrary will do, since other analysts lack the guru's unique interpretive methods.

"Clinton looked (to my eyes) as if she was drugged, tired, sick, or generally unhealthy, even though she was mentally alert and spoke well. But her eyes were telling a different story. She had the look of someone whose doctors had engineered 90 minutes of alertness for her just for the event. If she continues with a light campaign schedule, you should assume my observation is valid, and she wasn't at 100%."

Adams can 'just tell' — based on his private reading of what her eyes looked like — and if Clinton's campaign schedule continues as it is (which is likely!), we must assume his irresponsible and empty speculations are true because — because — well, because we just should..!

"Clinton's smile seemed forced, artificial, and frankly creepy. I'm already hearing on Twitter that mentioning a woman's smile is sexist. I understand the point. But when someone goes full Joker-face and tests the uncanny valley hypothesis at the same time, that's a bit different from telling a woman to "smile more." My neighbor Kristina hypothesized that Botox was making her smile look unnatural. Science tells us that when a person's mouth smiles, but their eyes don't match the smile, they look disingenuous if not creepy. Botox on your crow's feet lines around your eyes can give that effect. But whatever the reason, something looked off to me."

Here, Adams puts a fig-leaf over his completely arbitrary and childishly nasty insult by appealing to a 'hypothesis.' The specifics of the hypothesis are irrelevant; what's important is that he is able to appeal to one at all. A gross insult becomes somehow legitimate if the guru can attach a 'hypothesis' to it. It gives his insults the gloss of Science.

"By tomorrow, no one will remember what either of them said during the debate. But we will remember how they made us feel.

Clinton won the debate last night. And while she was doing it, Trump won the election. He had one thing to accomplish – being less scary – and he did it."

Really? No one will remember what they said? No one will remember what Trump said about his birther crusade, his tax returns, Rosie O'Donnell, his failure to pay contractors, or his obnoxious interruptions? Really? I suppose one mustn't doubt Mr. Adams...

I cannot say with any certainty whether Adams is not pulling one over on us. But there are throngs of intelligent and thoughtful people who take his writings at face-value. Most of them are Trump supporters enjoying rallying around a writer who keeps the faith alive that their candidate knows what he's doing and will ultimately prevail. They do not perceive themselves that way: they perceive themselves as having access to the special insights of a master analyst of a master of persuasion. This is clearly not true — again: Trump is profoundly unpopular, and Adams' reliance on pop-psychology and marketing rhetoric is impossible to take seriously once it's perceived for what it is. But whatever is at the bottom of things, Adams' act makes him the Donald Trump of punditry — a transparently phony con artist who relies on forcefulness, repetition, sleight-of-hand tricks, and marketing gimmicks rather than depth of insight. He saw Trump coming — but he was not the only one. Whatever he has said that's right is better expressed elsewhere, and what he gets wrong he gets horribly wrong. His wager that many people cannot tell the difference between his act and the real deal is, alas, at least to some degree, true.

Paul Ryan

Paul Ryan's New Budget: Ideological Wish-Fulfillment Fantasy

Huffington Post | 03.13.13

I have been a fan of House Budget Chairman Paul Ryan (R-WI) for several years now. I voted last year for Mitt Romney — nose held firmly tight — only because of Ryan's presence on the ticket. Quite simply, he is one of the only politicians in Washington who has demonstrated any sort of willingness to substantively address Medicare reform — and as both a young voter and a fiscal conservative, correcting that program's terrifying budgetary math ranks near the top of my priorities.   Our country's long-term debt crisis is really a crisis of an aging population coupled with rising health care costs. These factors will devastate Medicare if Congress obstinately insists on perpetuating the status quo into the decades ahead. As a society, we have agreed that the government should guarantee health coverage for senior citizens. If we are to guarantee coverage for future seniors, too, then comprehensive reform is essential. This isn't a controversial assertion — President Obama himself has publicly acknowledged it. He is right that this is the work of a generation: the system will go bankrupt if changes are not made, cheating millions of seniors out of coverage that they were promised. Ryan's voucher-style plan for Medicare reform — borrowed largely from ideas promoted by Brookings Institution scholar Alice Rivlin — would go a long way in correcting the structural fiscal issues that will otherwise sink the system in the decades to come.

Ryan's proposals are important less because his plan is the only viable one in Washington — Simpson-Bowles, of course, remains on the table — but because it is viable at all. It is crucial that competing entitlement reform ideas are discussed seriously and transparently. The GOP simply must have a credible plan on this issue. It is to Ryan's immense credit that he stepped forward on behalf of his party to address an issue that most Republicans have until recently refused to touch. Moreover, he has demonstrated that he is willing to compromise with his critics. Alice Rivlin initially opposed Ryan's plan, for instance, but warmed to it when he allowed for seniors to opt into traditional Medicare instead — a change that also brought Sen. Ron Wyden (D-OR) on board.

It is perplexing to me, then, that Ryan's new budget is premised on pure ideological wish-fulfillment: the repeal of Obamacare. There were always aspects of his plan that relied on rosy projections — an unrealistic rate of economic growth, for instance — but never anything so blatantly absurd. Obamacare is the law of the land, and it is not going anywhere. The new budget is dead-on-arrival if it insists upon repeal.

To be sure, I opposed Obamacare. Regardless of its merits as a universal coverage program, the law does nothing to control skyrocketing costs — without a doubt the number-one problem facing our health care system. It is also troubling to me that a supposedly progressive president would champion a law that mandates doing business with corporations as a requirement of citizenship. I was disappointed when the Supreme Court upheld the law, and I was disappointed that President Obama was reelected, thus securing the law's fate. Republicans poured their all into blocking and then overturning the law, but it was not to be.   Yet, Ryan can't let it go. He has adopted an uncharacteristic attitude: one that is more devoted to ideological grandstanding than to practical governance. Where is the man who worked with Sen. Wyden to make his reform proposals more palatable to the center-left? Where is the man who bucked the Tea Party and voted to raise the debt ceiling? Where is the man who voted for

TARP over the objections of right-wing populists who would have rather watched the economy burn? He was nowhere to be found when he unveiled his new budget.

I still admire Rep. Ryan and hope that he continues to make strides toward making serious entitlement reform possible. But if he wants to govern — rather than simply make an even bigger name for himself — then he needs to bow to reality and accept that elections have consequences — even elections that he lost.

Mitt Romney

Why I Just Can't Vote For Mitt Romney

Liberty News | 03.20.12

I look at Mitt Romney and I see a man dedicated to excellence, in the most conventional sense of the word: he has what, to most people, would seem to be a perfect life. He was born into a wealthy, influential family. He attended a prestigious university and graduated first in his class. He married a lovely woman and had five healthy, happy sons with her. He became a successful business executive, rose to prominence in his church, and then was elected governor of an important state. Now, as the final notch in his belt, he wants to become president.

But why?

Political philosophy is baffling to Mitt Romney because his lifeblood is efficacy, not ideas. People who work their way up the ladder of success like Romney has are too busy "being successful" to contemplate meaning and vision. They do what's expected of them, and they do it devilishly well. They color perfectly within the lines, creating pictures that are exquisitely drawn — but, because the outlines were already provided for them, are never very interesting or original. Thus, he runs in Massachusetts as a centrist and on a national level as a conservative. Not too hard to figure out. He wants to be an elected official because, well, it's what successful people do — not because he wants to put any philosophy into action. He doesn't really care about the issues all that much, and he's annoyed that others do. Romney wants to be president because it's the final check-box on his sublimely perfect resume. There's nothing else he hasn't done.

I can't vote for Mitt Romney because he doesn't want to *do something* — he wants to *be somebody*. Rick Santorum and other critics of Romney charge that he has no core, no guiding vision. But that's not entirely true: the core of Mitt Romney's campaign is that Mitt Romney really, really wants to be president. That's not enough of a reason to elect someone. And it's why conservatives just won't vote for him.

Judge Romney By His Religion

Frum Forum | 12.01.09

Before a defense of any kind of religious discrimination, one ought to make all of the necessary disclaimers: of course, I oppose government-sponsored discrimination, and I certainly would not support the kind of absurd treatment described by Steven Reinhart in his piece featured below. That being said, there is a legitimate case to be made for judging any candidate for office by his religious convictions. In late 2007, Mitt Romney made his somewhat-famous speech on religion, where he spoke the following words:

Freedom requires religion just as religion requires freedom. Freedom opens the windows of the soul so that man can discover his most profound beliefs and commune with God. Freedom and religion endure together, or perish alone.

Similarly, Romney has stated: "I believe in my Mormon faith and I endeavor to live by it… my faith is the faith of my fathers. I will be true to them and to my beliefs."

If freedom requires religion, if his Mormon faith sustains his life and he will be true to those practices, then I'm at an utter loss as to why we should ignore Romney's religious beliefs when evaluating his fitness for the White House.

We ask plenty of questions of any evangelical Christian candidate: what do his beliefs about the nature of God, the nature of the cosmos, and the meaning of man's life mean for his potential tenure in office? But for whatever reason, these questions are looked at as unnecessarily piercing and prejudiced when asked of a member of a minority faith.

When Sarah Palin gave her fumbling answer about Israel's settlements, several commentators jumped on her faith, wondering whether she subscribed to the bizarre but potent sect of modern Christianity that believes in the imminence of the End Times. Will anyone ask Mitt Romney about the oddities of the dogma of the Mormon Church? There are plenty of Mormon doctrines that may strike people as a bit odd — and rightly so. It is established in the church that the devout can reach the upper echelons of heaven and eventually become gods themselves, able to create their own universes and govern them as they see fit (all while supervised by the One True God). Why is it that when I bring this up to Romney fans, I am dismissed as a bigot?

As an atheist, I both understand and accept that in a predominantly Christian society, my thoughts on religion are necessarily going to open me up to questions. If I were to ever run for office (don't count on that, by the way), I would not expect that my supporters would try to ward off any questions about my atheism with the victim-card of discrimination. One's philosophy of religion contributes profoundly to his worldview and thus is a completely valid criterion by which to partially evaluate a candidate's fitness for office.

I view all religions as equally bizarre and irrational. But mainstream Christianity is often adopted as a cultural guise, meant for purposes of assimilation with the majority. Probe most self-described Christians and you'll find plenty of deviation from standard dogma. Devotion to Mormonism, which is completely outside of the American mainstream, requires a certain level of commitment. To what extent will Romney's faith influence his decision-making? I ask that question of devoted evangelicals and judge them accordingly, and I will do the same of a Mormon. And I am not going to apologize for that.

Gay, Republican, and Voting for Mitt Romney and Paul Ryan

Race 4 2012 | 10.30.12

Christopher Hennessey, a gay writer over at the Huffington Post, has penned a piece slamming Republicans who are supporters of same-sex marriage, yet support the Romney-Ryan ticket:

If I hear one more person explain how, even though they believe in gay rights, they're voting for Romney, I'm going to lose my mind. We need to find ways to reach these people who say they love us and call us friends.

Below I share the most salient moment from each post. The first is from Pulitzer and Tony Award-winning playwright Doug Wright, who said:

I wish my moderate Republican friends would simply be honest. They all say they're voting for Romney because of his economic policies (tenuous and ill-formed as they are), and that they disagree with him on gay rights. Fine. Then look me in the eye, speak with a level clear voice, and say, "My taxes and take-home pay mean more than your fundamental civil rights, the sanctity of your marriage, your right to visit an ailing spouse in the hospital, your dignity as a citizen of this country, your healthcare, your right to inherit, the mental welfare and emotional well-being of your youth, and your very personhood." It's like voting for George Wallace during the Civil Rights movements, and apologizing for his racism. You're still complicit. You're still perpetuating anti-gay legislation and cultural homophobia. You don't get to walk away clean, because you say you 'disagree' with your candidate on these issues.

The moment I read this I felt that it encapsulated feelings and ideas I'd been stewing in for weeks. "Yes!" I shouted at my computer screen. "I want you to face me! Tell me these are your priorities!" Can you imagine the cathartic moment? But more importantly, think about all the people who might not vote for Gov. Romney if they knew they had to look their gay and lesbians loved ones in the eyes after they did so.

Mr. Hennessey explicitly directs his post toward friends and family members of gays and lesbians, blithely assuming that no gay person could possibly have any interest in voting for Mitt Romney. Yet, here I am — I exist! — a gay man who is voting — well, voted early — for Mitt Romney and Paul Ryan, despite my support for same-sex marriage. Why?

Well, let's begin at the beginning: Marriage is not a "fundamental" civil right, and the comparison between George Wallace and Mitt Romney is demagogic and outrageous. The sleight-of-hand trick is this:

Gay activists have adopted marriage as a proxy war for the public acceptance of homosexuality, thus inappropriately smuggling what should properly be a cultural issue into the realm of electoral politics. Obviously, as a gay man, I believe that homosexuality should be publicly accepted — yet, I really do not think that electoral politics is the appropriate arena in which to conduct this argument. Astute Republican professionals have long recognized that same-sex marriage is inevitable and that, at this point, it is largely a matter of waiting for demographic shifts to take place. Can anyone recall any Romney-Ryan ad campaigns slamming the president's support for same-sex marriage? Of course not — they don't exist. Mitt Romney is a traditional man and opposes same-sex marriage, yet, he is not a fool: he understands that this is not a winning issue, and that embarking on a lost-cause crusade against same-sex marriage is not a particularly important issue during a time when we face a $16 trillion (and growing) public debt, the economy is stagnating for the middle-class, and a narrative is being written about American decline.

As a gay man, I'd like to call for a moratorium on comparisons between the fight for same-sex marriage and the Civil Rights Movement — are gay teenagers being forcibly segregated from their peers? Are gays and lesbians made to drink from separate water fountains? Are gay protesters being hosed by the police, or having dogs unleashed onto them? This is an utter farce. Liberals have a visceral urge to be "part of history," so they cook up these phony narratives so they can feel like they're "part of something." I voted for same-sex marriage on my ballot here in Maryland, and I hope that I'm fortunate enough to meet a man worth marrying, one day — yet, as a rational human being with a functioning brain, I find that cannot bring myself to engage in the kind of self-congratulation that is required to compare what I'm facing to what black people dealt with in the South during the era of segregation.

The fixation on same-sex marriage as a political issue, though, reveals a classic left-wing blind-spot. Over the past decade, public opinion has dramatically moved in favor of gay people and same-sex marriage — yet, which politician has taken the lead on this issue? Barack Obama has been utterly useless; he was officially opposed to it until he needed to whip up support among his gay supporters during this campaign season. No, the politicians have all but been silent. The prime movers here have been found in the culture. In 2004, when I was first beginning to recognize that I was gay, I faced a culture that, in my young eyes, seemed disapproving and wary. Here, just a decade later, the love that dare not speak its name has transformed into the love that won't shut the hell up!

From Lady Gaga to Glee, there has been an explosion of public support for gays and lesbians, especially in the youth culture. It is perplexing beyond belief to me that so many left-wing gay activists spend less time celebrating these gains than slavishly devoting themselves to the drudgery of politics. Politics is slow and messy — but when it comes to the social issues, the politics invariably responds to the culture. Again: If anyone can show me the Romney-Ryan ad campaign or stump speech slamming the president's support for same-sex marriage, I'd love to take a look at it. But no politician produced this sort of climate. Instead, it is the culture. Ironically, given their dominance in music, movies, and television, liberals tend to lack an appreciation for the role of culture in shaping society, instead pouring their devotion into political crusades. How can it be that a pro-same-sex-marriage celebrity can look into the camera and tell average people that the most important work that they can do on behalf of gay marriage is to vote for Barack Obama? These people are oblivious to their own influence. Left-wing obliviousness to culture — and my own classical conservative appreciation for its role — goes a long way in explaining the gulf between us on this issue.

Yet, given all that we face as a nation, what can explain the manic obsession with this issue? I look at my own lived experiences, for answers. I was obsessed with my sexuality when I was younger. As a gay man, I've had to devote an inordinate amount of time thinking about what straight people take for granted. Yet, the reason that I was so fixated on it was so that one day I wouldn't have to be so fixated on it. Once I'd figured it out, I could stop obsessing over it. Thinking about the basics of one's identity is like a ladder: You climb it so you can get to where you want to go — and then you leave the ladder behind. When I was 18, I wanted a gay roommate in college, I went to gay clubs, I had a GLBT button on my messenger bag (which is pretty gay in itself, no?), I posted on gay forums, I made sure that I met all the gay people that I could. Now, at 22 — Enough! Obsessing about my homosexuality is a relic of my younger years. As it is for heterosexuals, my sexual orientation is background noise in my mind at this point. Hence, when I walk into the voting booth, I'm doing it as a citizen, not as a homosexual. My homosexuality is a part of my identity, yes — but I'm also someone who holds a share of the public debt, a student, a worker, a patriot who values American global leadership, a taxpayer. (My gosh! — It's almost as if there were more to me than my homosexuality!) It seems to me that these activists are locked in an adolescent mindset.

I voted for Mitt Romney and Paul Ryan in the hopes that they might address entitlement reform, tax reform, and deficit-reduction. They may or may not succeed; what we know for sure is that Barack Obama is indifferent toward or incapable of addressing these issues. As an American citizen, I believe that these are among the most pressing issues of our time. Yet, I am supposed to cast aside these priorities of mine because the president personally supports — finally, in the heat of a campaign! — same-sex marriage? I am supposed to forget about everything but my sexual orientation when I enter the voting booth? And this is supposed to be...liberating? If same-sex marriage is legitimately the most important issue of our time, then let's hear the case for it — but for God's sake, with so much potentially at stake, with a debt crisis looming, with our international stature in decline, with the economy stagnating — don't give me this patronizing nonsense about my homosexuality being the be-all and end-all of my "dignity as a citizen of this country."

Why Romney Lost

Race 4 2012 | 11.11.12

Mitt Romney is a fundamentally decent man with conservative instincts. I think that he could have been a good president, had he been given the chance. But his temperament simply did not match the times.

Mitt Romney lost because the electorate did not trust that he actually understood their problems. He bested the president in the exit polls on questions about the economy, the deficit, managerial competence — yes — data points on a sheet of paper. Nobody in the world believes that Mitt Romney doesn't understand business. But ultimately, he's all business.

Consider his willingness to play ball with a man like Donald Trump, for instance. Donald Trump is a notorious self-promoter, a media tycoon whose claim to fame in the 2012 cycle was his bombastic insistence that President Obama isn't a citizen of the United States. Mitt Romney not only staged a spectacle of an endorsement by this man — but he actually went above and beyond, sponsoring a contest in which a donor could have dinner with the two of them!

In the conservative media bubble, we often brush these things off — Oh, Romney's doing what he has to do, kissing the right asses, covering the right bases. But consider what something like that means to the broader electorate. The election's over, so we don't have to finesse anything, right? — Donald Trump is a buffoon. He is a clownish, self-promoting ass who likely uses hundred-dollar-bills as toilet paper. And here was the future president of the United States, wining and dining this guy, this graceless ape of a man whose public political persona consisted of questioning the president's very citizenship. Donald Trump, this shameless, race-baiting, conspiracy-mongering clown — and the future president of the United States was at his beck and call, lining up his endorsement, kissing his ring.

Are we supposed to believe that these things don't matter?

In business, you most definitely can succeed while playing ball with the crazies. The CEO's playbook is one of being all things to all people — making sure everybody's happy, all the way up the chain. But the president is supposed to be a larger-than-life figure. He's supposed to rise above the absurdities and injustices of everyday life to represent something grand. So when the future president of the United States can't stand up to the Donald Trumps of the world — or those who call for "self-deportation," or those who call for using the Constitution as a political weapon against minority groups – it says something to people. And it creates a barrier of trust that prevents people from even beginning to examine extremely important conservative ideas about pressing issues. Entitlement reform, tax reform, restructuring the bureaucracy, shaking up education policy — all of these are ideas that Romney discussed in his campaign book, and which doubtless he would have liked to pursue had he been given the opportunity. But he won't have that opportunity, because he engaged in a cover-your-bases strategy that forced him to suppress those ideas.

Mitt Romney gambled his life's dream on translating his businessman's instincts to presidential politics. But successful presidential candidates don't analyze problems like data points on sheets of paper, and they don't court people in the same way that they would in a business venture. Successful presidential candidates speak to people's lived experiences — their dreams, their aspirations, their visions. They speak to the country as a whole — they see not only where the country is, but where the country is going. They refuse to play ball with the crazies. They have the ability to, somehow, rise above it all, and look like a leader. Successful presidential candidates present a shared vision for the future and persuade people to come in line behind them.

What conservatives need right now is leadership and vision — someone to to push out the clowns from the rodeo, modernize the party, and pull us into the 21st century.

Who's it gonna be?

Donald Trump

How Trump Put Reaganism On Death Watch

New American Perspective | 01.27.16

The indispensable Sean Trende of RealClearPolitics.com has repeatedly challenged my belief that Trump is the product of a base in revolt by pointing out that a surprisingly large portion of his support comes from self-described 'moderate' Republicans. The idea that Trump was attracting disproportionate support from supposedly moderate people made little sense to me, but I was not sure how to account for it. One popular argument used to be that Trump's success across all Republican factions was due mostly to his name ID and media domination. But Jeb Bush and Chris Christie for a very long time had much higher name ID than Ben Carson — and Carson was still frequently tying or defeating the former candidates among Republicans overall. Among conservatives, a less-covered, less-known conservative could beat more-covered, more-known 'center-right' candidates, so we would expect at least that these supposed 'moderates' would disproportionately break for Bush and Christie. But no: they liked Trump as much as anyone else.

I have come to a different conclusion: that 'moderate' Republicans since Reagan's presidency have never really been 'moderates' at all. Many if not most of them really are basically secular people who, just as much as self-described conservatives, have understood Reaganism — a mixture of pro-business and libertarian economics, religious advocacy, and a muscular foreign policy, with a nice helping of civic mythology — to be the foundation of the modern Republican Party. They call themselves 'moderate' because they de-emphasize issues like abortion, religion in public life, and same-sex marriage. They score only two out of three on the Reagan test, and they know it. Lest we forget beneath the recent torrent of positive coverage about homosexuality and feminism: the Religious Right was prominent and influential in the 1990s and through the early 2000s, during the 'culture war.' In polls, many secular Republicans will sooner identify as 'moderate' than 'conservative,' and 'somewhat conservative' sooner than 'very conservative.' But they are still tethered in Reaganism's assumptions and attitudes.

There's little that's 'moderate' about the modern Republican Party in the sense we ordinarily take that word. The truly centrist wing of the party abandoned it little by little in the 90s and the 00s, recognizing it was not welcome any longer — and now we can count their numbers in Congress using our hands. They were replaced by Jacksonian former Democrats, especially from the South, and Evangelicals new to politics. Reagan pushed out the old guard of moderate establishmentarians and brought in the populists. Reagan was not a populist himself, but he found room for them and promised them that his agenda would make them freer and more prosperous — and that it would take our down their enemies at home and abroad. And they accepted that.

Trump understood all this, but he also understood further: he wrote in his Art of the Deal that Reagan was a smooth talker who never delivered the goods. And he's right: Reagan didn't. Big Government kept growing. Christianity kept receding. 'Reaganomics' boosted growth, but, decades on, is no longer effective. Nobody feels freer for having elected Republicans. Even the revered Reagan could not reverse the intrinsic logic of liberal democracy. And what is worse: it turns out Reaganism is not actually very good at winning presidential elections. The nation as a whole was willing to send Reagan to Washington as a response to the excesses of liberalism in the 60s and 70s, but Reaganism as a positive ideology has never since been very popular, and Republicans have only won the popular vote once since Reagan's vice-president was elected in 1988 — and even that was during wartime, three years after the only attack on the American homeland since Pearl

Harbor.

About a quarter-century after the publication of Trump's book, the many political children Reagan fathered have caught on to the fact that two Bushes, Newt Gingrich, Tom DeLay, John Boehner, and others have repeatedly failed to deliver the goods — and are revolting. Many of them are intent on doubling-down on Reaganism and want to nominate a Reaganite with a radical temperament: Ted Cruz. Sen. Cruz, while taking on the 'establishment,' is still saying basically the same things conservatives have been saying for 40 years. But Trump is doing something different: he is implying their decades of ineffectiveness are the direct result of their dogmatic attachment to right-wing ideology. Siding mindlessly with elite business interests inevitably leads to acceptance or tolerance of policies like amnesty, unfettered free trade, and 'political correctness.' Hence Trump's Sanders-like attacks on Cruz's loans from Goldman-Sachs and his game-playing during the 2013-2014 immigration reform debate. Trump suggests, in essence: 'The aim is not to be a good disciple of someone else's belief system, but to deliver the goods to the people. The deals we should be making are deals where we get something we really want — not where we get only scraps while in the big picture our country keeps going to hell.' It seems there are more people open to this message than who are receptive to Cruz's message that what we really need is someone who really means it. Trump's shrewdness beats Cruz's sincerity. Reaganism as a doctrine is now in question.

Trump's attacks against his opponents, from Jeb Bush to Rich Lowry to Charles Krauthammer, are basically all the same, which is why they've all worked: 'Why should you listen to them? They're the same people who want to make a deal on amnesty. They're the same people who want you to shut your mouth about Islam while more Americans die. They don't want to admit that, so they criticize my tone, just like people criticize yours when you've tried to talk about these things honestly and have been called a bigot and a racist. We're not bigots or racists. We're good people who are going through hard times and nobody seems to care. I'm not gonna put up with the old guard's crap anymore, and neither should you. And the beauty of me is: I'm very rich. Unlike these other guys you've elected, I cannot be bought. I already have everything. I do not need anything they could give me, and I'm gonna change things. If you need proof, look at what's happened already.'

It seems the only way Trump can now lose the nomination is if his supporters fail to show up to vote. He made an audacious decision to make a play for the most alienated factions of the Republican Party. But even if he loses, there is no going back: the post-Trump Republican Party is not going to look like it did in May 2015.

The Trumpening

New American Perspective | 02.10.18

The outcome in New Hampshire could not have been more favorable to Donald Trump: Chris Christie's operatic kamikaze mission against Marco Rubio succeeded in spectacular fashion, humiliating the boy wonder for a second time by reducing him to a fifth-place finish in a state where just one week ago he had dreamed — plausibly — of finishing in second. But that is not all: John Kasich, roughly matching Jon Huntsman's 2012 total, was the one to snag Rubio's prize — and he will find himself utterly incapable of capitalizing on it. And because God has a sense of humor, Ted Cruz was able to block Jeb Bush from even claiming a spot in the Top 3.

With Rubio deflated and Kasich a poor fit for the state, Mr. Bush may win 2nd place in South Carolina — especially since he is finally wising up and bringing George W. Bush, beloved among the GOP base, to campaign for him. But even a strong second-place finish would be too little, too late for the unhappy warrior. And this result would only further muddle the prospects for the 'establishment lane,' besides. A relatively strong Iowa finish by Rubio, a relatively strong New Hampshire finish by Kasich, and a relatively strong South Carolina finish by Bush all amount to this: Donald Trump steamrolling the competition. (As for Ted Cruz, he is likely to meet the same fate as the last two 'winners' of Iowa.)   I am writing all of this not because I like it, but because it is true. One week ago, I endorsed the conventional wisdom that we had a three-man race on our hands. The race is now effectively over. Let's be blunt: Rubio had his shot to consolidate the center-right against Trump, and he blew it. Some will be tempted to blame Christie for spoiling a beautiful opportunity, but we should really be thanking him for doing us the favor of quickly exposing Rubio for the empty suit he's always been. Why the Republican 'establishment' ever tried to convince the center-right to rally around a hiding-in-plain-sight religious-rightist with no legislative accomplishments or policy heft is utterly mystifying. Since last autumn, conservative pundits have been trying to force Rubio down people's throats — maybe out of envy toward Obama, who knows? — but they somehow forgot that he had competitors who weren't going to just passively let that happen. The long-prophesied Rubio surge finally — finally — arrived, and it took just five days for an able prosecutor to snuff it out. (Maybe they should have tried to force Christie down people's throats instead?)   Given these dynamics, Trump is probably unstoppable. He is dominating the polls in every state that will vote over the next month, and he will only gain momentum from New Hampshire. There seems to be nothing he could possibly say that could alienate his current supporters.

As for the other personality-cult leader who triumphed last night: it is truly the height of chutzpah to declare that SuperPAC money corrupts our democracy on a night in which neither of the winners have SuperPACs, the second-place Republican finisher pulled it off via retail politicking, and the $100,000,000 man placed a distant fourth. Disciples of St. Bernie should enjoy the week in which their candidate leads the delegate count, because the race is about to shift to the South, and they will have to face the reality that not everyone in America is a white bourgeois-type aspiring to imitate the Swedes.

How Trump Represents the GOP

Facebook | 09.11.17

Proof that American democracy has mechanisms of representation hidden to the untrained eye: never before has a modern political party been so utterly at war with itself as today's Republican Party, and yet it still not only remained totally united against the Democratic Party in last year's election — but in doing so elected a Republican president who is ideologically at war with himself, the one man in the entire country who personally embodies with almost immaculate totality both the plutocratic and proletarian tendencies of the American right, and therefore is genuinely representative of the entire party, in all its mutated deformity.

Memo to Trump Opponents For the Next Four Years

New American Perspective | 12.29.16

As the dawn of the Trump era tiptoes ever-closer, many Democrats and skeptical Republicans have still not figured out what makes the president-elect 'tick.' It is fair to say that we have never known so little about the motives and core beliefs of an incoming president. Nonetheless, we know enough about him to cut through the noise and sketch an outline of what the opposition must note as it prepares for battle. If Trump's opponents want to effectively combat him, we will need to re-learn a lot of what we thought we already knew:

1. Remember: Trump Is Not an Ideologue, and He Has No Master Plan

Many vain attempts have been made to make sense of Trump by gathering the president-elect's various statements and attempting to discern a systemized ideology from them. But Trump has no ideology: he is more like former Chinese autocrat Deng Xiaoping, who declared that 'it does not matter what color a cat is, as long as it catches mice' — which is not to say that there are not discernible patterns in Trump's thought, but rather that they are informed more by 'gut,' instinct, or prejudice than by a coherent system of abstract principles.

This is a major part of his appeal. He boldly declared earlier in the year that, while he is a conservative, 'it's called the Republican Party, not the Conservative Party.' He does not attempt to justify his beliefs by appealing to time-honored principles: he defines what is politically good by its immediate practical effect — which is always hand-in-hand with increasing his power — and if existing theories conflict with Trump getting his way, then Trump insists on a new theory, rather than on accommodating his desires to pre-existing principles.

The Khan family wondered over the summer whether Trump had ever read the Constitution. The answer is that he probably hasn't but that it really doesn't matter. He is indifferent. He doesn't have contempt for it — he just doesn't care. He is motivated primarily by a desire to be the best, the most successful, at everything he pursues, whether it is money, celebrity, women, or political power. But he makes up the details as he goes along. He distrusts master plans.

Ultimately, ideological attacks against Trump are doomed to fail, as they did in both the Republican primary and the general election: his beliefs are instinct-driven, and his approach is transactional. Successful attacks against him must focus on a combination of his temperament and judgment on the one hand — and on the other, the practical, bottom-line effect of his policies.

2. Keep Your Eye On the Ball

Last month, progressive commentators made themselves dizzy with the idea that Trump was tweeting against the cast of Hamilton to distract the people from his political problems. Actually, Trump tweeted about Hamilton because he felt like it, and progressives were distracted by it because they found it annoying and vulgar. Progressives weren't played by Trump: they played themselves.

One reason Trump won was that his opposition, though united by hatred of him, could not agree on just what made him so odious. He floods the media with so much material that the practical effect is attacks against him can come across as having a scattershot character — as if his critics are throwing everything at the wall to see if something sticks. Again: there is no master plan at work here. Trump is histrionic: he was the king of the New York tabloids before he ever became a television celebrity or presidential candidate. He was acting manic on Twitter before he ever took a shot at the Bushes or the Clintons.

The lesson here is that the opposition must learn to keep its eye on the ball and resist being sucked into Trump's tabloid world of gossip, sensationalism, and noisy-but-meaningless conflict. If the goal is to resist a policy, then the correct response to, say, that tweet about Hamilton — is just to wave it off.

3. Learn How to Troll

We will never understand Trump or his supporters until we understand that, whatever their goal at-hand is, tactically all is subordinate to trolling the left. The entire Trump saga is, to a very large extent, a big joke to them — a master class in trolling — in part because they think liberalism has already transformed our culture into a big joke. To them, the real joke is that anyone is actually defending liberalism instead of trying to do something — anything — to remove the horrible status quo from power. And since they feel — correctly, to a large extent — that their demands are not taken seriously in ordinary discourse, they have made use of the tactics of the marginalized — to disorient, inflame, and win attention.

On the one hand, we should be wary of 'normalizing' these tactics. On the other hand, the genie is already out of the bottle to some extent. Critics should experiment with ways to confound Trump and his supporters. Irony, absurdity, ridicule, and playground teasing are all on the menu. Saul Alinsky was right: there is no effective response to ridicule. Trump's thin skin ensures there is plenty of material to work with, and that he is easily baited into self-destructive behavior — but opponents cannot deceive themselves that arguments with him can ever become like a collegiate debate society. We are about to enter a strange, post-modern presidency — and to some extent we have little choice but to play along.

4. Admit It When He's Right

One reason President Obama has retained a degree of sympathy even from people — like me — who opposed him is due to the sheer intransigence of his critics. If Obama discovered a cure for cancer, some of his opponents would berate him for looking down on people with Alzheimer's.

Trump's critics should not be like this. We should not want him to fail. We should cheer when he makes good decisions or successfully compromises a deal worth achieving. If he is able to get an infrastructure bill through Congress, that's a good thing. If he appoints a quality justice, that's a good thing. If he makes greater headway in the fight against ISIS, that's a good thing. Our interests are as Americans first and as Trump opponents second — and if we really want to effectively oppose Trump, we cannot allow ourselves to lose sight of that truth.

Everyone Needs to Calm Down a Little

New American Perspective | 02.05.17

A month after the election, I wrote this:

"There is no way around it: Trump is really bad. But I refuse to spend the next four years in perpetual disappointment, embarrassment, and outrage over what is likely to be a long series of unfortunate events."

I stand by that assessment. I have several friends telling me they are frightened by Trump, even personally frightened. They are frightened for women and minority groups, and they are frightened about the possible advent of a fascist regime.

The rhetoric driving these fears is out of hand. I firmly believe that some lamentable crisis is likely to take place in the next four years — probably in the foreign policy arena, where the president has his broadest powers — but once we cut through the clutter, the chaotic administration of the flurry of executive orders, and the rhetoric — we are most surely not there yet. The specter of fascism — a somewhat amorphous term that often just is invoked as a synonym for "extreme right-wing" — remains mostly inside progressives' heads.

Some of my social media commenters have suggested I am failing to appropriately speak out during a critical historical moment. But I have spoken out against Trump as much as anyone — repeatedly, and harshly. I have said that his election represents a turning point for our republic and an indictment of its current claims to greatness, that he has the soul of a tyrant, and that he is uniquely unqualified to be president. And unlike many people now complaining the loudest, I did all that was within my power to support the only person who could actually keep him from becoming president.

I don't trust Trump in the least. What I trust is our Constitution and the durability of liberal principles. We are not used to real instability and division in contemporary life; our Founders, however, were preeminently concerned with those matters. I trust in our system of separation of powers and checks and balances, I trust that we have good people in our courts and in the Senate — the judiciary will continue to prove its worth as the most reliable defender of individual liberty — and I trust that the voters will do the right thing in the 2018 midterm elections. And I perceive that, even though his presidency is a national disgrace, there is some truth to what my friend Tim Hulsey warned me about last year before the election took place: that it may be the case that the only thing worse than losing the election would be winning the election, given that whoever won was destined to enter office under a haze of illegitimacy and head up an almost-certain-to-fail administration under siege from all directions. Having lost the popular vote by a shockingly wide margin and entering office with historically low approval and favorability ratings, that haze is a thick fog.

The fact that Trump only won 45.9% of the vote — that a clear majority of Americans rejected him — also should be heartening for the long-term. It also may be good for America to "get this out of our system": if we must endure a moment like this, better it be now, sooner, and with a boorish, impulsive, self-destructive opposition leader, than later, after resentments have festered another 4-12 years, with, say, a young and articulate Pat Buchanan-type rather than a vulgar buffoon representing the right-populist/nationalist viewpoint.

And finally, not everything Trump says is simply wrong. The trajectory of "political correctness," especially on college campuses, has to be halted, and Trump has caused many progressives to engage in self-criticism on this front for the first time. He has brought attention to how imperiled is the consensus sustaining free trade: those on the left and right who believe in open markets will have to sharpen their rationales and their rhetoric. We talk as much about transgender restroom use as we do about the emptiness of the middle class recovery, and Americans will not stand for that forever. You can't just dismiss 46% of the country as fascist or ignorant. President Trumps do not come to power when people are not desperate and hurting. Instead of driving oneself insane with fears of fascism, people ought to use this opportunity to conceive of new political possibilities. Nothing else will make it possible to move on from Trump.

Sorry, Cinzia, But the Rot Comes From the Top

New American Perspective | 08.02.17

Cinzia's latest stream of columns are bold and full of confidence, despite a series of recent high-profile defeats for the president. They are best interpreted, however, as typical of the desperate blame-shifting occurring among Trump's core supporters as his presidency falls into disarray.

She has convinced herself that the blame for the humiliating Obamacare repeal fiasco rests at the feet of Mitch McConnell and Paul Ryan, and that they must go — as if any Republican on the planet is capable of uniting the Cruz-Paul-Lee faction of the GOP with the Collins-Murkowski one. The simple fact is that the Republican Party, despite its recent electoral successes, is still very much confused about its direction and very much internally divided — and its Senate majority, while real and useful, is simply too narrow to pass truly controversial legislation. One would think that Cinzia would look to our president — the man who styles himself as the master of 'the deal' — the man who united the national party in last year's election — the man who launched his campaign with a rousing speech in which declared that we needed a president "who wrote 'The Art of the Deal.'" But the man who 'wrote' 'Art of the Deal' was nowhere to be found when he should have been leading the way. He was a follower, not a leader — but Cinzia prefers to blame Reince Preibus for advising Trump to dance with the ones who brought him — Republicans, who also elected the Republican Congress — rather than blaming Trump for taking on a job for which he was obviously not prepared.

Cinzia blames the media for focusing on gossipy leaks, which Trump incompetently cannot stop — even as she spent months in 2016 justifying the constant press coverage of illegal WikiLeaks hacks on the basis that what's really important is not the leaking itself, but the information contained in the leaks; that, since Clinton is an important public figure, the people deserve to know about what's in them and that therefore her campaign and supporters had no right to complain. The point here is not that Clinton was treated unfairly — the point is that Cinzia has one set of rules for Trump and another, completely different set of rules for everyone else. She relies on ad hoc logic to defend Trump because he cannot possibly be seen in a positive light if he is judged by ordinary standards.

Instead of focusing on leaks and legal troubles, Cinzia would rather the media cover Trump's supposed accomplishments. Of course, Trump cut his teeth in the campaign season by going to war with the media, so it's sad and ironic that she would blame the press for not trying to prop him up in his hour of need. But more importantly, he really has not accomplished much of anything. To my mind, the only substantive policy shift so far has been his backing out of the Trans-Pacific Partnership: a win for China, which can now make a legitimate claim to forthcoming economic supremacy in that zone of the East. Backing out of the non-binding Paris Accord was all noise since it had no enforcement mechanism to begin with. The piecemeal chipping away at regulations are more about quantity than quality, and it is telling that Trump loyalists never offer any specifics. The ban on transgendered people in the military is completely made-up (the Pentagon does not consider a tweet a policy order). The vaunted 'travel ban' was so thin as to be practically non-existent. There has been policy change regarding NATO or NAFTA. We continue to be hostile toward Russia, Obamacare stands. Rates of illegal immigration were declining long before Trump took office. It is absurd to give the young Trump Administration credit for positive economic news (the president gets too much credit or blame for the state of the economy generally, besides). His management style is perceived more as that befitting his reality-TV past than as 'modern-day presidential.' His approval rating is in the toilet. He appointed a quality conservative justice in Neil Gorsuch — but that is no different than what Jeb Bush or John Kasich would have done, so there's nothing Trump-specific to report in that instance.

Devoid of real accomplishments, Trump fans can speak of his ability to 'change the conversation.' I suppose he has done that, but it has not been for the better. Never has this country seen a major party taken over by people so utterly indifferent to governing, so obsessed with petty fights with media personalities, pundits, and activists, so proudly policy-ignorant. The tragedy of Trump, as I have said, is his ability to drag everything and everyone down to his level. He is living proof that the problem of excessive polarization and tribal loyalty in politics is not destined to simply resolve itself.

I maintain that Trump is sincerely ignorant about the overwhelming majority of policy issues that do not directly affect his businesses. I think he really meant it when he asserted his belief that "no one knew healthcare could be so complicated." He really thought it was going to be "so easy" to pass a repeal bill. He sat on the sidelines during the policy fight because he knew that if he got involved, he would be stepping into an area in which he had no idea what he was doing and would probably make things worse. He doesn't really understand how Obamacare works. I think Cinzia will not realize the depth of trouble the failing Trump presidency is in until she accepts that Trump is a genuinely ignorant person, an entertainer who knows how to put on a good show and knows how to win an election — but does not know how to discern a good, viable policy, and does not know how to govern.

If Trump fans are really content with what he has done, though, then maybe we should be glad. If Cinzia thinks Trump is winning, then I say: good! We can endure three and a half more years of what has so far amounted to more of an embarrassment than a danger — so when this strange, sad saga is done, let's declare victory and get out.

Is Trump More Dangerous Or Embarrassing?

New American Perspective | 11.21.17

I fell in love with presidential politics during the 2004 race and have been writing about it ever since. I love the presidency. I love presidential campaigns. I think the president is always a vital player in corralling his party behind a coherent, purposeful agenda.

Since the inauguration, I been caught in a lull as a political writer, largely because, as I suggested in previous articles, President Donald Trump makes me less angry than depressed. Unlike all but a couple of past presidents, Trump is anything but a vital player, and is incapable of becoming one. He is worse than useless; he entered office as a lame duck and still has nothing to brag about but his victory over Hillary Clinton, whom Republicans quite obviously miss very much. Trump has spent the entirety of the last six months wielding his unique reverse-Hand-of-Midas ability to turn everything into shit — which he then proceeds to fling at everyone. It's "damn good for CBS"! But I didn't get into politics to cover it like a paparazzo.

A president who maxes out at a 45% approval rating and is stuck mostly in the 38-42% range is incapable of wielding leverage. He is neither feared nor loved. Leaders of Trump's own party casually dismiss his proposals, and he has so alienated the other party that he cannot possibly form viable non-traditional coalitions, despite running last year, in a sense, against both parties. For the last half-year it has been almost like America doesn't have a president. At best, Trump can hope to become a bill-signing machine for the Congressional GOP. But with nearly every plank of the Republican agenda stalled despite the party controlling nearly every conceivable part of government — the presidency, the Senate, the House, the Supreme Court, governorships, state legislatures — there is in a sense little to write about. Each time I try to write something about an event like Trump's classless, clownish speech to the Boy Scouts, I am stopped by the sentiment I expressed at the end of last year that I refuse to spend the next four years in perpetual anger and irritation. The healthiest way I can react to Trump's hijinx is to ignore them.

It depresses me that my opinion of the President of the United States is such that I can do little but roll my eyes at him and ignore him. But I would rather be depressed than fearful. I stand by what I wrote in February:

"I don't trust Trump in the least. What I trust is our Constitution and the durability of liberal principles. We are not used to real instability and division in contemporary life; our Founders, however, were preeminently concerned with those matters. I trust in our system of separation of powers and checks and balances, I trust that we have good people in our courts and in the Senate — the judiciary will continue to prove its worth as the most reliable defender of individual liberty — and I trust that the voters will do the right thing in the 2018 midterm elections. And I perceive that, even though his presidency is a national disgrace, there is some truth to what my friend Tim Hulsey warned me about last year before the election took place: that it may be the case that the only thing worse than losing the election would be winning the election, given that whoever won was destined to enter office under a haze of illegitimacy and head up an almost-certain-to-fail administration under siege from all directions."

So far, this has more-or-less come to pass. Even the vaunted 'travel ban' is mostly for show. That is the Trump brand, after all: little light, but lots and lots of heat. For now, Obamacare looks very much alive, and plans for a border wall look very much dead. In Neil Gorsuch, Trump has appointed a reasonable and accomplished justice. NATO and NAFTA are untouched, we finally bombed the Assad regime in Syria, the Iran Deal remains, and the United States not moved any closer toward a warm relationship with Vladimir Putin.

The most dangerous facet of the Trump presidency is his fans' cultish devotion to him — and their willingness to shrug their shoulders or even cheer as he inclines toward slashing or burning some new norm. The most strident among them carry a revolutionary mindset — witness Cinzia's desperate battle-plan to quell the obviously-legitimate questions surrounding Russia. She conflates collusion and puppetry, denying the latter as if it vindicates Trump from the charge of the former. She suggests shocking breaches of traditional protocol, including finding a way to sack Robert Mueller as special counsel — probably because she knows the Trump family's taxes are almost certainly a minefield of legally dubious practices. And she calls for too little, too late on trying to convince Americans that Russia is our friend — which coming from Trump would have no credibility whatsoever and which would be a terribly difficult sell from any politician, even a popular one, or one who is effective at something other than campaigning.

The other danger, which should not be understated by any means, is the potential for Trump to overreact to some crisis. I am fearful when I imagine some new 9/11 taking place under Trump, and how he might react: what fearful, angry, outraged Americans might authorize him to do. I do not wish to speculate, but we cannot dismiss or downplay the very real threat of his militaristic, hyper-security-oriented side rearing its head.

With his agenda stalled, his antics more-or-less successfully contained, and his daily agenda consisting mostly of shit-flinging, Trump is so far more of an embarrassment than a threat to the republic. There are still some days during which I am bitter that a deserving, hard-working nominee lost to this graceless pretender to the presidency — but if what we have seen so far is the worst Trump is capable of, then, between silent thank-yous to the Founders for their foresight, we should be grateful for every moment we feel merely embarrassed.

Why Does Trump Treat His Subordinates So Disgracefully?

New American Perspective | 03.13.18

President Trump has fired now-ex-Secretary of State Rex Tillerson. Although the timing of Tillerson's public execution is something of a surprise, it has been clear for some time that Tillerson's relationship with the president had become — how should we put this? — icy, which, coincidence of coincidences, is exactly what has become of his relationships with Attorney General Jeff Sessions, Chief of Staff John Kelly, and others. The common thread to these frayed relationships is the presence of the president. What is Trump trying to accomplish by firing Mr. Tillerson? I am not sure he knows, himself; the decision seems born more of restlessness than of deliberation. What Trump does think he knows is that he can get what he wants through sheer force of will — that, after enough lashing out, the dust is likely to settle in his favor. This has been, to a large extent, the story of his life. But there is little evidence so far that Trump's borderline-caricature personality has functioned well for him as ostensible Leader of the Free World.

The ancient conception of a tyrant could be paraphrased as one who insists on having through one means what he can only have through another. Trump thinks he has a hammer, and he has shaped enough external obstacles into nails that he has become to believe that all of life is like this; that all that limits him is an absence of will. What has made him this way? I think the key to understanding Trump's tyrannical soul is the simple observation that, since his brief stint in military school as a teenager, he has never been in a position in which he has had to be held accountable and does not know what accountability looks like. Owing to a convergence of peculiarities, he has never been required to significantly modify his speech or behavior in the face of external resistance, as almost all politicians have at some point in their lives. Quite understandably, after the experience of perpetually 'winning,' Trump came to view antisocial behavior as a viable strategy to fulfill his every whim. (One might say he has adopted a perverse version of the

Ayn Rand quote 'The question is not - Who is going to let me?, but rather - Who is going to stop me?')

Beside the effects of his considerable inheritance, which has allowed him to buy his way out of several legal situations in which he has left others holding the bag — as well marry beautiful and charming women like the First Lady, who would never otherwise have had an interest in him — the Trump Organization is structured like a family business, not a publicly-listed company like Amazon or Google. He has never had to issue quarterly reports to an executive board; he has never faced the risk of being fired for making a bad decision. And even in the context of his family business, he has not really served as the 'boss' of anyone else in a meaningful sense, given that his main commodity has always been — almost uniquely — himself, and an extension of himself, his luxury-lifestyle branding. Britney Spears' manager once said her job was to Be Britney Spears; one could say the same of Trump's larger-than-life persona. He was rewarded for his PT Barnum act with a popular primetime reality television show in which he acted out the plebeian fantasy of being the all-powerful Big Boss. But it did not resemble any of Trump's reality.   What we can speculate, then, is that, the primary lesson he has learned from all this — which is the lesson he brought to his 2016 campaign and has tried and failed to impose on the presidency — is that if he wants something badly enough — if he is insistent enough on it — then he can get it, and that it is due to the unique force of his personality that it is possible for him to get it. But he has finally reached a position in which lashing out will not secure for him what he wishes to secure: a successful presidency. The only way he can do this is if he can let go of some of the bad lessons he has learned from his life experiences. But as La Rochefoucauld said, 'there's no fool like an old fool,' and what seems more likely is another 34 months of the circus-freakshow.

Barack Obama

Obama's Cabinet Picks Clash With Message

CBS News via UWire and the American University Eagle | 11.22.08

Now that he no longer has to pretend to be a tax-cutting, corruption-busting, lobbyist-defying, bipartisan agent of reform, our illustrious president-elect, Barack Obama, has decided that he's more interested in bringing together a team of people who will ensure that he doesn't do anything stupid than he is in bringing about any sort of fundamental change. Perhaps he's realized that he's not quite sure what exactly he's supposed to do, given that he spent almost his entire time in the Senate running for the presidency. But let's give the man a break. After all, who better, really, to ensure integrity in the White House than Bill Clinton's friends?

Let's review: our next Attorney General looks to be Eric Holder, a former No. 2 in the Clinton Justice Department. Our next secretary of state? Possibly Bill Clinton's wife. Joe Biden's chief of staff, Ronald Klain, also served as Al Gore's chief of staff. John Podesta, the man heading up Barack Obama's presidential transition team, was Bill Clinton's deputy chief of staff. Rahm Emanuel, a former senior Clinton adviser, will serve as Obama's chief of staff. Obama's chief counsel will be Greg Craig, a former Clinton lawyer. Other former Clinton cabinet members that have found their way into Obama's team so far include: William Daley, Carol Browner and Federico Pena. It's not known at press time whether Monica Lewinsky will serve as an intern.

And what about those wicked lobbyists? On the campaign trail, Obama declared decisively "they won't find a job in [his] White House." Now that he doesn't have to tell people what they want to hear anymore, he's sounding a whole lot more like Hillary Clinton, who famously defended the role of lobbyists in front of MoveOn.org's annual conference. The Obama team has instituted a weird, arbitrary rule that says: if a lobbyist hasn't worked on behalf of any particular interest in more than a year, he is free to join the administration. I suppose this would help explain why Biden's chief of staff is a former lobbyist for Fannie Mae.

Of course, to anyone who has actually paid attention to Obama's record, this isn't particularly shocking: before he ran for president, he gladly dealt with lobbyists, taking plenty of money from them, including those of large insurance corporations. So now we know exactly how long Obama opposed lobbyists for: from the day he began running for the presidency until the day voters elected him. Obama's knee-jerk opposition to lobbyists and weird, undefined fetishism for change was never one of his stronger intellectual selling points; to a Republican observer such as myself, these developments are actually quite welcome. Obama's clearly a smart — if incredibly deceptive — fellow and these appointments should make the American people more comfortable with him than they were. If the worst that happens to this nation is a retread of the Clinton years, then the potential for redistribution of wealth should be a whole lot less terrifying than eye-rolling ourselves to death over the years to come.

But what should the Obama Cult do now? The man has turned off the switch on the 'Hopenosis' and has revealed the 'Change Brigade' for the useful idiots that they were. Even Obama's early opposition to the war in Iraq is looking increasingly meaningless, given that his vice-president and probable secretary of state were among the biggest Democratic cheerleaders for it. What should the cult do, then? Take it as a wonderful lesson about how fundamental change isn't the name of the game in American politics. In D.C., the more things change, they more they stay the same.

Obama Stands Up For the 9/11 Mosque

Frum Forum | 09.14.10

Somewhat shockingly, Obama's approach to the Ground Zero mosque issue has emerged as a libertarian one. In prepared remarks about it on Friday, he didn't feel the need to assert any (false) platitudes about "interfaith outreach" or defend the particular Muslims behind the initiative — he simply pointed out that people are free to build what they please on their own property: ...[A]s a citizen, and as president, I believe that Muslims have the same right to practice their religion as anyone else in this country. That includes the right to build a place of worship and a community center on private property in lower Manhattan, in accordance with local laws and ordinances," he said. The critics of the mosque weren't called racist or "Islamophobic," and the mosque was not defended on the merits of its goodness. Obama merely asserted that our laws grant people the right to do what they please with their own property.

Rep. Peter King's response was puzzling for its irrelevance: "It is insensitive and uncaring for the Muslim community to build a mosque in the shadow of ground zero. While the Muslim community has the right to build the mosque, they are abusing that right by needlessly offending so many people who have suffered so much." King and Obama, then, seem to agree that they have the right to build the mosque, which is really the key issue at hand here. Obama didn't ground his support for allowing the mosque to be built on the basis of the upstanding character of the imams behind it. The only relevant factor in allowing the mosque's development, as Obama correctly pointed out, is whether the property was acquired legally. Whether one is personally offended by its being built — as I am — has nothing to do with whether it should be permitted. One's rights don't evaporate upon the majority taking offense. Our rights exist primarily to defend not the majority, after all, but the offensive, the radical, the shocking, and the outlandish. Obama and I diverge drastically when it comes to the nature of Islam, and his respect for property rights has not always been particularly stellar. But on this issue, he is absolutely correct and the right is absolutely wrong.

Obama's Measured Gulf Spill Response

Frum Forum | 06.14.10

We can safely classify most of our nation's political commentators as partisan automatons who would cast a ballot for Pol Pot if he had the right letter behind his name. If the economy is performing poorly while your favored party is in power, then there's little that the ruling class can do about it. If the economy is booming, then it's thanks to the ruling class. And so on.

With that in mind, one should consider that the conservative response to the BP oil spill has been roughly the same as the president's daughter's: "Daddy, have you plugged the hole yet?"

Dick Morris — who, in his post-Clinton career, has metamorphosed into Stephen Colbert without the jokes — has declared that the administration's response is proof that Obama "doesn't have a clue," and that the spill could end up turning into the equivalent of the Bush Administration's response to Hurricane Katrina, if not Jimmy Carter's response to the Iranian Hostage Crisis. Rush Limbaugh has been shouting from the rooftops that the situation has turned into "Obama's Katrina," which could actually be read as some kind of tacit admission that he believes that the Bush Administration was truly incompetent during the response — even though he, like Sean Hannity, spent most of 2005 blaming Ray Nagin and Kathleen Blanco for the failure. Even the normally-reliable Rudy Giuliani, who has commendably refused to join the anti-banking lynch mob, has lunged at the president, stating that he has "made every mistake he could possibly make."

Now, President Obama is not a Certified Expert like James Cameron, but he at least has the brains needed not to overreact. He has soberly sat back, allowing BP to do its job. He is to be commended for what he hasn't done: he has not engaged in rabble-rousing, he has not called for the heads of corporate officials, and he has not bumblingly involved the federal government. This incident should also definitively put to rest the lunatic idea that the president is some kind of closet socialist: the Socialist Party USA has declared that the spill is a corporate crime proving that the industry should be nationalized. Obama has correctly pointed out that only the oil companies have the technology and expertise to get this done.

The truly conservative response to this — and by conservative I mean *temperamentally* so, not ideologically so: skeptical, sober, and realistic — is to say: shit happens; don't freak out, don't expect overnight solutions, and don't expect the president to be able to wave a wand and make it all go away. That this type of demagoguery remains the norm amongst the right is proof that we're not going to see any substantive change in focus if the GOP takes back the House this November.

Why Obama Lost the First Debate With Romney

Race 4 2012 | 10.05.12

Barack Obama is unique among American presidents in that he has spent his entire career successfully avoiding being directly questioned by a competent adversary from the opposing political party.

In 2004, he faced only token opposition in his race for the Senate, and once elected he immediately ran for the presidency — against a man possessed by the idea that to take the nation's probable first black president to task would be inappropriate. Obama walked into the other night's debate with Mitt Romney with the same attitude that he brought to his battles with Alan Keyes and John McCain — against whom he could simply run out the clock with impunity. In 2004, Barack Obama ran as a symbol: He represented the future; he was The One, an exciting new figure for the next generation. He repeated this act at the national level in 2008, offering the famous hope-and-change routine to a nation weary after eight years of controversy and division under the Bush Administration. Obama's presence on the stage against John McCain was an implicit proposition to America: Are you really going to let this guy get in the way of dynamic, generational change? John McCain wants to get in the way of this historical moment — *Can you believe this guy?* It was a role that McCain was all too willing to play.

In 2012, for the first time in his life (!), Barack Obama is an incumbent with a record. He can no longer live in the world of mere symbolism and potential. He has to deal with the realities of an unemployment rate he has failed to tame, inflation that can no longer be denied, deficits he has failed to control. Appeals to sentiment and symbolism alone are no longer an option. For once in his life, he must run on facts and figures — for once in his life, his opponent is the man who lives in the realm of potential. So what can Obama do? He can't run on his record. He doesn't have any new ideas. And he knows it: His body language oozed annoyance — *How dare this man? How dare he not behave like John McCain? Can you believe this guy?*

But America can believe that guy. Mitt Romney refused to roll over for the sake of a phony narrative — and Obama didn't know how to fight back. It was literally the first time in his life that he'd been held to account for his ideology, face-to-face, by a competent, prepared member of the Republican Party. It is simply astonishing to reflect upon this fact. Liberal pundits expressed shock that Obama was so utterly unprepared to be challenged — but why? What in the president's history could have prepared him for such a moment? There is nothing. And did it ever show: CNN's post-debate poll showed that Obama was simply annihilated — judging strictly by public response, it may very well have been the worst debate performance by a sitting president in modern history. And the ratings for the event were the highest since 1980.

If the president didn't find Wednesday night to be adequate preparation for the debates ahead, then he should gird his loins for something else he's not used to: Defeat. Because Mitt Romney wants to win. And for the first time in weeks, he has reason to believe that he can.

Why Barack Obama Deserves to Lose Re-Election

Race 4 2012 | 11.05.12

Barack Obama deserves to lose this election.

As Republicans, we spend a lot of time mocking the president's 2008 message of hope and change. But we should not forget that, to tens of millions of Americans fed up with how Washington conducts its business, candidate Obama was promising something rather specific — and rather thrilling, too. It wasn't about policy, really. It was a high-minded, idealistic vision about changing how we approach the business of politics. What was missing from our system, Obama said, was a unified sense of purpose. And here he stood, an outsider, untainted by years of assimilation to the system, who seemed to "get it." In his famous 2004 convention speech, he declared that Red State voters have gay friends, too, and that Blue State voters go to church and worship an awesome God. The pundits liked to slice and dice America into competing demographic groups, he said, but the president should unite us. He promised to go to Washington and fight not just for new policies, but for a new kind of politics; a clean break from the divisive Bush years. That's what change was supposed to mean. Does anyone remember that? I didn't vote for Obama, but it was easy to understand his appeal. His platform was big — it meant something.

That promise rests in utter ruins. The manner in which the president has conducted his re-election campaign is simply disgraceful. His campaign has accused Mitt Romney of thinking that soldiers and senior citizens are worthless bums. We have been told that Romney wants to drag civil rights back to the 1950s and "turn back the clock" for America's minority groups. That he "bets against America." That he harbors a deep-seated loathing toward women and wants to "wage war" on them.

These are not policy arguments. Nobody actually has a clue about what policies the president wants to pursue in his second term. These are not arguments about Mitt Romney's professional style, either. The president has virtually ignored Romney's record as Governor of Massachusetts. Instead, the focus of the Obama campaign has been a constant, calculated, deliberate attempt to ruin Romney's reputation and paint him as not just unworthy of the presidency, but as a fundamentally bad person unworthy of even basic respect.

Welcome to politics, right? This nastiness is as old as the republic. But there's something particularly jarring about a man whose main qualification for the presidency was his outsider status — his promise as a change agent — becoming the poster boy for that perennial division and nastiness. Without that promise, without that qualification, why did we put him into office in the first place? His proven executive skill? His deep record of legislative accomplishments? The premise of electing him in the first place was that maybe, just maybe, this guy was different. But he's not different. He's just like all of the useless politicians he railed against four years ago.

The president's policies have been ineffective. He is in over his head. This country needs new leadership. But the proposition I am making here goes beyond that. President Obama's re-election campaign has been disgracefully small and petty. And for that reason, not only does America deserve a new president, but Barack Obama personally deserves to lose this election.

Farewell to Eight Years of Adriftness

New American Perspective | 01.12.17

Except in comparison to Donald Trump, I can't say I'll miss President Barack Obama. From the very beginning of his first presidential campaign, I was deeply suspicious of what I viewed as a cult of personality: the slick, too-cool cultural phantasmagoria eliciting orgiastic joy from my peers: I was a freshman at American University in 2008, after all. I supported the moderate-but-hawkish Rudy Giuliani in the Republican primary contest (and Hillary Clinton against Obama) and eventually voted in the general election for John McCain, despite serious reservations over his temperament and the Palin pick, simply because I did not trust that someone such as Obama, with so little experience, could really have a successful presidency. Unlike my frightened conservative colleagues, I did not fear he would be a radically anti-war president, a wild-eyed socialist, or what-have-you, once he actually stepped into office and surveyed the tasks at hand. I merely believed that, despite being an intelligent, charismatic, capable man, the scope of the office and its responsibilities are overwhelming, and he had never been in charge of anything other than his campaign. You can have all the potential in the world, but experience counts — it takes more than a vision to force an idea to life. Moreover, hailing from safely blue Illinois and waltzing to his Senate victory, Obama never had to endure the full force of conservative opposition, and had no clue what he was in for.

I think for the most part that assessment was basically right. Obama often seemed outflanked by clever foreign adversaries, whether it was being caught off-guard by ISIS or our humiliation at the hands of Russia in Syria. He frequently adopted a sanguine attitude toward emerging threats, often seemed harsher with Israel than with Iran, and was embarrassed by Vladimir Putin more than once, owing most of all to his overestimation of his willingness to act in good faith. Beyond this, he punted the details of his major legislative achievements to Congress — which fortunately for him started out with a Democratic supermajority. As he campaigned across the nation for health care reform, he spoke only in the broadest terms and left it to Congress to hammer out an agreeable consensus-bill. He did not rally the nation around a particular vision, because he had none other than that he wanted to reform health care.

Really, Obama should have never focused on health care reform at all — not when the nation was fixated on jobs and the economy, which somehow took a backseat to reforming the sector that comprises nearly a sixth of our output during already-turbulent times. But this was not all: the bill that ultimately became law was premised on popular lies, pushed through with procedural gimmicks and individual buy-offs of senators from Nebraska and Louisiana, and was passed on an unprecedented party-line vote. Once that Democratic supermajority disappeared, Obama never again maneuvered a major piece of legislation through Congress. Obama mistook the repudiation of George W. Bush in 2008 for an endorsement of his vision of progressive social and economic change. He was never any kind of radical, but he was distinctively comfortable with progressive economic and social goals, and the progressive movement — and unsurprisingly, Republicans fought ferociously against every major piece of Democratic legislation from the start of his tenure. The economic policies he did undertake — bailing out the auto industry, Dodd-Frank — were meaningful as far as they went, but there should have been more concerning pocketbook issues. It is inexcusable that he chose to compromise on the woefully under-sized, pork-ridden stimulus, of all bills — the one bill that directly impacted citizens seeking work. Yet Obama seemed to have a kind of contempt for the ugly-but-necessary game-playing that takes place in Washington — clinging to a belief that he had a special ability to appeal to our higher angels. In the case of health care reform, he gave in to those tactics at the last minute, but otherwise he seemed to foolishly hold to the false hope that he could convince moderate Republicans to support progressive-lite legislation.

His domestic policy legacy is a grab-bag of half-measures and parlor tricks: Obamacare, designed to frustrate us into demanding single payer; feckless attempt after feckless attempt to shove through all-but-symbolic gun control legislation, executive overreach on immigration, moving too slowly on same-sex marriage and then too quickly on trans acceptance. The potential for an economic depression was removed by the much-despised, wrongly-despised bailout before Obama came into office, so we cannot credit him for averting that disaster.

His foreign policy was simply incoherent, and America looks right now as if it is not interested in setting the moral tone for a liberal world order, but rather is unsure of itself and its purpose, and in its own judgment. Our enemies are emboldened — in Russia, in Iran, in China, and across paramilitary Islamist networks. For the first time since the end of the Cold War, liberal democracy and its institutions are playing defense.

What, then, in eight years has been accomplished in which Obama was an essential player? What has he moved that any other Democrat could not? Why did we elect this man in particular? Would Hillary Clinton have accomplished more or less than Obama did with a Democratic supermajority at-hand?

Obama is facing the distinct possibility that his will be remembered as a decidedly average presidency, at best. I would happily accept Obama for four more years against the alternative of Trump — my standards have truly lowered! — but instead, we do get Trump, and he is also part of the Obama legacy, insofar as part of it was built on overreach and hubris. History will not forget that, either.

The Alt-Right

Alternative Right's Ugly Racism

Frum Forum | 03.13.10

Tim Mak is right: the website Alternative Right is run by a white nationalist, for white nationalists.

I happen to intermittently know Richard Spencer, the site's director. Through a couple of mutual contacts, I met him in the midst of CPAC 2009 and received a ride from him from Washington DC's Dupont Circle, where we were each protesting the censorship imposed upon Dutch parliamentarian Geert Wilders, to the Marriott Hotel where the convention was being held.

Along the way, things got a little testy. We somehow got into discussing biological differences between the races. Our ideological differences soon emerged, though, because, simply put, I am an individualist and he is a collectivist.

"Show me one black nation that's ever been run competently," he challenged me.

"That's a ridiculous methodology. I'll accept that claim for argument's sake and still say that it's bogus: African nations have not failed because the skin color of the people is black. The skin color is just a coincidence. It's the culture that's the problem."   "Not   true,"   he said. "You look at Liberia, where ex-slaves went back to Africa, tried to bring American ideals to the country, and failed, because the blacks wouldn't accept them."

"This is not Western," I said. "How can you possibly claim to stand for Western civilization? What's brilliant about our values is that they stand for the individual, not the supremacy of the group. You come to America, you're judged by your merits — not by what you look like."

After a few more back-and-forths, we arrived at our destination, and as our car-mates went ahead, he told me to stay with him for a minute so he could talk to me. As the others faded into the background, he moved just inches away from my face, gave me a menacing look and yelled: "You little child. How dare you talk to me — me! — about the West! You don't know the first thing about the West! You're a little twelve-year-old who thinks he knows shit. Don't you ever talk to me like that again or I will beat your face into the fucking ground!"

As with my infamous argument with gay-basher Ryan Sorba, my confrontations with collectivists always tend to end up degenerating into threats of physical force. Richard Spencer is a fairly tough guy, and I'm, well, kind of scrawny. So I kept my mouth shut. But I was frightened. I let him walk ahead of me, and it ended there. But that is the real Richard Spencer: a white nationalist, a bully, and an intellectual coward.

Richard Spencer's Nordic Supermen

Frum Forum | 03.14.10

Before one proceeds with an article explaining what goes on in the white nationalist world, it's probably important to explain exactly how one knows about it.

I have always been intrigued by the bizarre. I'm familiar with every weird movement in the book: from astral projection to suppressed Nazi technologies to black magick — yes, with a 'k', if it's loony, I've probably studied it. (With apologies to John Avlon, anyone who thinks that Glenn Beck and Keith Olbermann represent the lunatic fringe of America is not being very adventurous.) Why exactly I take such an interest in the field is something of a mystery even to me. I suppose that, to a degree, I'm attracted to the creepy, mystical aesthetic surrounding it. It's also continually fascinating to explore the outer regions of the human experience.

Now, anytime one researches this area, he's sooner or later bound to come across what I call the Nordic cult. Its dominant branch is 'Odinism,' which seeks to revive ancient Pagan tribal religions from Northern Europe, with a special focus on the warrior-god Odin. Alternative Right's Richard Spencer — who is also a former employee of The American Conservative, one might add — is in a Facebook group called the "IrminFolk Odinist Organization" (and another called "Society for the Re-Definition of the word 'RACISM'"). Odinism is typically — though not always — racialist in orientation, usually emphasizing the bloodline of the adherent. A white nationalist text I once stumbled across put it thus: "It's not you, it's the chain, the chain, the chain…"

Strictly speaking, they are not white supremacists. When white nationalists use the word "racism," they are not calling for the subjugation of other races. They simply want them to live somewhere else, with their "own kind." The races naturally do not intermingle well, they maintain, and inborn biological differences make it impossible to form a cohesive mixed-race society. As an article on Alternative Right puts it: diversity is a "siren song." This is by-the-book collectivism, no matter how much Spencer protests to the contrary. Contra Charles Johnson, none of this has anything to do with the Republican Party or mainstream conservatives. This is a fringe movement that gladly declares itself reactionary. One ought to understand it, though — to differentiate it from rank-and-file right-wing beliefs, and to grasp the beast as it is, rather than as one supposes it to be.

In the course of my readings, I picked up contacts within this bizarre movement, and was once invited to a white nationalist gathering by an acquaintance of mine who lives in the area. I'll call him John. I don't ask for John's conversation, nor did I ask for him to invite me to this event, but he's thirty years old and lives with his mother, so his social skills are a little lacking. He was told to bring someone he knew, and for whatever reason, he thought to ask a gay, atheist, classical liberal. I wasn't told the location — it was a secret! — so I just gave him my address and told him to scoop me up. After being hopelessly lost for about an hour, he finally arrived. Coincidentally, my mother was making her way home (I'm in college) at this very moment and wondered where on Earth I was heading and who on Earth I was with. Trying to explain it to her, John informed her, without looking her in the eyes, that it was a Northern European cultural festival. Fine, good enough explanation for her, she said — and as we drove off, he explained why he couldn't look at her in the eyes: she's a MILF! (Even the most manly and racially pure get nervous around pretty women.)

Sadly, when I arrived, the festival was already over. All that remained were four or five stragglers and the head honcho: a fat, hairy, shirtless man bearing a Thor's Hammer necklace. Now, I'd planned my day around this event and I didn't intend to leave without some good anecdotes, so I asked some of them for information about their ideology and their organizations. One of them handed me a business card promoting the "Wolves of Vinland," a "folkish heathen" organization that revolved around ancestor-worship, Nordic pagan imagery, and racial purity.

In the meantime, I'd seen the wife and children of the master of the house going back and forth. All of his young boys sported neo-Pagan Thor's Hammer necklaces, and their father proudly announced to his guests that he was raising his children to be warriors. Even at school, he said, they're proud of their ancestry. When students ask them why they wear the hammer, they'll explain that they are proud to be Nordic. (The subtext of the conversation was: 'I intend to live vicariously through them, for I am one hundred pounds too heavy to be any kind of warrior.')

I sat and watched in morbid curiosity. The conversation soon shifted to the direction of the movement, and three of them discussed who counted as legitimate members of the folk. The first man, whose ancestry could apparently be traced back to Northern Europe, thought that the folk, properly conceived, was strictly a Nordic venture. Norway usually gets top billing among subscribers to this line of thinking, but

Sweden and Denmark are almost always approved. Iceland and Finland are usually good to go, too. But to preserve the purity of the folk, there should be action toward excluding those of impure, non-Nordic ancestry. Another man, whose heritage was German, argued that the blood of the folk actually extended to central Europe and the surrounding areas. Conveniently enough, the third man, whose ancestry was Irish, believed that anyone of any European ancestry should be included in the folk. The folk are a pan-European movement, not a Northern European one — even though, he admitted, the purest folk were of Nordic descent.

They also discussed an event from earlier in the day, when a white woman apparently brought her racially impure boyfriend to the event. Many of the folk approached him, telling him that his presence made them uncomfortable. Not surpisingly, he was acquiescent and left. (What he was thinking by showing up in the first place, I have no idea.) John sat back in silence for most of the time, although I did provoke him by saying that he had a rather Jewish-looking nose. He was livid while driving me home: "You can't say things like that! They might think I'm a Jew! Please don't ever say anything about me looking like a Jew!" I suggested that he try to find friends who aren't going to judge him based upon whether he has a "Jew nose," but I somehow don't think the message hit home.

The 'Alternative Right' most diverges with American conservatism in the way that it takes a sledgehammer to classical liberalism. A crude 'might is right' philosophy is applied to human action, with the understanding that group loyalty and self-preservation within the collective is the only way to prosper. Richard Spencer seems to have picked at least part of it up after a hideously poor reading of the works of Friedrich Nietzsche — he is a self-proclaimed Nietzsche fanatic (although, like most wannabe-ubermensches, Spencer is little more than a scribbler). Christianity is abhorred because of its inclusiveness. Nietzsche's attack on the 'slave morality' of Christianity — which is a swipe at altruism, mostly — is extrapolated to an understanding that Judaism and Christianity are too racially impure. Anyone can become a Christian — all that's required is faith in the divinity of Jesus. This is what sparks the impetus to Odinism: it's more selective, and one's membership is determined by his genetic makeup, rather than individual accomplishments or personal beliefs.

Even one's musical tastes must be examined through the lens of race. White nationalists tend to pass over American pop culture in favor of Norwegian 'black' metal — bands such as Burzum, Emperor, and Immortal. Some of the musicians are racists, some are not; all are nihilistic and aggressive. Black metal is characterized by a depressive, hopeless sound, featuring thrashing guitars, inscrutable bass-lines, screamed vocals, and lyrics glorifying mystical fantasies and the icy landscapes of the North. If one keeps a certain distance from the music, it is actually quite gorgeous at times — if a bit of an acquired taste. (Burzum's "Dunkelheit" and Emperor's "The Acclamation of Bonds" are both excellent.)

Many of the musicians are infamous for church-burnings. Burzum's Varg Vikernes — or, as he prefers, 'Count Grishnackh' — was imprisoned fifteen years ago for the brutal slaying of a rival musician and was only recently released. A former drummer for the band Emperor was imprisoned for the murder of a gay man who propositioned him. Aggression, aggression, aggression. As a brief perusal of the comments at the website "Occidental Dissent," which reprinted my confrontation with Richard Spencer, will show, the attraction toward the violent nihilism embodied by these bands is hardly an accident.

While not all of the Alternative Right contributors subscribe to this silliness, a good portion do. Richard Spencer sympathizes with it, at the very least. But whatever the makeup of the sympathies of the contributors, one must not mistake Richard Spencer and the Alternative Right for conservatives. They're not, and they don't pretend to be. More of a cult than anything else, these proud reactionaries are primitivists, tribalists, and racialists. They despise modernity, classical liberalism, individualism, and any attempt to suppress what they view as the natural right of the hammer to tell the nail whether it stays up or gets pounded down.   The far-left has its deconstructionists and postmodernists, and the far-right has its reactionaries and tribalists. Neither camp is intellectually serious, neither has any real influence; both are composed of pseudo-intellectuals who think that they've stumbled onto The Real Truth that's being suppressed by an elite power structure (that's why they both hate the Jews!). The trouble comes when Spencer and his ilk try to wrap up their excrement in bows and ribbons. The fringe needs to stay confined to the fringe: that's why articles about these, er, folk, by me, Tim Mak, and David Frum are necessary.

Notes On the Alt-Right – Part II

New American Perspective | 09.16.17

Since the rise of Donald Trump, media interest in the 'alt-right' has spiked, and, understandably, Spencer has emerged among reporters as one of its favorite representatives. Since the Trump campaign took off, Spencer has made the rounds as a speaker on college campuses, notoriously led an audience in a Nazi-style salute of his Trumpenfuhrer, and participated in last weekend's already-infamous 'Unite the Right' march in Charlottesville, VA. (Although he may be most famous for being punched in the face.)

Since 2010, I developed *my* interest in the preservation of Western civilization by completing a Great Books graduate program at St. John's College — Annapolis, where I wrote and presented papers about Plato, Hobbes, Burke, and other great thinkers from our inheritance. Richard Spencer's pretend-interest in the West as a whole is merely a smokescreen for his real interest in a certain version of the West — a narrow vision rooted only in modern European history. Through his limited historical perspective, which is enabled by his ignorance of the Western canon, he can perpetuate the lie that 'whiteness,' rather than Christianity, is what bound Europe together. It was not so long ago that the notion that Swedes, Italians, Poles, and Irishmen were all of the same racial stock would have been met with laughter. But a combination of American liberalism — a universalist creed insofar as it proclaims that our rights are rooted in nature rather than convention — and opposition to blackness made the concept grow and stick.

As one of the leaders of last weekend's march in Charlottesville, where he held up his tiki-torch and joined in chants of 'Jews will not replace us!' alongside the likes of Mike Enoch, David Duke, Augustus Invictus, troll-haven writers from The Right Stuff, and some guy ranting about 'fucking Jew-lovers,' Spencer has affirmed that, yes, these are 'his supermen,' and these are the people he counts on to lead his movement and lead a resurgence of the West.

They have been emboldened, of course, by President Donald Trump. While the president is not a white nationalist, and Spencer and his ilk know this, they see him as moving the goalposts forward a little bit, shifting the terms of the conversation, and making it possible to ask questions that once seemed forbidden to ask — about immigration, race, nationality, and more. They hope that history will come to look at Trump's election as the beginning of a racial awakening among white Americans — a new recognition that, owing to policies pushed by a heavily-Jewish (that is: non-white, non-European, 'rootless,' 'deracinated,' etc.) media-financial-political empire, they are being racially displaced by non-whites while being manipulated into fighting amongst themselves over relatively minor issues like gender, sexual orientation, and class.

The 'alt-right' remains a small movement, largely limited to internet hideaways, and in a sense, Spencer and the people who attended the 'Unite the Right' rally don't represent anyone but themselves. They are trying to force their way into the conversation by arching their backs, attempting to appear stronger and bigger than they are. Like the president/troll-in-chief they admire, they have a keen sense of how to manipulate the media: how to push the right buttons to win press coverage, how to dissemble and equivocate — this was the point of the seemingly-innocuous 'alt-right' moniker in the first place — and how to hijack news stories to insert themselves into them. This raises the question of whether it is better to ignore them, or whether to adhere to the maxim that 'sunlight is the best disinfectant.' Charlottesville made clear that this movement is not ready for primetime, and such overt public displays, attracting such intense media coverage, are likely to backfire. I certainly decided myself many years ago that the 'alt-right' ought to have been nipped in the bud rather than ignored. But still — last weekend's so-called 'unity' march featured just a few hundred people — compare against 2010's 9/12 March on Washington, D.C., which attracted about a million people. Local Tea Party events routinely attracted more people than this march. Why should the world's eyes be upon them, looking at them as a looming threat rather than a repulsive nuisance barely worthy of consideration? Again, we must wonder whether these people even represent anyone but themselves.

In the end, the 'alt-right' white-nationalist set's tendency toward excess and self-destruction is likely to do them in, regardless of what reporters, writers, and activists choose to do. The movement's appeal is too narrow, its tone too vicious and hostile, its people too divided, its ideas too shallow and illiberal, and its strategy too scattershot. Spencer is what I said he was seven years ago, along with everyone else who attended that noxious gathering in Charlottesville: a white nationalist, a bully, and an intellectual coward.

Richard Spencer Replies

Richard Spencer, Alternative Right | 03.16.10

"Evidenced by his constant use of "collectivism" and "altruism" as cusswords, my guess is that Alex [Knepper] is really a devotee of a philosophy followed by many a 20-year-old, Ayn Randianism. (Most everyone I know was a Randian at some point during their undergraduate years. Thankfully, there was no David Frum around at the time to publish our embarrassing polemicizing.) And I don't think it's a coincidence that Alex's writings about me have taken the form of the typical Randian fantasy of the principled intellectual being persecuted by the irrational, violent mob."

Musicians

The Truth About Lady Gaga

Truth About Lady Gaga Blog | 01.02.11

Lady Gaga has been described as "a voice for our generation." She is a woman on the verge of releasing *Born This Way*, a potentially world-changing record which one person has called "the greatest album of this decade." The lead single of the same name has been dubbed the "anthem for our generation." Her concerts have been deemed "youth churches," and, as someone once put it: "the bitch can sing."

Oh, right — just so you know: all of those quotes are Lady Gaga talking about herself.

The Truth About Lady Gaga

Lady Gaga's favorite subject is Lady Gaga. She envisions herself as an enigmatic riddle wrapped inside a mysterious paradox. For my inability to understand this infinitely complex figure, I'm constantly being bashed over the head by her Monster Cult: I simply "don't 'get' her," they say. Browse YouTube comments or Twitter flame wars: her detractors are told that they fail to understand Gaga's deeper points about celebrity, fame, and art. If we understood what she was aiming at, we're told, we'd stop aiming our bayonets at her and proclaim ourselves Little Monsters, too.

In this essay — which will be ever-growing — I intend to chronicle, in fairly comprehensive fashion, why I totally do "get" Lady Gaga — and why to understand her is not to embrace her.

2010 was a watershed year for her — but for all the wrong reasons. Having achieved fame, she has shed the arty, self-knowing persona of her early period and has come to embody all of the pop life's worst attributes: egomania, pretension, and self-importance, topped off with a big, steaming pile of histrionics.

Let's begin by examining what exactly a 'Little Monster' is.

The Sociology of the Monster Cult

The first notable point about the term 'Little Monster' is that it did not evolve organically, as was the case with, say, Justin Bieber's equivalent, the 'Beliebers.' Lady Gaga herself decreed that her followers were her 'Little Monsters,' and they obediently followed suit in adopting the terminology. It was not a creation of the fans: 'Mother Monster' simply started calling them that during her concerts (or 'youth churches,' as she has called them) and they adopted the moniker without protest.

No big deal. But why 'monsters'? Let's allow Gaga to explain herself. Here, in her own words: the full text of the 'Manifesto of Little Monsters.'

There's something heroic about the way my fans operate their cameras. So precisely and intricately, so proudly, and so methodically. Like Kings writing the history of their people. It's their prolific nature that both creates and procures what will later be perceived as the "kingdom." So, the real truth about Lady Gaga fans lies in this sentiment: They are the kings. They are the queens. They write the history of the kingdom, while I am something of a devoted Jester. It is in the theory of perception that we have established our bond. Or, the lie, I should say, for which we kill. We are nothing without our image. Without our projection. Without the spiritual hologram of who we perceive ourselves to be, or to become, in the future.

The first thing that's notable about this startlingly incoherent manifesto is that it's actually not a manifesto. A manifesto is a body of work outlining the intentions and core components of an ideology or movement. Gaga's two-paragraph brain-droppings can be described as many things, but 'manifesto' is not a term that comes to mind. Second, if the manifesto is of Little Monsters, then it ought properly to be written by Little Monsters, not Lady Gaga. (And the word 'prolific'? I don't think it means what she thinks it means.) A proper fan community should be allowed to grow organically. But from the naming of the community to the expression of its ideas, the Monster Cult seems to be a strictly top-down operation: Lady Gaga issues the decrees, and the Monsters follow suit.

Gaga's inscrutable ramblings aside, the common explanation seems to be that 'monster' is a tongue-in-cheek reference to what is allegedly the nature of the typical Lady Gaga fan: eccentric, a bit freakish, maybe a bit of a misfit. Mother Monster thus styles herself as the Queen of the Misfits; a public representation of the positive, artistic role of the outcast. She diligently thanks her Monsters in all of her public speeches and appearances, declaring them her reason for living and even the true writers of *Born This Way*. In October 2010, Lady Gaga even took to her Twitter to announce that, for Halloween, she was going to dress up as a Little Monster. It takes a special kind of egomania to dress up as a fan of yourself for Halloween. But then, Lady Gaga's arrogance — already thoroughly documented in the first paragraph — is pretty extraordinary.

Breathtaking Arrogance

"The funny thing is that some people have reduced freedom to a brand. They think that it's trendy now to be free. They think it's trendy to be excited about your identity. When in truth, there is nothing trendy about Born This Way."

Gaga spoke those words as November 2010 drew to a close; the statement was a seeming allusion to a recent duo of #1 pop hits: Ke$ha's "We R Who We R," and Katy Perry's "Firework," both of which emphasize self-expression and individuality.

Gaga's statement is perplexing on a couple of levels. Somewhere along the line, this woman seems to have convinced herself that her music is about personal liberation, individuality, and self-expression. A cursory glance at Gaga's small catalog of music reveals that she has written a grand total of zero songs emphasizing this theme. And her most visible songs undercut the message on a grand scale: her major hits have been about getting wasted at a party ("Just Dance"), having sex ("Poker Face"), and ignoring your boyfriend while you're clubbing ("Telephone"). Who exactly, then, is Lady Gaga to be lecturing anyone else about lyrical themes?

The point I'm making here is not that there is something wrong with singing about booze, boys, and parties, but rather that if Lady Gaga is going to parade herself around as an exemplar of personal liberation, she really ought to write a song about something other than, well — booze, boys, and parties. There's nothing wrong with the topic, really: but can we please try not to pass it off as high art?

Worse, still: if Lady Gaga is serious about encouraging young people to embrace their identities, why on Earth would she be spitting upon others' efforts in furthering this message? Ke$ha and Katy Perry are high-profile pop singers, after all. One would think that Gaga would want to thank them for embracing a positive message. One would think that she would view them as allies in helping others. But alas, this is not the way that Lady Gaga operates: the disgusting truth seems to be that she simply wants the stage to herself. (Perhaps, one might venture, she'd recognized that the music she'd released to that point had absolutely nothing to do with individual expression — and was thus angry that other artists beat her to the punch.)

The obvious retort here by the Monster Cult is that Lady Gaga has been hard at work on an album full of songs about individual expression, self-acceptance, and personal liberation. This is, at least, what I've been breathlessly informed of by the Monsters: she's using mindless pop to get her foot in the door, or so goes the line — and then she'll unleash her high art. Fine. Maybe so. (Although, given the asinine inanity of the lyrics of "Born This Way," I highly doubt it.) But right now, we've heard nothing but talk. It would be bad enough if she'd released a song or two about individuality and then hit the road as a one-woman hype machine for her own brilliance. That's color-by-numbers, par-for-the-course industry arrogance, and it's never becoming. But Gaga's arrogance is virtually unprecedented: it takes a special kind of audacity to take cheap shots at others for putting out allegedly inferior versions of art that you have yet to even produce!

Strange Lies

MTV reported that Lady Gaga made this strange remark during one of her London shows: "Now, I don't know if you know this, but for those of you who don't know, I write all my own music. Every single lyric, melody and note was created by me. I am not manufactured. I'm a bad cat and coming for you 'cause I believe in you and I. It's not that I don't like to be humble, it's just that pop music has a pretty bad rap..."

Jacques of The Prophet Blog says all that needs to be said: "I wonder what RedOne, Darkchild, Fernando Garibay, Rob Fusari, Akon, Martin Kierszenbaum, and about fifty other engineers, backing vocalists, producers, writers, musicians, marketing assistants and A&R reps would have to say about that?"

In summary: Gaga's statement is objectively, provably false. This is not an opinion.

Some fans, mentally rejecting any negative information about Mother Monster that arrives at their desks, have rationalized this bizarre statement by claiming that Gaga comes up with all of the lyrics and melodies to her songs, and that the producers just add the instrumentals. It's easy to understand why this explanation is appealing to the Monster Cult: since nobody has specifically claimed credit for individual sections of each song, the melodies and lyrics can be chalked up to Gaga and her integrity, statement and all, remains roughly in tact. (To the Little Monster, the alternative — to admit that she's such an egomaniac that she feels that she can openly take credit for others' work in front of the world — is unthinkable.) Alas, the contention is too far-fetched to hold water. First of all, unless we are to dismiss the production as unimportant, irrelevant, or otherwise not notable, this still doesn't explain why Gaga would claim credit for "every note" on the album. (The album kicks off with "Just Dance," for instance, which begins with a synthesized "E." That qualifies as a note, yes? That's part of the production, yes? Which is credited to — why, I believe it's...RedOne.)

But furthermore, there is a marked quality difference between her work with marquee-name producers and the B-listers she chose to play around with. "Summerboy" is a passable pop song, but it's no "Boys Boys Boys." Left to her own devices, Gaga seems to prefer to write rock ballads, such as "You and I" or "Speechless." The intense, driving dance-pop sound that has become Gaga's signature is virtually all RedOne's doing.

Manufactured This Way

It's easy to forget it, but there are several videos that exist of a young woman named Stefani Germanotta performing soulful, smooth-jazz ballads for eager New York audiences. Germanotta — the woman lurking underneath the layers of "Lady Gaga" that have been applied to her — never felt the need to adorn herself in bras made out of meat, collect gay men as fashion accessories, or declare her concerts "youth churches" for politically active students.

Rob Fusari, the man behind "Paparazzi," has felt compelled to dish on Gaga's manufactured personality. Explaining that she'd initially been discovered in a New York nightclub as a promising prospect for a Strokes-style rock record, Fusari recounts his work with Gaga throughout 2006 on just such a project, but says that he felt like a fish out of water working on anything but R&B. After showing Stefani an article about how Nelly Furtado was launched back to superstardom after ditching folk-pop for pulsating dance music, he convinced her that club beats and performance art might actually be the way to go to achieve stardom — despite her preference for a more stripped-down sound. "Beautiful, Dirty, Rich" was the first dance song they recorded together, and the song caught the attention of Interscope. Sometime in 2007, she was introduced to RedOne, and the rest, as they say, is history. What to make of this? The Monster Cult dismisses Fusari out of hand as a bitter ex-boyfriend trying to steal Gaga's money in a frivolous lawsuit. He may very well be bitter, and his exorbitant lawsuit strikes me as a bit quixotic. But the kind of scenario Fusari describes is par-for-the-course in the business, and it's not as if Gaga's recent actions don't confirm his version of events: as noted, when Gaga is set loose, she prefers to pen songs like "Speechless" — songs that are fairly close to the kind of sound she'd originally been going for. There is certainly nothing shameful about adopting a new persona. But the hypocrisy reeks to high heavens: Lady Gaga has cast herself as the champion of misfits, eccentrics, and weirdos, telling them to embrace their identity, no matter what the costs; no matter what others might say to them. But she is particularly ill-equipped for such a role, given that she herself compromised her identity to win stardom! Stars like Ke$ha and Britney Spears happily admit that they wear masks on stage for the sake of performance. Lady Gaga, on the other hand, defiantly insists that nothing about her is an act; that her stage persona is a pristine representation of who she really is:

Alexander Fury: What do you think is the biggest misconception about you?

Lady Gaga: That I'm a character. Or that Gaga is separate from Stefani. We are one and the same, there is no difference...

Puh-leez. Go watch Stefani Germanotta perform. She's fantastic at what she does, and she loves doing it. "Lady Gaga" is nothing but a character played by that woman.

The Thinnest Skin In the Business

Given that she's not who she claims to be, it should probably not come as a surprise that she's got such a massive chip on her shoulder. Indeed, I have never seen a pop star as concerned as Lady Gaga about what her critics are saying about her. Never have I seen someone with such thin skin; who felt so strongly that they had something to prove. In addition to the above-documented statements where she (falsely) claims to write all of her own music and whines that there's actually nothing trendy about her music, consider this obnoxious video, where, in a grating tone, she yells "Surprise! A pop show — and the bitch can sing!" And when her mic cut out one night, she felt the need to intone: "I told you I don't lip-sync! My fucking mic just went out!"

Yeah, and? Virtually nobody in the industry except Britney Spears blatantly lip-syncs their way through entire concerts. Even the weaker singers — Katy Perry and Rihanna, for instance — give it their all, even when it comes up a little bit short. That Gaga feels the need to announce the fact that her vocals are live on such a repeated basis seems evidence to me that she's — oh, let's just put it politely: very insecure. It's absolutely baffling: she's on top of the world — what does she care whether some anonymous critic is accusing her of lip-syncing? In this sense, Gaga's public outbursts remind me of Sarah Palin. Both women are attractive divas; both of them think they're far more important than they actually are; both of them let their critics get to them; both of them wrongly believe themselves to be voices for their generation — and while both of them are beloved by a base of hardcore fans, it's hard to overlook the fact that they're both just a lil' bit nuts.

A Horrid Role Model

The following episode was a defining moment in the evolution of my thoughts about Lady Gaga. If we are to believe her that her Monsters are comprised primarily of misfits and lonely hearts — she notes that she has received plenty of letters from gay kids who had been kicked out of their homes, for instance — then what can we call her except foolish, irresponsible, and destructive — when she admits to dabbling in cocaine? She did "bags and bags" of cocaine when she was younger, she confessed, and implores her fans to not go down that road. But, well, that being said, she still admits to "occasionally" dabbling in cocaine since achieving superstardom! (Please try to imagine what people's reaction would be if Britney Spears told the world that she dabbled in cocaine.) Cocaine isn't like marijuana. It is not a falsely-stigmatized drug that does little more than send a person into a small high for a while. Cocaine is very dangerous, and Gaga, as a self-appointed spokeswoman for vulnerable young people, has a responsibility to transmit the right message. (And for the record: "Do as I say, not as I do" ain't that message.) She might be playing with fire, here: her fans absolutely worship her. At the very best, what we're now dealing with are thousands of people who are, at the very least, apologizing for or excusing her cocaine use. This is totally unacceptable. We cannot just excuse this as "Gaga being Gaga." Despite her claims to the contrary, she is a human being — one with immense influence over a lot of young people. Her breathtaking irresponsibility here is shameful. At the very least, she could have kept her damn mouth shut.

Queen of the Gays

For some reason, Gaga's Monster Cult always seems to think it has me trapped, here. "You love Britney Spears so much," Little Monsters say to me. "But when's the last time Britney Spears did anything for the gay community?"

First of all, I completely reject the notion that celebrities are somehow morally required to "speak out" on political and cultural issues. That singers are public figures is a byproduct of the widespread appeal of their craft, not their political aptitude. If Britney Spears just wants to perform, let her perform in peace. We don't demand that carpenters, teachers, or even lawyers become public advocates for political positions. Why should we expect the same of performers? Moreover, even if they're inclined to speak out, I believe that they should always weigh their options prudently: celebrity activism always serves as a double-edged sword. The headlines surrounding Gaga's Don't Ask Don't Tell activism were never, for instance, "Lady Gaga speaks out for gay rights," but rather "LADY GAGA!!!!! speaks out for gay rights." The celebrity always ends up overtaking the issue, rendering their efforts, intentionally or not, somewhat self-indulgent.

Second, how utterly patronizing is it to ask me such a question in the first place? Do Lady Gaga fans look at me and see nothing but a homosexual? Might it have occurred to the Monster Cult that I have other considerations in mind than my sexual orientation; that my life doesn't revolve around the fact that I'm gay? When Lady Gaga thanks "the gays" in her speeches, I wonder: would anyone thank "the blacks" for their support? Would any other minority group ever be lumped into such an undifferentiated, stereotypical mass? I have always maintained that Lady Gaga's affection for gay men is little more than glorified fag-haggery. She simply strikes me as someone whose first reaction to a gay friend's coming-out would be "Oh my gosh! I love gays! Can we go shopping?" Gay people, to Lady Gaga, are bunch of pink, glittery, fashion-obsessed queens. There's not a lot of difference between Christian conservatives' stereotypical views of gays and Lady Gaga's: the key distinction seems only to be that she likes that stereotype. It's incredibly condescending — and it's really a shame, given that she could be using her platform to empower young gay people to be truly individualistic, trailblazing, and self-empowered. Instead, she sends them down the path of the same-old same-old political nonsense, with a liberal dosage of trite cliches about "loving yourself."

The truth is that being gay doesn't have to be "about" anything. I think I speak for most gay people when I say that our sexual orientation is not a central part of our identity. Lady Gaga is positively obsessed with our homosexuality — and it's condescending, not liberating.

Miscellaneous Bullshit

Gaga is well-known for her living her act, but it's no accident that her meat dress is the top suggested search result on Google when one types in "Lady Gaga." Somewhat intriguingly, though, she appears strangely self-conscious about her sensationalist tactics. In a rambling, incoherent attempt to justify the artistic merits of her meat dress, she fumbled around awkwardly to Ellen DeGeneres, jumping from one piece of nonsense to another, none of them connected to the other in any discernible way:

"However, it has many interpretations, but for me this evening ... If we don't stand up for what we believe in and if we don't fight for our rights, pretty soon we're going to have as much rights as the meat on our own bones."

...What?

"And I am not a piece of meat," she added.

...Yeah, that too!

And, infamously, Gaga declared to Vanity Fair that she feared sex with men, lest they rob her of her creativity through her vagina. (Imagine if Taylor Swift had said this.)

How much absurdist bullshit does Gaga have to spout before we finally declare her nutty, rather than merely eccentric?

We Arrive at the Real Problem

I don't want to dislike Lady Gaga. The heart of the problem is not what has truly made her a star: her music is intense and driving, her fashion sense is interesting, and much of her showboating is entertaining and part of a long tradition of pop divas, inherited from the likes of Cher, Madonna, and Britney Spears. And it's mostly those aspects that are appealing to the public. The key problem is the utter disconnect — even discord — between perception and reality amongst her and her fans. I can always enjoy Ke$ha's music, for instance, mindless and carefree as it is, because she never pretends to be anything other than what she is: a pop artist who makes fun party music. There's little substantive difference between the topical themes of Ke$ha and Lady Gaga's music, but Ke$ha isn't out there pushing her work as high art. Gaga and her fans present her as an avant-garde, politically-conscious revolutionary, single-handedly bringing art, style, and sensibility back to the pop arena. She is not doing that. Since the release of The Fame Monster, she has been a cancer on the pop arena, epitomizing everything that people loathe about showbiz. She is a narcissistic egomaniac running amok on the world stage, unleashing havoc on the pop world, and talking down to anyone who gets in her way.

I wonder what the Lady Gaga of 2008 would have to say about the Lady Gaga of 2010. That was the Lady Gaga I once loved: the self-knowing, humble, fun-loving Lady Gaga who I requested at the clubs, rooted for at awards shows, introduced to my friends, inspired me to take fashion risks, and saw in concert. Wherever she is, I want her back. The pop music fans who once rooted for her but just couldn't swallow the Monster Cult bullshit are still out there. And we are eagerly awaiting her return.

Nicki Minaj: My Kind of Feminist

The Re-Examiner | 11.01.10

Her debut album won't be released for another two weeks, but Queens rapper Nicki Minaj is already shaking up pop culture and reminding us what a truly independent, pro-sex feminism looks like.

Minaj made the rounds with guest features on tracks by the likes of Ludacris and Christina Aguilera — not to mention the riotously dumb hit "Bedrock," a collaboration with her home base, Young Money (headed by the inexcusably-overrated Lil' Wayne). She's impacted the culture like an electric current by actually being what Lady Gaga only pretends to be: independent, super-stylish, and not afraid to inject some eccentricity into the scene.   Pro-sex feminists and gay men must embrace Nicki Minaj. Her arty, self-reliant femininity holds a magnetic pull over the latter, and should give the former much cause for celebration: she is defiantly open-minded about sexuality. While the likes of Katy Perry playfully toy with sex, Minaj wields it like lightning. She raps about girls, but rejects media attempts to pin her orientation down: "I just don't like that people want you to say what you are, who you are. I just am. I do what the fuck I want to do…you've got to let people feel comfortable with saying what they want to say when they want to say it. I don't want to feel like I've got the gun pointed at my head and you're about to pull the trigger if I don't say what you want to hear." No 'solidarity' here; no intense moment of revelation, just exploration — this defiant brand of sexuality is a gigantic middle-finger to the identity-politic culture.   Minaj combines her ambiguous sexuality with a fierce sense of beauty and a keen, street-smart attitude. Refreshingly, she doesn't take herself too seriously: she self-identifies as a comedian, calls her own songs stupid, dismisses her beefs as the equivalent of a schoolyard basketball game — that is: a self-contained bubble — and has concocted a handful of self-knowingly silly alter egos, including a "gay man who lives inside of her." She heaps praise upon herself for being hot enough to make gay men want to impersonate her raps online.

She's taken some heat for embracing Barbie in her image. On her *Pink Friday* cover, Minaj appears as Barbie, with over-sized legs and plucked-off arms, and, in an echo of Britney Spears' "Gimme More," has been known to randomly shout "It's Barbie, bitch!" All of this has prompted criticism from certain corners, concerned with Barbie's 'plasticity' and phoniness. But Minaj is too confident for that: "Once I figure something is irritating people, I'm going to do it more — because I like to get on your nerves until you realize how fucking stupid you are." Boom! Indeed, Barbie is the perfect icon for Minaj to identify with: she has an endless number of personae, none of them necessarily connected, all of them dependent upon the mood of the master at the helm. Minaj is the master of her personae, from the uppity British woman to the gay man who lives inside of her (preposterously named after Roman Polanski). She might wear a different mask tomorrow than she did yesterday, or care about a different issue: you'll get none of Lady Gaga's childish bromides about "God loving everyone in their own special way" from Nicki Minaj. Her persona is too playful and inconsistent.

Her flow is admittedly average, but her swagger — and her flair for the dramatic — is undeniable. She shoves it in the face of the old guard of feminism. Nicki Minaj, whether she means to make a statement or not, is pro-art, pro-sex, and anti-identity politics. The world needs that, and is moreover ready for that — and that's why she's found such a receptive audience. I can't wait for *Pink Friday.*

Review: Epica – The Quantum Enigma

Metal Archives | 01.27.18

I am a supreme fan of Epica, having seen them live four times in the last decade and evangelizing their work to any willing listeners. Since The Quantum Enigma, Epica seems to be at their critical and commercial zenith, and yet I find myself feeling totally unsatisfied. How can this be?

Although they have crept closer and closer to a glossy, modern-metal sound on every album since the start of their career, making their first decisive break with 2009's excellent *Design Your Universe, The Quantum Enigma* finally sees the fulfillment of Epica's long evolution. The production on this album is so full of slickly mixed and compressed sound that it sounds virtually flat at times; it threatens to, and often does, sap every drop of character out of the recording. Every band member does their job well, but nothing crackles.

The band has buried an incredible fact in its liner notes: Mark Jansen is no longer its primary songwriter. Jansen had always been responsible for the vast majority of Epica's output, and his exchange of energies and ideas with vocalist Simone Simons gave Epica its unique characteristics, including its dialogic lyrics and push-and-pull between the universal and the particular. On even its previous outing, 2012's *Requiem for the Indifferent,* Jansen is credited as the primary composer (not lyricist) on nine of thirteen tracks, and as a secondary composer on one additional track. On *The Quantum Enigma* he has composing credits on only four songs, although his lyrics — which are far inferior to his music and often preachy and overly speculative — show up on seven. Sure, there are highlights, but none of them hit the desired emotional highs: "Omen (The Ghoulish Malady)" and the lengthy title track, both written primarily by Jansen, have their moments, and the first track-pair,

"Originem/The Second Stone", is worth a listen — but overall, the album showcases all of what I have always believed weakened Epica's music: melodies that chase down the runway but never take off, orchestrations that try to make up for with size what they lack in character, and lyrics that are alternately preachy and just plain lame — take this sing-songy silliness from the title track: "New perceptions keep us inspired/Ingenuity is required!"

What is most insulting about this album (as well as its follow-up) is that emotionally and thematically it offers nothing but more of the same to listeners who have been engaged from the beginning. If I knew nothing of *Design Your Universe*, I might be entranced or at least highly intrigued by *The Quantum Enigma*, with its exploration of psychedelic, mystical, and philosophical themes, propelling guitar work, and grandiose orchestrations (which actually take more of a backseat on this record than any previous one). But by this point, these songs are retreads of retreads; everything explored on this album has already been explored on *Design Your Universe*, and better.

If you are new to Epica, this could provide a gateway to their better, earlier-and-mid-career works. But don't let the hype around this one deceive you: this is Epica minus its heart.

Review: Emperor – IX Equilibrium

Metal Archives | 01.27.17

On the back cover of their second record, *Anthems to the Welkin at Dusk,* Emperor pompously proclaimed that they play "sophisticated black metal art exclusively." By the time *IX Equilibrium* dropped, at least, that was actually true, and the black metal kiddies no longer could make sense of what the band was trying to accomplish. As I stated in my review of *Prometheus*, it is a real shame that so much of the fan community has so egregiously misunderstood the band's later works, which are clearly superior to their older works, but since — there is no way of saying it without sounding pompous myself — the themes of the album are necessarily accessible only to a few, that was probably inevitable.

Despite its greatness, an atmosphere-reliant record like *In the Nightside Eclipse* is infinitely more accessible than *IX Equilibrium*, which demands attentive, active listening. It insists that you learn the lyrics to each song, since they are not, as on an album like *Nightside*, just a random smattering of evil, fantasy-based word-strings — however good — that are more-or-less interchangeable with the lyrics of any other song on the album. *IX Equilibrium* takes its cues most of all from *Anthems*' "With Strength I Burn" and its lyrical turn toward philosophy and self-criticism. The lyrics and the music are deeply intertwined, and the pacing and intensity ebbs and flows with the movement of the words. A prime example is the magisterial "Decrystallizing Reason," one of Emperor's most remarkable accomplishments, which speaks back to Reason as a demi-god who demands allegiance from seekers and inflicts suffering as the cost of knowing. The music visits all of the emotional marks of this theme: steadiness in inquiry, manic excitement at discovery, the depressive self-awareness of realizing a little too much. This theme is revisited on "Of Blindness and Subsequent Seers," an excellent note on which to end the album, as well the soaring "An Elegy of Icaros," whose titular character stands next to Prometheus as one of mankind's representatives of seekers.

Not that this record is devoid of raw power: opener 'Curse You All Men' captures the same feeling of majestic aggression found on the best tracks of *Anthems,* 'and 'Sworn,' which is the thrashiest track the band has ever recorded and features one of their most undeniable riffs, epitomize this tendency. Indeed, in some ways, *IX Equilibrium* is Emperor's most purely metal record. But the raw feeling of power is not the center that holds the record together, as those looking for it have all discovered. The most striking downside of the album is the same as on all of Emperor's other records: sometimes there are too many ingredients in the pot, and there is a failure to recognize that this section does not naturally flow from that section, leaving certain songs feeling patched-together at times; at other times, I find myself turning on songs only to wait for a certain part to play. Another reviewer noted that there is a kind of pop gloss to *IX Equilibrium*, and he was not wrong — there is a 'catchiness' to certain parts of the record that is undeniable: 'Sworn' seems to me to be the most obvious: no wonder Ulver thought it was the prime candidate to be given a strange modern remix.

This is not the band's best album — that title goes to the towering masterpiece which is *Prometheus* — but those who cannot make sense of it and embrace it really do not understand what Emperor was really all about.

ABBA Is Reuniting. Is That Really Such a Good Idea?

New American Perspective | 05.22.18

That ABBA is reuniting after nearly 40 years comes at an uncanny time in my life. Last autumn I had a major ABBA phase, during which I listened to all of their albums in-full several times and gained an appreciation for them rivaling my other pop favorites, like Madonna. I like their standards — like 'Dancing Queen' and 'Lay All Your Love On Me' — and their deep cuts — like 'Kisses of Fire' and 'Like An Angel Passing Through My Room.' I love their final three albums in particular (and their final pair of stand-alone singles), especially the disco-fest 'Voulez-Vous' and the bittersweet 'The Visitors,' on which a mere three songs can be called uptempo. I've seen 'Mamma Mia' in D.C. and in Las Vegas, and grew up with the incredible ABBA Gold album. So it's as a hardcore, lifelong ABBA fan that I say: I would really rather this not happen.

Now, this is not a 'true' reunion; the four of them will not be performing as the senior citizens they are, but in hologram form, one of the industry's latest fads. They will therefore be 'performing' as their young selves — keeping their promise to not make a farce of their old material, nor try to recapture old live magic that isn't there anymore. And the reunion special will focus almost entirely on contemporary performers singing old ABBA songs.

But ABBA has promised over the years that they would not reunite, even going as far as to turn down a billion-dollar tour offer. They have been fiercely protective of their legacy in many ways, rarely granting permissions to sample (Madonna and the Fugees excepted) or cover, and only very rarely releasing any unreleased material — just a decent song from the vault in 1992 for 'More ABBA Gold' and a fascinating string of demos for 'Like An Angel Passing Through My Room' in 2012 for a new edition of The Visitors. This has made me appreciate them that much more: so many bands don't know when to hang it up, and end up spoiling their legacy with an endless stream of ill-conceived projects, reunions, and new music that just doesn't have the old spark. I liked that ABBA was above that.

It's been clear for a while, however, that ABBA is not too proud to cash in: although 'Mamma Mia' is fun, it's worthless as art, and the fact that they are going through with a sequel film is rather embarrassing. It isn't hard to imagine that the group just couldn't resist the paycheck any longer. 'Mamma Mia' has been an extremely lucrative enterprise for the group, but much of the public thinks it 'knows' ABBA through hearing those songs in that movie or stage production. Granted, I am glad that songs like 'Slipping Through My Fingers' and 'Honey Honey' got a second chance at life — but the original recordings are exponentially superior to the Broadway and movie recordings. And although I like that they embrace their fun and carefree side, it makes it harder for people to appreciate their songs as art — and so many of their songs are great pop art.

At any rate, I won't write the entire endeavor off too soon: if the new song, 'I Still Have Faith In You', is good, then all will be forgiven. ABBA knows better than anyone that all is forgiven in the name of a truly catchy hook. Some of their corniest songs lyrically are some of their most relentlessly catchy, like Arrival's 'Dum Dum Diddle', which is found between smashes 'Dancing Queen' and 'Knowing Me, Knowing You' on the track list, and Waterloo's dreamy 'Honey, Honey'. At the very least, God knows I will be tuning in: I will be too curious. The participation of the band makes it a capital-e Event — and ABBA is the greatest pop group of all time (yes), so it will be gratifying to see younger artists paying tribute to those who blazed the trail. The pop I love best descends from ABBA: they pioneered the variety of female-fronted pop music mastered in today's scene by fellow Swede Max Martin, the true King of Pop, who has written hits for Britney Spears, Kelly Clarkson, Taylor Swift, Pink, Ariana Grande, and others.

Don't expect to catch me at the tour, though.

At any rate, here are my favorites:

Favorite ABBA albums, in order: The Visitors, Voulez-Vous, Super Trouper, Arrival, The Album, ABBA, Waterloo, Ring Ring

10 favorite songs, roughly in order: Lay All Your Love On Me, Dancing Queen, Gimme Gimme Gimme! (A Man After Midnight), Chiquitita, Kisses of Fire, The Day Before You Came, When All Is Said and Done, As Good As New, The Winner Takes It All, Under Attack

Gay Issues

The Rise of Liberal Homophobia

American University *Eagle* | 01.13.10

What happens when prejudice doesn't die but merely changes its form?

The burgeoning cliché amongst the younger, ostensibly pro-gay set is that we're just waiting on the crotchety old homophobes to die off. The upcoming generation supports equality for gays, we're told. At last, gays and lesbians will be liberated as these citizens change the policies of the government.

Forgive me for crashing the party, but I'm one of those who doesn't view the federal government's acceptance of my sexuality as the end-game. If we're really taking the same route as the Civil Rights Movement of the 1960s did — that is, through the state and through the courts, rather than through the culture — then I'd like to channel William F. Buckley, stand athwart history, and yell, "stop!"

The dirty little secret of the Civil Rights Movement is that the lives of actual individuals were swept under the rug. While the policy of the state is that blacks have equality before the law at every level — that is, abstractly, we are integrated — we are more segregated than ever as a culture. Whites and blacks live in different neighborhoods, attend different schools, watch different television stations and vote for different political candidates. Overt racism is virtually dead, but in its place, we have the patronizing "look-at-my-black-friend" phenomenon.

Already, this is manifesting itself in how straight people interact with gay people. We get gay characters on television, but they're Gay Characters, not characters who are gay. We get "Queer Eye for the

Straight Guy": your friendly neighborhood homosexual who wants to redesign your house and give you a makeover. We get young women who learn that we're gay and exclaim, "I've always wanted a gay friend! Can we go shopping together?" At last, liberation!

This disgusting phenomenon, which I call liberal homophobia, is a symptom, not a cause. An article in the Eagle last semester covered the National Equality March by remarking excitedly about a "new civil rights movement." The reader could gather that it was an exciting opportunity for young people to get involved, to get down on the ground with the oppressed. Not a problem, right?

Not so fast. These "enlightened" youth emphatically do not view gay people as individuals who have been unfairly singled out for their sexual orientation. Rather, they view them as people who must be honored for their group membership. There is a monumental difference.

Once we start viewing people in terms of their group identity, we inevitably descend into tribalism. When I penned a column last year decrying the university's new Women's Resource Center, several campus feminist leaders lambasted me for "betraying" the feminist community, which had done so much for "my people." Apparently, these "people" are those who are similarly attracted to the same sex. This attitude is appalling, but hardly surprising: these women had been trained by the culture to view people as members of identity groups, rather than as individuals, with their complexities, personal interests and singularities.

In the final analysis, identity politics is hoisted by its own petard. Instead of liberating minorities, it ensnares them in a cage built with the same steel used to construct the walls keeping them from the mainstream. The gay man is reduced to his sexuality, the black man to his race. That is the new face of liberation. Boy, am I excited for this new generation.

How 'Different' Are Gays and Lesbians?

Personal Website | 11.22.14

I strongly doubt that the advent of same-sex marriage or near-universal social tolerance of gays and lesbians will prompt straight people to seriously examine the experience of being gay any more than racial integration spurred white people to seriously investigate the experience of being black. Although the importance of equality under the law and widespread social tolerance can hardly be overstated, I am concerned that liberalism (in the broad sense) is going to rush to do to homosexuality what it has done to race relations: cover up the continuing tensions, complexities, and difficulties under a gloss of high-sounding rhetoric.

I think gay people's lives are probably destined to be different — and more difficult — than straight people's lives, and that there is little that politics can do to change this. Getting the politics right can make our lives a lot less difficult by protecting us from persecution, but the threat of persecution is not and has never been the only difference between being straight and being gay.

At its core, homosexuality seems to me to be a quintessential 'outsider' identity trait, by its nature. It is not comparable to race, class, gender, or religion: people who grow up as minorities in those categories are usually surrounded by their own. Black people grow up around black people, Jews grow up around Jews — but gay people usually have to wait until early adulthood to meet more than a couple of other people like them. Moreover, we are not simply informed from birth that we are gay; even in the best-case scenario, it is a years-long process of discovery that involves a lot of serious self-questioning and self-analysis — and this process comes to a head during the already-difficult adolescent years. Moreover, nature, not culture, determines how many of us there are: being a racial or religious minority is relative to where you live, but in every nation on Earth, only about 2-3% of the population is LGBT. So, no matter what, gay people experience at least some sense of isolation while growing up.

In my experience, gay people, considered as a whole, relative to straight people, seem to have a distinct sense of humor — with a greater emphasis on wit and snark — are more world-weary, more aesthetically androgynous, more sexually adventurous, more theatrical, less surprised by people's idiosyncrasies, more skeptical of convention, and have a deep longing for some 'je ne sais quoi' that will make them feel more at home in the world. I do not believe that homosexuality is just a 'gay version of being straight,' to put it a certain way — the way liberalism seems to be encouraging people to think of homosexuality: 'They're really no different.' But I think we are different. And I want people to investigate and appreciate those differences — not pretend, in the name of sociopolitical ideology, that they don't exist.

Gay Party, Not Ken Mehlman, Should Apologize

The Daily Caller | 08.26.10

George W. Bush's former campaign manager, Ken Mehlman, has announced to the world that he's gay, and, predictably, the shrieks of outrage are fast reverberating. The gay blogger Joe Jervis, among many others, slammed Mehlman as a "quisling," and the comments in his blog call Mehlman a Nazi, an Uncle Tom, and a self-hating sleazeball. The explicit message is basically that Mehlman, upon a singular urge for male flesh, is supposed to discard his feelings about every non-gay issue in the political arena and march into battle hoisting the rainbow flag.

It may come as a shock to the maladjusted children who enjoy throwing temper tantrums in front of the White House, but the experience of homosexuality is not monolithic, nor is there any cosmic decree mandating that it be a monumental, revolutionary identity shift. Mehlman, whose sexuality is probably far more ambiguous than his caterwauling critics can relate to, is one of millions of gay men whose values and life experience simply do not align with Gay Party dogma. In all likelihood, Mehlman doesn't understand why gay people care about marriage so much. I'm gay, and I certainly don't. Am I supposed to feel like less of a human being until some bureaucrat validates my existence? Is this the message I'm supposed to internalize? Out of one closet and into another.

The Gay Party apparatus closets just as many gay men as the Religious Right does. Less-effeminate gay men, as well as those with conservative dispositions, look at television shows like Glee, pop stars like Lady Gaga, gay activists maligning the merely misguided as hateful Nazis, and think: Is this what I'm supposed to relate to? Am I supposed to stop caring about economics and foreign policy simply because I'm attracted to men? Am I supposed to despise my Republican friends? Am

I supposed to care about irrelevant nonsense like the Westboro Baptist Church? Am I less 'authentically gay' for not subscribing to this line of thought? Sane, tempered gay men like Bruce Bawer and Jonathan Rauch notwithstanding, the Gay Party is setting the tone for what it means to be gay in America. People like Mehlman undoubtedly believe what I do: that homosexuality, like skin color and anatomy, should be irrelevant, not celebrated. Identity politics keeps people closeted, and it has to go.

Mehlman says that he wants to become an advocate for same-sex marriage. I pray that he isn't doing this out of some misplaced sense of obligation to "make up for" his past sins. Ken Mehlman has nothing to apologize for. His critics, who are as narrow-minded as they slam Republicans for being, do.

Gay Party Jihadists On the Attack!

The Daily Caller | 10.01.10

Yesterday, I posted a piece in The Daily Caller about Tyler Clementi, the Rutgers student who committed suicide after being secretly taped having gay sex. Predictably, a gaggle of Gay Party jihadists started hyperventilating about my "insensitivity" (never heard that one before, guys). I'm not retracting anything, but since certain sectors of the blogosphere are erupting, I'll tack on a few points of clarification.

Before continuing, I ought to clarify something contentious: there seems to have been some confusion among certain people — perhaps in bad faith, but I'll let it slide — about my prose, which is, admittedly, partially my fault: it is my job as a writer to keep my syntax crystal-clear. I never intended to imply that Clementi's death was not tragic. What was not tragic, I meant, was *the public broadcasting of the sex tape.* That, I contended, and continue to contend, was a basically frivolous matter, certainly a preposterous rationale for suicide, and not something that the other students could have or should have anticipated.

Why Clementi has turned into a *cause célèbre* amongst the gay left is perplexing. The evidence that he was being viciously targeted for his sexuality is dubious at best. The deluded fantasies of the far left paint our nation's college campuses as hotbeds of anti-gay bigotry, but in fact they are just hotbeds of immature pranks. It says more about the far left than about the Rutgers community that Gay Party jihadists are rushing to fill in the blanks of the case with their own ideological narrative. As a gay man, I have never felt safer than when I am on college campuses.

More saliently, though: it is disturbing and depressing that Clementi's immediate reaction to this incident was to throw himself off of a bridge. He had his dignity violated, yes, but he didn't have his life destroyed. His life wasn't threatened, his family wasn't harmed, and his livelihood was not at risk. It appears that we are raising our children to believe that the cosmos is a benevolent, peaceful place, and that insensitivity and thoughtlessness are bizarre deviations from the natural order of things. This is an absolutely insane view of life. Why did no one ever instill a realistic view of human nature into Clementi? If the culture had equipped him with the proper philosophical tools, he'd still be alive today, dealing with this in a healthy manner. And I should hasten to add that there is no "wrong" time to bring this fact up — unless we have collectively decided that it's a truth we'd rather hide from ourselves, in order that we may continue to sport our Good Guy Badges.

No rational person could have been expected to foresee Clementi throwing himself off of a bridge over this incident. Thoughtless pranks occur all the time; shame and humiliation are an inevitable part of life. The kids who broadcast the tape bear zero culpability for his death. They're stupid, not monstrous. And there's certainly no evidence at hand that bears out the claim that they were motivated by hatred toward gay people. We have got to understand this — before this narrative gets even further hijacked by ideologues.

Thoughts For Pride 2017

Facebook | 06.22.17

When I was younger, I was hung up about the language of 'gay pride,' and I definitely still have plenty of reservations: why be 'proud' of something that does not intrinsically merit pride or shame? But the concept arose as a reaction to gay shame and self-loathing, and I can appreciate it more from that perspective.

When I was a young teenager, I believed it was simply not possible to be both openly gay and meaningfully integrated into society. I actively tried to suppress or negate my same-sex attractions — not to mention hide them from all but a few — and I was nothing if not creative about it. Why? Well, to be blunt: sometimes I feel like in middle school I was called a-word-that-gets-me-banned more often than my actual name. So, imagine you're just hitting puberty, you're trying to come of age normally — and every day your same-sex peers are making it very clear to you that you aren't one of them. Not because you're a dweeb or weird or whatever, but, essentially, because they don't consider you legitimately male. Obviously this wasn't everyone — but it was the sort of experience that popped out at me many times each day. So, by high school the message was clear: if you're one of 'those people,' you're going to have a hard time. And even if people aren't overtly ridiculing you — you know what they feel inside. And I was pretty sure that I at least wasn't not one of 'those people.'

It was never so much that I thought there was something intrinsically shameful about my desires as much as I was fearful of how I would be treated by others if I were to be honest about them. The dangers seemed to come not only in the forms of harassment — mostly verbal, but not only — but also of being patronized to death, caricatured, 'objectified.' I was grappling with these feelings first when the most visible representations of gay people in the media were Queer Eye for the Straight Guy and Queer as Folk. So: you can either serve as a fabulous accessory to bourgeois women, or you can live a gritty, troubled life among your own, in an essentially separate culture. Or — you can hide.

What makes coming of age so peculiarly difficult for gay people is that we have little choice but to deal with these feelings alone; during an already tumultuous time in life, someone throws an anchor onto my lap — and I don't know anyone I can trust to talk to about it. My parents? No, they won't understand, and I don't want to worry or disappoint them. My peers? I'm sure some among them are also questioning, but how can I know who? (I let a few know over the course of high school before coming out.) A teacher? No — I can't talk to a teacher about my sexuality. There was no mentor figure, no family figure, no 'role model' — nobody I could really talk to. The internet was a godsend, although it also added more to the confusion in some ways, too — but it made me feel not so alone, at least. But no other minority group goes through this: racial and religious minorities grow up among their own, at least. Not gays and lesbians.

It's also extraordinary to learn just how much straight people can take for granted: it was just a few years ago I was still commonly met with arguments in favor of Don't Ask, Don't Tell to the effect that gay people don't need to 'shove it in people's faces' — even though, say, having a picture of one's boyfriend on one's desk, or casually remarking that you find a celebrity attractive — reveals your sexuality. Straight people take it for granted that heterosexuality is the norm, the default — and do not realize they are revealing their gendered desires on a very frequent basis. (You learn to put up with a lot of bullshit after years of this, too!)

I didn't feel comfortable 'coming out' until I was 17, when I finally found a good place to talk to other young gay people — people who seemed normal, smart, funny — people I could actually see myself in. I guess that made the difference to me: feeling like I didn't have to deal with it all by myself, that it wasn't my struggle and mine alone like it was in high school. Since then, I've been totally out to everyone and refuse to self-censor. I have even identified myself as gay on national television and in nationally-published op-eds. Once I decided I was ready to embrace that I was gay, I told myself I wasn't going to let anyone inhibit me anymore.

To be sure, it's not all society's fault: political and cultural changes cannot fully erase the difficulties inherent in the nature of things. I have said before and will insist again that being gay is not just a 'gay version of being straight.' There are important big-picture differences in how we think and feel, and at the end of the day, the best data indicates that only about one in fifty of us are gay or lesbian. There will always be difficulties and struggles that accompany being part of a small, weakly-understood (by ourselves as well as others!) minority. But society can do a lot to make things easier — and, thankfully, has done a lot. I 'just missed the boat' as an adolescent — the real sea change seemed to start happening just around the time I graduated high school. In most areas of the country, there seems to be a night-and-day difference between now and even 15 years ago — let alone 30 or 40. So I feel pretty good about the future for gay people — while difficulties remain, I think for the most part we've successfully made our case to society at-large and have room to live basically normal, secure lives.

Gay. Republican. And Not Confused.

Independent Gay Forum | 02.19.09

I am a gay Republican. I am not "self-hating." I am not confused. I am comfortable enough with my sexuality to think of myself in terms of traits other than simply my sexual orientation. I believe that my attraction to the same sex should have no bearing to my thoughts on tax policy, trade, foreign affairs or abortion. I believe that my sexuality is merely an incidental part of my life and should not be a major factor in my decision-making.

I am aware that there is a rich tradition of intellectualism, secularism and equality within the Republican Party outside of the Religious Right. I am aware that Hillary Clinton and Dick Cheney hold the same positions on gay rights. I am aware that Bill Clinton signed into law the last major anti-gay piece of legislation passed by Congress, the so-called Defense of Marriage Act. I am self-respecting enough to know that the words of the Democrats on gay rights are no substitute for their lack of action.

I believe that the virtues of classical liberalism — individualism, self-reliance and a rejection of cultural relativism — help gay men, just as they do all of mankind and are better exemplified by the Republican Party than by the Democratic Party. I am furthermore woefully confused by gay men's ambivalence toward radical Islam, which holds them in a particularly low esteem.

I believe that the gay subculture is destructive. I am not completely sure why a person should be "proud" of his sexuality, which is not an accomplishment. I am confused by the discord between a group of people who insist that they're just like everyone else on one hand and then on the other refuse to assimilate into mainstream society.

I am unable to relate to the faction of gay men who revolve their lives around their sexuality: their neighborhood is gay, their friends are gay, their music and movies are gay, their academic interests are gay, the stores that they frequent are gay - their lives are gay. I am not interested, though, in living my life as a gay man, but simply as a man. I envision a future in which a person's sexual orientation will be an afterthought. I do not in any way whatsoever see the Democratic Party furthering that.

I have been discriminated against more by Democrats than by Republicans. I have been shunned and mocked by Democrats, many of whom will not accept me as a gay man unless I fit into their neatly packaged view of what a gay man is "supposed" to be. I have yet to encounter, on the other hand, a Republican who has rejected my presence in the party, shunned me on a personal level or refused to engage me on the issues.

I have come to understand on a very personal basis that the stereotypes and caricatures of the parties are no substitute for experiencing their members up close. I see that the "tolerance" and "compassion" of the left only extend as far as a person is willing to further their ideological worldview.

I am not Alex Knepper, the gay man. I am Alex Knepper, a man who just so happens to be gay. I believe that my chosen virtues and the actions that I take, not my unchosen sexual orientation, defines me as a person. I am a man who chooses to think for himself and shape his life on his own terms.

I don't think that makes me so radical.

To The Anti-Gay Right

Facebook | 06.16.16

Dear certain right-wingers expressing outrage toward the left for not acknowledging that there is nasty Islamic bigotry against gay people,

Thanks for your newfound concern with religious bigotry directed against us — it seems like just yesterday that when we complained about bigotry, we were told to stop being so damn PC, or that we were a bunch of fascists against the religious because of some homo cake jihad or something.

Or could it be that you only give a damn about us as a group when you can use us to shit on Muslims?

I'm certainly all for criticizing religion and religious believers — I take part in a lot more of it than most of you — but some of you are pretty transparently opportunistic. Just — please stop pretending you care about us rather than about dividing the left.   PS - Yes, I know this doesn't apply to *all of you*.

Thoughts On God and Homosexuality

Facebook | 03.27.18

In a sense, reconciling my homosexuality with belief in God and the reality that God is all-loving, all-forgiving, and all-knowing was the last obstacle to self-acceptance in that regard. I am not a progressive or a fool: I can see male and female in Nature's design, how they fit together, and why they are made for each other. I also cannot deny the authenticity of the sexual outsider's experience and perspective — the reality I have lived. I think homosexuality results either in a special closeness to God or else an especially intense alienation from God, at least as far as the consequences of sexuality are concerned — and I do believe the desire for God is embedded, if you will, in human sexuality — and that mystical union with God requires an emptying of sexual desire — gay, straight, or otherwise. But homosexuality does not in itself prevent either the worldly entering of the 'kingdom' nor the ascent of the soul after death; the coming into the world of Jesus signaled the reconciliation of man and God, which covers *all* sexual desires.

Gay people who come to God are actually at a major advantage in one respect, I think, which is indicated by the Gospel of Thomas and the partially-lost Gospel of Mary, both of which indicate that a kind of transcendence of maleness and femaleness has to come about as part of the work of achieving union with God and achieving a genuine second birth — as a consequence of the work of the emptying of self. One is not 'born' gay, but in free societies, certain people, with certain inborn inclinations toward gender-nonconformity, are highly likely to end up adapting to a same-sex-loving identity that it is not possible to change after puberty. If one can trace back the whys and wherefores of one's gay identity, he can both understand where it came from and affirm it without being obstinate about its characteristics nor denying who he has become. There is no single profile of homosexuality, but there are typical, or 'classic' characteristics that mostly correspond to gender non-conformity. Insofar as erotic love is a searching for a 'missing piece,' there is usually some sense in which gay men, deep down, feel they are lacking what they understand as the masculine within them and seek it out in an image of a person. This corresponds to the myth of Aristophanes in Plato's *Symposium.*

Campus Affairs

American University: A Campus of Victims?

American University *Eagle* | 01.31.10

Hearing the complaints of college students, one might imagine himself to have wandered into the ghetto. Now, it may be confusing at first glance to think that one of the most expensive universities in the country harbors anyone other than the luckiest 20-year-olds on Earth — or, in their own words, the most "privileged" - but this is silly talk. To understand the collective psyche of university political culture, one has to realize that one walks among the oppressed, the damned, the downtrodden.

Most of us who have managed to remain grounded in something resembling sanity are familiar with someone who walked into college a political moderate and emerged as a radical one year later. It's inevitable, really. From the second the freshman stumbles onto campus, he is introduced to a million and one reasons why he should feel slighted by fate. The mild-mannered DLC Democrat is transformed into a postmodern radical once he learns that the world is out to get him; the mainstream liberal woman becomes a "radical queer feminist" once she understands that she is about to get raped (if not physically, metaphorically). The vicious offenders at hand - The Man? - are everyone and no one; the problem is "institutional," not anyone's fault in particular. (Huh?)

For some reason inexplicable by standard logic, people *want* to be victims. When I explain the statistical fallacies of feminist grievances, one would think that this would be a relief to the activists. Well, it's not. Example: It is objectively incorrect to claim that women make 25 cents fewer than men for the same work. It is not a "debate." One side is correct, and the other side is incorrect. The figure at hand is obtained by averaging the annual incomes of all men and comparing the result to the average income of all women, the problems of which should be obvious to anyone who has ever taken STAT-202 — or has a functioning brain. The proper response to such a revelation should be: "Oh, I didn't realize that. Thank you for clearing that misconception up." Right?

Alas, that would remove the impetus to march. One must understand that campus activists are not fighting for social justice, but for ice cream socials. Campus activists stand for the interests of campus activists, not of the oppressed. Piñatas are constantly being constructed to hit: smash them and your guilt gets relieved! Feminists march for "a world without rape" because they know — as well as everyone who witnesses their march — that a world without rape is impossible. But this assures that their club — and their grievances — will never perish. The war against human nature doesn't end. (On second thought, concealed-carry laws would assure that rape becomes at least improbable, but feminists hate guns, the one Great Equalizer of the sexes).

Little gets done for people who have real problems. More money is spent on gaudy drag shows and the Vagina Monologues than on education — the one thing that can actually improve people's lives. The rationalizations that they make — "it raises awareness!" — are as cynical as they are transparent. I might — might! – have a modicum of respect for them if they just came out and admitted that this is a giant charade to allow them to immerse themselves in identity-based subcultures. That's no great evil in itself. But please, please, let's stop this patronizing nonsense about "social justice" being the impetus behind the recreation.

"This Is Not a Debate":

The Authoritarian MO of Campus Jacobinism

Personal Website | 11.14.15

You cannot reason with leftist identity politics ideologues on campus. They do not want to have a debate or a conversation with you.

They are certain you are suffering from some combination of unconscious prejudice and unchecked privilege, and they will not legitimize the oppressor by engaging in 'dialogue' with him as if he were their moral equal. In their eyes, the topic at hand is *not* a debate, and you cannot understand them until you grasp the implications of that.

I would certainly know — at American University, while I was a columnist for the school newspaper (I identified as a 'classical liberal'), I tried repeatedly for over a year to convince representatives from both Women's Initiative and Students for Justice In Palestine to participate in their choice of one-on-one or multi-person panel debates with me and someone else from the College Republicans. I was the most-read and most-responded-to writer in the paper and I wrote constantly on identity politics and campus matters, so it's not like I didn't have standing to propose a student debate. Time after time: No, no, no, no, no — "This is not a debate," "We won't treat this issue as if there's your side and my side."

In essence, these are the moral assumptions of war. If it's not a debate, the enemy must be destroyed. Their methods of 'debate' against me were always attempts at character assassination: I was a 'reactionary,' a 'sexist,' an 'elitist,' a 'rape apologist,' etc., despite the fact that I was an openly gay libertine atheist who publicly bashed social conservatism and bourgeois values. No matter — the nature of the event is that you are either with them or against them.

Consequently, explanations about why they are wrong should only be addressed to fence-sitters. Don't even try to reason with the campus fanatics. Just pronounce swift, unequivocal judgment. Their attitudes are incompatible with liberal democracy. They are censorious. They are arrogant and dismissive. They are not emotionally or spiritually prepared for human life. And what they stand for absolutely must be stopped, because the state of education in this country is already dire enough.

Why Is Campus Culture Tribalist?

American University Eagle | 02.17.10

The contemporary university is defined by its culture, not its curriculum. It is a conscious, deliberate effort to drain students of meaning, self-confidence and intellectual discernment.

The classical ethos demands of students a transcendence of base instinct into the realm of moral judgment. Community, nationhood and notions of value, in this vision, are based upon ideas. This great tradition stood for the emergence from barbarism, the liberation of man from his animal passions and urges and the order of a structured world. The new ethos, exemplified by relativism, uproots morality and replaces it with identity. In its quest to free men from the duties of moral judgment, the academy has reverted to its sole alternative: tribalism.

What does it mean when the student of international affairs is more likely to encounter Edward Said's Orientalism than Edmund Burke's Reflections on the Revolution In France, or when the future educator reads Paulo Freire's *Pedagogy of the Oppressed* rather than Aristotle's *Nicomachean Ethics*? As the classical tradition fades, something needs to take its place. If moral judgment is out, something else must be in. But there is no third way between open inquiry and natural instinct. Debase that great tradition, and there is nothing left. Our institutions remain, but our virtues do not. And with that, we get a distinctly modern tribalism. The postmodern ethos looks a lot like the primitive one.

The contemporary student has no idea what to do with the materials he is handed. He quickly comes face-to-face with cultural relativism, postmodernism, feminism, and myriad other radical causes — in which time he is bombarded with claims about the depravity of the Western tradition. But being completely ignorant of it, he has no context in which to analyze claims against it.

Is traditional Western culture bad? Students say that it is, due to the immense pressure from the university establishment, but the truth is that they generally have no idea whether it is or not. They are ignorant, not malicious. With no background in the great tradition, they have empty minds, and so are drawn to the first passionate cause they encounter, glad that there's something to live for. The radicals, being manifestly the most passionate, are thus in control of campus culture.

Alas, those who do not think cannot escape the siren song of tribalism. Because I am gay, I cannot speak out against a proposed Women's Resource Center without being accused by feminists of betraying "my people." Whoever are "my people?" "My people," insofar as they actually exist, are those who subscribe to the same virtues as I do; those who aspire to excellence. But the product of relativism cannot begin to understand the notion that "my people" might not share my minority identity. He cannot conceive of communities based upon moral judgments because he does not believe in communities based upon moral judgments. When the campus activist decries Pat Robertson for judging gay men based upon their sexual desires, he is not condemning him for the motives of his judgment —he is condemning him for the fact that he is judging. The point is not that he is incorrect, but that he is daring to inquire. The product of classical virtue and intellectual inquiry can safely and rationally rebut Robertson; the relativist descends into emotional hysteria and knows only how to chant against "hate," "discrimination" and other incoherent buzzwords.

There are only two real alternatives presenting each new generation: constructive, rational virtue—and primitive identity tribalism. The latter's campus incarnation, in its attempts to live without using reason, is a parasite feeding off of the gains of the first—but it's a parasite that kills the host. All men who value the rational mind must unequivocally condemn these modern-day tribalists morally.

It's Time to Lift AU's ROTC Ban

American University *Eagle* | 03.03.10

This week's column was difficult to write. Not because of the content, of course - but because of what I had to leave out. I could have written this column about the Women's Initiative's new venture, the "Vagina Men" campaign (can I start a "Penis Women" counter-campaign?). But alas, I've spilled too much ink whining about feminist follies; this column, instead, will address something of actual consequence.

Twice a week, campus ROTC recruits have to wake up early in the morning to engage in physical training, which will prepare them for their eventual deployment. This task would normally be performed on campus, but our esteemed student government has exiled them to Georgetown. The explanation is thus: AU's official code prohibits funding to any discriminatory organization. And with the military's official "don't ask, don't tell" policy still in place, alas, what are we to do but ban the presence of the U.S. military?

Leaving aside the fact that the U.S. military has done more to make the world safe for gay people than any do-gooder college activist, let me state emphatically that yes, the military's policy is asinine. Every civilized country on Earth allows for openly gay soldiers, and it's a shame that our own military has been slow on the uptake. But it makes little sense to punish our perfectly honorable campus recruits for a policy they have nothing to do with. The only people punished by the student government's policy are our recruits—most of whom oppose "don't ask, don't tell," anyway.

Really, it is a perfect testament to the fact that the student government is filled with kids playing politician that they think that they're "sending a message to Washington" this way. Washington's not listening. Those of you in the Student Government ought to figure out what everyone else on campus knows: you're not important. Leave our recruits alone and get back to doing what you're supposed to be doing. Some of you, with your inflated egos, might actually get to be members of Congress one day. Right now, you're just college kids in a student government. Stop trying to send the Defense Department a statement.

Fascinatingly enough, there actually is something that the SG could do about anti-gay campus culture that falls within their proper purview. If it really wants to cut off funding to campus organizations that promote anti-gay policies, I've found one that objectively violates this policy: Students for Justice In Palestine.

This week has been "Israel Apartheid Week" on campuses across the country. Groups such as AU's own Students for Justice In Palestine have taken part in smear campaigns against the—well, I guess I'm supposed to call it the "Zionist entity" this week—instead standing up for a government that is about as friendly to gays as your humble columnist is to feminists. But I have yet to hear a senator propose cutting off funding to Students for Justice In Palestine, despite the fact that there is only one country in the Middle East where gay men can serve openly: Israel. Try holding a gay pride parade in "Palestine" and see if you can get two feet before your life is endangered. There is simply no comparison between the policies of the two governments toward gays. I'm not saying that the U.S. military's policy is fair. I'm just saying that if the student government is going to banish the army from campus, we ought to banish Students for Justice In Palestine, too.

Also Women's Initiative.

Politics, Society, and Foreign Policy

Foreign Policy

Yes, Mitt Romney Was Right About Vladimir Putin

Race 4 2016 | 04.16.14

Writing at the *National Interest,* Robert O'Brien joins a chorus of conservative commentators happily reminding the world that Mitt Romney was right to tag Vladimir Putin's Russia as America's top geopolitical foe, even going so far as to compare Romney to Winston Churchill. This has elicited eye-rolling from Daniel Larison, who in 2012 dismissed Romney's criticisms of Putin's Russia as "bizarre" and "outdated":

Romney assumed that Russia was an inveterate foe of the U.S. on everything because Russia sometimes opposed U.S. policies. This took an unremarkable observation–Russia strongly disagrees with the U.S. on a few high-profile issues–and turned it into an absurd, discrediting exaggeration. He seemed to think that any kind of diplomatic engagement or accommodation with Russia on any issue was equivalent to appeasement. It didn't matter that he couldn't ever explain how the U.S. had "appeased" Russia (or any other government)–he was just reciting from an ideological script that he picked up from other people in his party.

In light of this year's events, it is perplexing that anyone could any longer reduce the moral and diplomatic chasm between the United States and Russia to "disagreement on a few high-profile issues" — as if the clash between the two nations is nothing more than a petty ideological shouting match.

One may question the wisdom of Romney's particular policy prescriptions — and it is no great surprise that the leader of a national political party would "recite from an ideological script" — but the question at hand is not about Romney per se, but about President Obama's blindness toward Vladimir Putin's imperial ambitions. In the campaign against Romney, Obama mocked him for being stuck in a "Cold War mentality." But the so-called "Cold War mentality" is little more than a recognition of the stubbornly persistent primacy of power politics in foreign policy.

As Robert Kagan has cogently written, liberal internationalists have long dreamed of a Kantian world of 'perpetual peace' in which reason, diplomacy, and economic incentives will finally replace the need for projections of power — but this is a seductive illusion. The self-congratulating American narrative is that, as a threat to the prevailing liberal order, authoritarianism was vanquished at the end of the Cold War. To acknowledge that Russia is once again a geopolitical threat would be to admit that the 'End of History' has not arrived after all — and a war-weary public, tired of the burdens of global leadership, is loath to confront yet another imperialist autocrat who provides moral and material support to the world's bloodiest dictators, seizes foreign territory, criminalizes dissent, and makes a fool of our president on the world stage. But this year's events have decisively proven that Vladimir Putin intends to reassert Russia as a great power — and that his vision for the world is unquestionably hostile to American interests — and to the moral vision of classical liberalism.

At the bottom of Larison's ambivalence toward Vladimir Putin is a sort of benign neglect; a lazy moral relativism that, while well-intended, cannot reliably distinguish between good and evil, seeing in Obama and Putin just two sides of the same belligerent coin. But the distance between the United States and Russia is not simply a "disagreement" over "a few issues" — it is a fundamental conflict of visions about the world order. In 2012, Larison approvingly quoted Heather Hurlbert, who argues that the 'Cold War mentality' is a sort of psychological need to rely on the "comfortable certainties" of the 1980s. But it is those who would ignore or dismiss Vladimir Putin who are retreating into the mirage of certainty; the implicit assumption that the existing geopolitical order will persist for all time if we would only leave well enough alone.

But America's enemies will never accept the unipolar order — it must be constantly, vigorously defended. If we choose to shirk from our responsibility to uphold the world order, others will step in and remake it in their own image. Vladimir Putin is taking the long view in his pursuit of power. America must do the same.

Reporters' Russia Remorse Rings Hollow

New American Perspective | 12.13.16

Although I am glad to finally see the topic receive the acknowledgment it deserved two months ago, I must confess that I find media hyperventilating over the not-news that Russia meddled in our presidential election to be a bit perplexing. Little new information has come to light: it was clear in the fall that Putin was working to disrupt our electoral process — to weaken a likely President Clinton, and to exploit the crisis of faith in our institutions. Both candidates thought the specter of Russian interference was important enough to at least mention — although — alas — predictably, one of them thought it was actually a wonderful thing that Putin's lackeys could be willing to hack into the private communications of Clinton associates. So it is no great shock that Russia is likely behind the WikiLeaks e-mail leaks.

It is clear that some would like to take advantage of these non-revelations to promote the belief that Trump's victory was somehow illegitimate. In my mind there is little doubt that Clinton received a raw deal during the general election, with the e-mail leaks being among the most unfair obstacles she faced. But our Constitution stipulates when elections are held and how they are conducted, and Trump won — fair and square. Nobody — not the FBI or CIA, not the president, not the press, not the people — can guarantee that the timing of events and fortune will always be simply fair to the nominees. Clinton is embarrassing herself by endorsing the imprudent and unprecedented idea of delivering intelligence briefings to presidential electors regarding Russia in advance of the official presidential vote. Her frustration is palpable. But if the so-called mainstream press is feeling a bit of remorse, they should blame themselves twice for every time they blame

Putin: if reporters had treated the WikiLeaks saga as intolerable criminal foreign meddling in the first place rather than as an opportunity to engage in scurrilous gossip about the woman they thought would be the next president, we might not be having the kind of conversation we are having right now.

The Moral Bankruptcy of Israel-Hatred

Race 4 2016 | 07.25.14

In his indispensable book *The Case for Israel*, Professor Alan Dershowitz posits that, besides being the Jewish state, Israel is also the "Jew among nations" — constantly held to higher moral standards than its peers, and consistently singled out for one-sided, disproportionate criticism. The United Nations' Human Rights Council — whose members include human rights dignitaries like Cuba and Saudi Arabia – voted this week to investigate Israel for war crimes while shrugging its shoulders as Hamas uses young children as human shields for their weaponry — which, as all but the most willfully ignorant among us know by now, is frequently hidden in hospitals and schools. The United States cast the sole vote against coercing Israel into a show-trial, while Europe cowardly abstained from distinguishing between good and evil.

Instead of utilizing ordinary logic and blaming Hamas for setting up children to die and using their corpses as war propaganda, for perpetuating the violence that will lead to the deaths of countless more innocents, and for refusing to recognize Israel's right to exist, Israel-haters assert either that Israel has brought Islamist terror upon itself, or that it simply shouldn't give in to Hamas' provocations — since, after all, defending its citizens will only invite more hatred and blame. The former throw their lot in with Hamas by fundamentally denying Israel's right to exist, but the latter, like teachers who tell bullied students that they ought to stop making themselves targets for their tormentors, are no less reprehensible. For these people, Israel has two choices: stand by idly in response to unprovoked terrorist attacks, and allow its civilians to die — or fight back, only to be informed that it is not allowed to fight back unless it is willing to bear responsibility for the outcome of

Hamas' disturbing tactics. The Jews, then, must either allow themselves to die, or they must accept responsibility for the fact that they are hated. Heads, Hamas wins; tails, Israel loses.

Israel exercises force against Hamas rather than attempting to negotiate with it because Hamas simply cannot be negotiated with. This is not an opinion: it is in the words of its charter, which begins by approvingly quoting Hassan al-Banna, the founder of the Muslim Brotherhood: "Israel will exist and will continue to exist until Islam will obliterate it." The charter then declares that this interpretation of Islam is its worldview, and declares that "our struggle against the Jews is very great and very serious." Current Hamas leader Khaled Meshaal explicitly denies Israel's right to exist as a Jewish state. Peaceful coexistence is impossible with people who wish only for your extermination.

Virtually all of the criticisms of Israel that deny its right to self-defense rest upon standards to which no other nation would ever be held. We are told that Israel's response to Hamas is 'disproportionate,' the evidence for which is usually presented in the form of a t-ledger comparing the two sides' respective body counts — as if the fact that Hamas has killed few Israelis in recent years is due to a lack of effort, rather than Israel's vigorous efforts to defend itself — or, even more nauseatingly, as if Israel has a moral duty to let more of its own die before fighting back. We are told that Israel cannot legitimately conduct military operations in which civilians are likely to die — as if Israel does not go above and beyond to minimize civilian casualties, or as if some number of civilian deaths are not a tragic — but unavoidable — part of any military operation, just or unjust. Countless innocent German civilians, including young children, died in World War II. Are we to condemn as unjust every war conducted in the history of the human race?

Ultimately, the debate over Israel figures so prominently and arouses such passion because it serves as a proxy argument about morality and legitimacy in international relations. The world has increasingly turned against Israel. Is morality a popularity contest? Civilians, including children, die both in terrorist attacks and in military operations conducted in response to them. Is there no moral difference between the two? Hamas has explicitly stated its desire to exterminate the Jewish people — and the people of Gaza voted them into office —

while Israel is an outpost of liberal democracy and individual liberty in a region that is otherwise a political wasteland of chaos and oppression. Must we view Israel and Hamas simply as two bickering sides?

All states are imperfect, and it really ought to go without saying that there are countless legitimate criticisms that may be leveled at Israel, its government, and its military. But Israel-haters and their fellow travelers' ignorant propaganda masquerading as concern for children is a thin veil for the ugly relativism — and sometimes worse — inherent in any ethical perspective that is so morally enervated that it cannot reason beyond emotionally evocative photographs of dead children and t-ledgers of body counts.

Kerry and the Two-State Solution Hallucination

New American Perspective | 12.29.16

John Kerry has let loose against Israel, hot on the heels of American abstention from a United Nations vote condemning its settlements: "The US secretary of state sounded the warning on Wednesday in a final plea outlining the outgoing Obama administration's vision for peace between Israel and Palestine.

> *"The settler agenda is defining the future in Israel. And their stated purpose is clear: They believe in one state: Greater Israel,' Kerry said. 'If the choice is one state, Israel can either be Jewish or democratic, it cannot be both, and it won't ever really be at peace,' he added."*

It is as if the events of the last 25 years never occurred. From the days of the original UN partition, Israel has tried again and again to meet the Arabs halfway — two-thirds of the way — and constantly receives nothing but blame in return, ostensibly for not trying hard enough; for not being *really serious* about peace. The Arabs, meanwhile, are met with the soft bigotry of low expectations — as if everyone just knows that we cannot expect them to be reasonable; that Israel is the adult in the room who has to maturely hold its tongue so as not to inflame the child constantly on the verge of a tantrum. Let us remember that at the 2000 Camp David summit, Israel variously offered the overwhelming majority of the West Bank and Gaza, the dismantling of existing settlements, a shared capital in Jerusalem, and tens of billions of dollars in aid money to what would be the nascent Palestinian state — and was repeatedly turned down by Yasser Arafat, who refused to put forward a single counter-offer, and launched a new *intifada* just months later. Today, Gaza is run by a literal jihadist organization — but Netanyahu is held to be the extremist right-winger.

Peace with people who hold your annihilation as an indispensable goal is neither possible nor desirable — and even those Americans most craving peace must face up to the utter futility of all past attempts at brokering a deal. We really cannot be all that surprised that Israel should finally grow impatient with thousand-times-disproved Western fantasies that it holds the power to make jihadists stop hating Jews so much, if only they would swallow their pride and be magnanimous: nobody wants to forever play Charlie Brown to Lucy with the football. The Jews are hated for *who they are*, not the particulars of what they do. It is no wonder so many Israelis have come to believe that, since they are going to be hated and held to impossible double-standards anyway, they might as well pursue their own interests with little regard to what the rest of the world might think.

Nothing has changed: it is always easier to blame the Jews — a tiny minority — for their inconvenience than it is to face the depravity of their numerous, relentless antagonists who were equally devoted to the destruction of Israel before, during, and after the rise of the new settler movement. Arab rejection of the legitimacy of any Jewish state is the essential problem, and there will be no chance at peace until this changes.

Intervening In Libya Was the Right Thing to Do

New American Perspective | 06.01.16

It is ironic that foreign policy interventionists are so frequently accused by our critics of overestimating the reach of American power. Since the disappointments of the 'Arab Spring,' it has become commonplace to lay the blame for the ongoing chaos in Libya at the feet of President Obama — and especially then-Secretary of State Hillary Clinton, who was decisive in pushing the president to intervene — as well as those who have generally pushed for greater American intervention since 9/11. Non-interventionists are sure that Libya is their ace in the hole: how can anyone defend Clinton's urging to force out Qaddafi, given that ISIS has found a foothold in Libya and there is no resolution in sight? Haven't we learned our lesson by now?

Despite non-interventionists' foolish overestimation of the reach of American power, is not always simply up to the United States whether a tyrant stays or goes, and it is seldom within our power to prevent a badly deteriorating political situation from collapsing into chaos. Often we are given the choice between — to paraphrase Lindsey Graham on Ted Cruz — being shot or being poisoned. Of course, it is easy for pundits to declare that we should seek health — but if a nation's political culture is sick to the core, then recovery will take decades — not years, and certainly not months — and pretending we can avoid the problem simply by keeping our hands from getting dirty is nothing but kicking the can down the road.

From North Africa to Syria, the 'Arab Spring' was first and foremost a revolt against secular authoritarianism. We have learned that the removal of tyrants in the Arab world is likely to open a path for Islamists. This was relatively predictable, and many did predict it at the time. But when the will of the people is overwhelming, there is little the United States can do to contain the situation in a way that is tantamount to anything but a short-term fix. Looking at Egypt, for instance: if we actually had successfully propped up Hosni Mubarak — who, unlike Qaddafi, actually was 'our bastard' — we would have necessarily given Islamists many more years to spread their ideology, giving them a fresh chance to appeal to festering resentments and new fuel for anti-

Americanism in response to our meddling in propping up Mubarak. Instead, we accepted the inevitable and watched his regime collapse. Islamists have since had to attempt to turn their preaching into policy. Today, we see the many failures of Islamists in Egypt — and so do Egyptians. In the short-term, America is put into a more difficult situation in the Middle East for what has happened in Egypt — but in the long-term, we may have avoided something far worse, and helped to open up the path to new alternatives for the Middle East by allowing Islamists to put their limitations as rulers on display for all to see. The alternative — Mubarak-style secular tyranny in perpetuity — is inconceivable. Something had to give, and it's better to deal with it upfront than to let the situation fester.

Unlike Mubarak, of course, Qaddafi was a sworn enemy of the United States and its allies. In 2011, the situation in Libya was not radically different from the one in Syria today. There are no obviously 'good' actors involved, the few 'moderates' involved are moderate only in a relative sense — and hence there is no easy choice for America, especially in the short-term. But as with Assad in Syria, it had become blindingly evident in 2011 that Gaddafi had become intolerable to a large enough segment of the population that to assist in propping him up would be nothing but a short-term fix. Let's consider the alternatives: if we had not intervened and Qaddafi mercilessly slaughtered his people, Assad-style, Obama and Clinton would be blamed for that mess, too. If we had not intervened and Islamists were successful in ousting Qaddafi, Obama and Clinton would be blamed for that mess, too. The USA didn't 'break' Libya; Libya was bound for chaos, and the only question was how we were going to respond to it.

There is no excuse — on the part of the Obama Administration or our NATO allies — for not attempting to do more to follow up on its actions not only in Libya, but also in Syria and Iraq. ISIS will eventually have to be wiped out, which means there will need to be not only boots on the ground but a long-term commitment from a grand coalition of NATO allies, led by the United States, to oversee the maintenance of a new provisional government. But the need to destroy ISIS was going to materialize regardless of whether we intervened to take out Qaddafi — and Libya would still be chaotic, too. It is convenient for non-interventionists — and for opportunists like Donald Trump — to blame the the United States for every mess in the world — but sometimes all we can do is swallow the poison instead of taking the bullet.

The Big Lie: George W. Bush Caused the Rise of ISIS

Race 4 2016 | 08.12.14

The Big Lie in the debate over the chaos unfolding in Iraq is that somehow, the rise of ISIS would not be occurring were it not for President George W. Bush's ostensibly indefensible 'war of choice'; that by removing Saddam Hussein and participating in an ill-fated 'nation-building' project, we fostered instability and created a vacuum for ISIS — now called the Islamic State — to fill. Take away the Iraq War (and bring back Saddam Hussein), and, according to the likes of David Axelrod, we wouldn't have to deal with this problem, since it wouldn't exist.

It is simply a lie. Saddam Hussein, one of history's bloodiest tyrants, was never a source of stability, and, unlike other former Arab autocrats like Egypt's Hosni Mubarak, he was never 'our bastard'; he was a longtime geopolitical nemesis and a clear threat to peace for as long as he remained in power. Saddam Hussein invaded two of his neighbors, fired SCUD missiles at a third, used chemical weapons on Iraq's Kurdish minority, and funded regional terrorism. In 1998, President Bill Clinton signed the bipartisan Iraq Liberation Act into law, making regime change the official stance of the United States toward Iraq. (As non-interventionists never tire of pointing out, yes, we did cooperate with Saddam Hussein — once, in the 1980s, when we simply determined him to be the lesser of two evils in his war against Islamist Iran).

Iraq under Saddam Hussein would have been a breeding ground for the likes of ISIS. Like Syria's Bashar al-Assad, Saddam Hussein was a Ba'athist, a secular strongman who sometimes allied with Islamists against common foes, but had little in common ideologically with them. Like Assad, he would have been a ripe target for Islamist ire during the Arab Spring, and would have likely responded in a manner much like

Assad. Hillary Clinton is right that Syria poses a 'wicked' problem to the United States. Right now, Iraq does as well — but Assad's fate — and his willingness to use chemical weapons against the people he claims as his — mirrors what an Iraq run by Saddam Hussein would surely look like right now, holding all else equal.

Of course, it is not necessary to hold all else equal, because, upon the recognition that the Maliki government clearly was not equipped to deal with terrorist threats to Iraq, the United States should have never abandoned the country. It is true that the government wanted us to leave — but that should not have mattered; Iraq owes the existence of its government to us, and our mission there was not primarily a humanitarian one, but was conducted for national security purposes. Do people suppose that Angela Merkel wants tens of thousands of U.S. troops stationed in Germany, or that Japan likes being denied its own military? Surely not. But Germany and Japan posed a threat to the United States and to the world order once, and we decided that it should never happen again — and we meant it. So it should have been in Iraq — but President Obama decided that his desire to fulfill an ideological campaign promise entitled him to suspend the reality principle. The 'facts on the ground' made it clear that Iraq was not ready to assume total responsibility for its own defense. This does not make Obama in any way responsible for the rise of ISIS, of course — ISIS alone bears responsibility for its own primitive savagery and inhuman barbarism — but it does make him short-sighted, perhaps foolish, even. His former Secretary of State certainly seems to think so.

The Case for Engagement In Syria

New American Perspective | 04.11.18

Although I had originally planned to write a response to Cinzia's frustrating call for her native Italy to abandon a central pillar of the most successful military alliance in world history, the world had other plans. Now in my social media discussions, I find myself swatting Putin's flies, who keep buzzing in my ear that Bashar al-Assad is either the subject of a disinformation campaign by the wicked 'Deep State' or, more innocently, that he is the only viable option for keeping Syria in one piece; that all of his opponents are insane or theocratic. More importantly, they want to know what is at stake for the United States in Syria. Why does the Syrian Civil War call for an American response? And what would be the goal of an American response?

I am not sold on the wisdom of toppling Assad, primarily because I believe Americans currently lack the stomach to commit to a long-term project like assembling and helping to sponsor an interim government; we saw in the Iraq War that a large and vocal segment of the population is ready to pull the plug on a military venture at the first sight of trouble. Our history is short, our geography renders us uniquely secure, and the wars we have been drawn into have been short, conventional ground wars with conspicuous signs of unambiguous victory. Our nation has no frame of reference at all for what an unconventional, asymmetric war should look like, and thinks wars should be short, sweet, and simple. I think America can accomplish what it wants to accomplish, if it knows what it wants to accomplish — but our people must understand that there will be no instant gratification. At a time when we are plagued by so many problems of our own, it is a lot to ask of Americans.

But there are reasons for the United States to take an interest in the conflict. The fate of Syria matters to next-door Iraq, whose government once again shows a fighting chance of functioning, owing to the long-awaited near-defeat of ISIS. (Let us note that the old argument that toppling Assad opened the door for ISIS to rule is no longer valid.) It matters to our allies in Israel and Saudi Arabia, and our friends the Kurds. It matters for our enemies Russia and Iran, who are far more tangibly invested in the conflict than we are; the longer we keep the conflict going, the more we can bog them down and keep our options open. It matters for the sake of punishing chemical warfare rather than allowing a tyrant to show the world that he can use these weapons without fear of retribution — a strategy of both punishment and deterrence.

Some bestow relative praise on Assad for his secularism. It is time to recognize that the dream of a stable Middle East ruled by secular strongmen is as delusional as any neoconservative fantasy circa 2003. From the days of Nasser, secular autocracy has been heralded as a potential solution to the problem of a fractured Middle East, and it has failed again and again, most recently in the wave of revolutions called the 'Arab Spring', which was really a series of revolts against secular rulers. How many times must the imposition of secularism fail before we abandon this fantasy? How much longer will we deny the Middle East's 1,200-year legacy of Islamic rule? And this is to say nothing of the moral emptiness of settling for tyranny for the sake of convenience — to endorse despotism because it is easier to sit on our hands.

Many people who flee into Assad's arms believe they are fleeing Islamic mobs: they assume that any Islamic government is going to be tyrannical; that the rebels all want to institute Saudi Arabia on steroids in Syria; that we can't trust any group advocating religion in government to be anything but radical or militant. I cannot guarantee that this is not the case; no one can gauge what potential exists in some of these groups to compromise until we try. If we do decide to topple Assad, we will need to, with a large international coalition, sponsor a coming together of representatives from among the various factions to hammer out a semi-liberal pluralistic system that allows for several elements of sharia in government but recognizes Allah alone as sovereign over life and death, and does not allow individuals to take the law into their own hands. This must include representatives from the Assad regime, since they know much of importance about what various factions among the people want and what they will tolerate. This is an important lesson we must learn from Iraq: that purging all elements of the old regime is counterproductive.

Again: I am not sold on the wisdom of doing that. But I am afraid that President Trump, determined to turn his presidency around, upend expectations, and divert attention away from his scandals, might, under the advisement of militarist John Bolton, rush into Syria to topple Assad without any plan for what comes next: our fatal mistake in both Iraq and Libya. America can accomplish what it wants to accomplish militarily, but it must avoid acting reactively and have a tangible sense of what it is trying to accomplish before going in. If we aren't prepared to do that, then we ought to just take the path of least resistance, lob some missiles at Assad when he's especially bad, but otherwise allow Russia to prop him up.

Lil' Kim and the Donald's Surrealistic Singapore Trip

New American Perspective | 06.14.18

Pinch yourself — the *Apprentice* guy and the thirtysomething-year-old son of the man who was once the most psychotic despot on the planet have come together to negotiate nuclear arms. Naturally, a lot of people think this is a really cool — and really strange – event. It is strange enough that a lot of people seem to literally not understand what is happening.

How can I put this gently? Some among us appear to be confused about the nature of this event. I can't go ten minutes on social media without a Trump supporter telling me that North Korea is on the verge of 'denuclearization', or that there is a perceivable path to genuine peace between North and South Korea (at last!). Some intrepid commentators even discussed sanctions policy with me. As usual, President Trump's lack of preparation and lack of a concrete objective make this possible. His play-it-by-ear approach gives rise to a free-for-all media environment. Nobody at the White House can impose any order onto the discourse, because there is no clarity to be obtained. This Bigly Yuge Historic meeting is entirely open-ended; everything and nothing is on the table, and nothing has been promised by anyone.

Objectively, this meeting is a diplomatic coup for Kim Jung-un, who followed through on his father's ambition of pursuing nuclear weapons. Kim Jung-il reasoned that if North Korea acquired nuclear weapons, the world would have little choice but to accept the Kims as legitimate rulers, and little choice but to deal with North Korea on relatively normal terms. It clearly has worked.

Let us recall, as we did in my earlier piece on North Korea, that in 1994, President Bill Clinton, in America's first crack at treating the slave-drivers like real rulers, crafted the 'Agreed Framework' with Kim Jung-il. That failed 'framework' promised that the Kim regime would never pursue nuclear weapons. At the time, the deal was made with a very pleasing commencement, and the anointed ones — the realists, the liberal internationalists, the journalists and pundits — all told us that the deal represented progress toward peace, that nobody should root against it, that the hawks were proven wrong again, that those telling us we are being conned are rooting against peace, that it really is useful to talk to our enemies. The real mystery today, then, is: Why do people think we have never tried simply talking to the Kim regime before? And why are skeptics of this entire endeavor treated as cynics?

Kim Jung-un will have a story to tell to North Koreans about his meeting with President the Donald: "My grandfather, the Eternal and Supreme Leader whose vision guides my own, passed down his political know-how to my father, who pursued this nuclear program to bring the American imperialists to their knees. My father was right. Once I showed the world that North Korea was a nuclear power, the American president came running to talk to me without asking any questions or making any demands first. In fact, he seemed eager to make life easier for me, just for a few assurances. How can anyone now doubt that the Kim regime is legitimate? It has dealt with the American regime and brought it to its knees!"

What does Trump think he — America — is getting out of this? What is he going to tell us? I don't think he knows. He has openly said he has not prepared for the meeting. He wants to play it by ear and let the chips fall where they may. As far as particular items go, he has floated the idea of ceasing joint military drills with South Korea. If the Kim regime managed to extract that in the form of a concession in return for nothing but promises of later denuclearization, it would be a massive victory achieved by a small, weak state against a superpower without firing a shot.

As I mentioned in my previous piece on North Korea, we should have heeded the warning of Hillary Clinton in 2008, when she rebuked then-Senator Obama for intending to meet with tyrants without preconditions. She cautioned Obama that he needed to gauge the intentions of these people very carefully before rushing in, lest the office of the presidency be exploited for propaganda purposes. In this case, it is probable that all that will come of this meeting are a lot of priceless images that the Kim regime can use to show the submissiveness of the American imperialists before Dear Leader (who is now armed with nukes). I pray I am wrong. I would be very happy to be wrong. But I don't think I am.

A Teenage Prediction About the Iraq War

The Politics of Treason | 2006

In 15 years, when the Middle East is filled with democracy, when Iraq and Afghanistan are shining lights of how a society can function, when it perhaps spreads to Lebanon, Syria, Libya, and Iran, history will be more than kind to President Bush...Assuming that his Middle East policy has the great repercussions it looks like it will, as we've seen in Lebanon's massive rallies for change against Syrian rule, Libya cooperating in giving up its WMD program, Saudi Arabia allowing a limited vote for the first time ever, and Jordan joining the call for a war against terrorism, I do not hesitate to say that George W. Bush will be judged as the country's greatest president.

Islam

Can The West Modernize Islam?

Frum Forum | 08.19.10

Should the West be at war with Islam? In a critique of the hard-line stance against Islam, John Guardiano rebukes David Swindle, who has called for the "eradication" of Islam. Marine officer Guardiano is applying his firepower against a low-value target. Let me suggest to John that he turn his attention to some brave and thoughtful people who also stand against Islam with no less vigor but with much more sense: the Human Rights Service, located out of Norway. Contributors to HRS's website are secularists of the left and right, including Ayaan Hirsi Ali, Ibn Warraq, and Bruce Bawer. These writers are at war with Islam too – a war of enlightenment ideals against a fundamentalist faith, exactly the kind of war that Hirsi Ali's hero, Voltaire, waged against the Catholic Church.

The Human Rights Service writers (and I am one of them) reject the postmodern proposition that the plain words of a text are endlessly malleable; that they allow for any interpretation the reader wants from them. When the Qur'an states that the testimony of a woman is not worth as much as a man's, it is not to be read as an esoteric, arcane piece of apocrypha that secretly holds a feminist message: it is instead simply to be taken for what it obviously says – and then condemned. There's no hidden message beneath the contempt for women. It's just sexist.

Like the Enlightenment tamed Christianity, Islam too must be moderated. But Volatire, Hume, Montesquieu, and Madison have not yet found their Islamic equivalents, perhaps because certain clearly specified Qur'anic values that simply cannot be reconciled with Enlightenment ones.

The great thinkers of the past tried to undermine the values of the Church. They did not do this by treating it with awed reverence and solemn respect. The entire point of Voltaire's critique of Christianity was, indeed, to undermine the religion and drag it into the modern world. The Enlightenment was, at its core, a war on faith in the name of reason. It was a century-long process that involved much kicking and screaming, a lot of excess, and a few tragically misguided philosophies. But the glory of its end result can hardly be denied: the crowning achievement of the American project, and its secular, capitalist culture – the first country on Earth that placed full legal primacy in the individual.

Islam has not yet gone through that messy process. It must. To say so is no more "Islamaphobic" than Thomas Jefferson was "Christophobic."

Some may concede that above point – but argue that criticisms must from "insiders." Apostates like Hirsi Ali and Ibn Warraw, infidels like Bawer and me and achieve nothing. But why can we not speak for ourselves? If even Europeans won't condemn the misogyny of the burqa, how can someone who's grown up with it fight against it? The West cannot hope for Islamic reformers to come forward unless we affirm our confidence in our own values. Debates about tone and rhetorical approach are completely appropriate, but our fundamentals must be clear.

Does Islam Need Its Own 'Reformation'?

Personal Website | 03.07.15

I used to believe Islam needed to go through its own 'reformation.' It is a popular opinion — and a comforting one, too, since it is premised on the notion that History functions in the same way in all places, and thus Islam is just 'a little behind' the West and will soon 'catch up.' But this narrative is deeply problematic, because the concerns that motivated the likes of Martin Luther are not present in contemporary Islam. The Protestant Reformation was an intellectual rebellion against a powerful centralized authority in an era in which few laymen had actually read the Bible for themselves. But there is no centralized authority in Islam right now, and it is quite common for laymen — even illiterate ones — to have memorized the entire Qur'an. Islam's central authority was dissolved about a century ago — and no imam is discouraging lay Muslims from knowing exactly what the Qur'an says. How and why, then, would Islam need something akin to the Protestant Reformation?

What people really mean when they say things like this, it seems, is that Islam direly needs some kind of movement that will plant the seeds of liberal change. But here in the West, the process of liberal change took centuries, not decades. Besides, if the likes of ISIS, al-Qaeda, Hamas, Boko Haram, etc., are not legitimately Islamic and are therefore rebelling against traditional interpretations of Islam, then perhaps they are the *sola scriptura*-oriented 'reformers,' interpreting Islam in a fundamentalist manner that will, over the course of centuries — again, not decades — help the Muslim world overpower the hegemonic West rather than passively accept or submit to the ideology of its conquerors. Surely the Islamists have at least as much a claim to being legitimately Islamic as those who think the Qur'an is somehow a precursor to the American Declaration of Independence and progressive notions of universal human rights.

The Media and Islam: An Inconvenient Truth

Introduction by Bruce Bawer

Human Rights Service | 03.05.2010

"Alex Knepper, an American college student who has recently made headlines around the U.S. by challenging reigning ideas about "date rape," agrees to a telephone interview with a columnist for a major Dutch newspaper – only to find himself represented in the resulting column as a bigot and ignoramus on the subject of Islam. Never mind that he is, in fact, a student of Islamic history who plainly knows a good deal more about Islam than his interviewer. But in the mainstream Western media these days, with few exceptions, the knowledge he possesses is forbidden knowledge, and, through a weird Orwellian alchemy, is magically transmuted in the pages of politically correct newspapers into ignorance and bigotry." - Bruce Bawer

The West's primary conceit about religion is the idea that any legitimately-practiced faith must necessarily be a force for good. This noble lie is what causes Westerners — particularly those weaned on a diet of multiculturalism and cultural relativism — to imagine Islam as a kind of exotic version of Christianity: that is, not necessarily pure, but basically benign.A reporter for a major Dutch newspaper recently interviewed me by telephone for her regular column, which is devoted to recent developments in Washington, D.C. Her article was originally meant to be about a controversial piece I had written about date rape for the college newspaper at American University in Washington, where I am a student. But the subject of our conversation quickly turned to Dutch politics — specifically, Islam and Geert Wilders.Although the reporter's piece, as it turned out, treated me gently enough in regard to the controversy over my date-rape column, when it came to Islam I was stunned by her sheer dishonesty and misrepresentation. In line with the almost consistent effort by the mainstream Western media to depict critics of Islam as sputtering caricatures, my views of Islam and Mr. Wilders were presented as essentially narrow, ill-informed, and based on crude stereotypes. You would never have known from reading the Dutch journalist's column that I am, in fact, a student of Islamic history and that the journalist, who presented our interview as a brief and shallow chat, had in fact conversed with me for nearly an hour – and that during that hour, far from spouting shallow, ignorant comments about Islam, I had informed her about details of Islamic history of which she was manifestly unaware.

For example, she mentioned nothing in her column about my explanation of the Treaty of Hudaybiyyah, a pact Muhammad made with the state of Medina. This treaty was intended to be a ten-year truce between the two warring camps, but Muhammad broke it as soon as he had amassed enough power to conquer the city. (Incidentally, this episode contributed significantly to the rise of the Muslim practice known as *taqiyyah* – lying for the sake of the faith.)

I also suggested to the Dutch reporter that she read any randomly chosen sura of the Qur'an word for word, and explained that this was the fastest way to understand just how ghastly the Muslim faith is. I also cited Muhammad's farewell speech, in which he declared that he had been "ordered to fight until all men say 'There is no god but Allah.'" Then there was the small matter of Islam's institutionalized pedophilia: Aisha, Muhammad's child bride, had sex with the purported prophet, the perfect Muslim, when she was just nine years old. And these are just starting points. Because of all of this, I maintained, Islamic values are antithetical to Dutch pluralism. "But that's just it," the reporter objected. "We're a pluralistic society. Shouldn't they be allowed to live out their cultural values in Holland?" I said that it was not tolerant to tolerate the intolerant. "That's what Wilders always says. He's always saying things like that to the West. But then he turns around and defames Muslims in Parliament. Not Islam, but Muslims." She brought up a nasty statement that Wilders allegedly made that the Western media supposedly refuses to cover (the specifics escape me, unfortunately), and asked me if I knew that he tried to ban the Qur'an. "No, he didn't," I replied. "He was making a point about hate speech laws. He said that if Mein Kampf can be banned for its hateful language, then the Qur'an can, too. And he's right. The point of what he did is that religion should not be above criticism. He doesn't want either of them banned." (If this is spun as «trying to ban the Qur'an,» how reliable can one assume her statements about Wilders' "demagoguery" to be?) In her article, the Dutch journalist raised my point – a solid fact – that gay men can no longer walk hand-in-hand in the city of Amsterdam as safely as they once could, only to dismiss it cavalierly as an absurd falsehood that had been fed to non-Dutchmen like me by Dutch demagogues like Wilders. "Come to Amsterdam. You can walk with your boyfriend," she assured me. What could I say except, "No, I can't"? I mentioned the attack on gay American publisher Chris Crain, who was assaulted by a group of Muslim youths in an Amsterdam street. But she waved it away it as a non-story.

Disturbingly, the Dutch reporter may in fact be something of a prophet. For it is not unlikely that attacks on gay men will decrease as they increasingly self-censor their behavior. There may not be many more Chris Crain incidents, in short, simply because gay people will be more and more aware of the risk factors. The Dutch article quoted my comment that I would hesitate to hold another man's hand in certain parts of, say, Mississippi. It simply isn't safe, so gay people just don't engage in the behavior. Is Amsterdam – the capital of the country that first granted marriage equality to gay couples – tomorrow's Mississippi? On the phone, the reporter actually contended that Ayaan Hirsi Ali was essentially a media whore who lied on multiple occasions about her life being threatened. Before the famous incident involving Theo van Gogh, she insisted, Hirsi Ali had tried to provoke radical Muslims into threatening her life so that she could become a media critic of Islam. Hirsi Ali's life had never been threatened before then, the reporter claimed, but she knew that if she provoked radical Muslims, then she could become famous. Hirsi Ali's father, according to the reporter, had confirmed this to her.What can one say about such repulsive nonsense? Even a bare-bones outline of Ayaan Hirsi Ali's life reveals nothing but bravery and integrity. She both understands and accepts the risks inherent in speaking out against the totalitarianism of Islam, and she soldiers on even as she is obliged to live a guarded life. In a sane world, she would be universally commended as a shining example of intellectual heroism. Women like my Dutch interlocutor, however, look at Ayaan Hirsi Ali's courageous life and actually – incomprehensibly – see Muslims as the victims of the story.The Dutch reporter and her relativist kin like to imagine themselves as enlightened elites who have moved beyond the bourgeois morality of yesteryear. That's all well and good. But the trouble with this postmodern nihilism is that everyone else, including the Muslims, has to follow the same path to enlightenment and transcendence – or else the postmodernists will simply get crushed. Islam has responded to all this foolishness by correctly diagnosing it as a symptom of a moral and cultural vacuum in Europe, and it's rushing to fill that void. Even as my Dutch reporter and her colleagues, those maggots eating away at the corpse of Old Europe, cheerfully reassure everyone that we have no basis by which to judge the cultural values of others, Dutch values are being swept away. Dutch people are being fed the bizarre line that Sharia law is no better or worse than the Dutch constitution, and that the Qur'an is no better or worse than the Nicomachean Ethics. Imperialism? Pedophilia? They're just fine, as long as they're committed by "people of color" in the name of traditional religion.

Perhaps what the postmoderns really admire Islam for is how alien it is. Existential dread has not found its way into the Muslim consciousness. Allah's not dead; Islamic culture is still cohesive. There's no Allah-worshipping Michel Foucault because there's no Allah-worshipping Nietzsche. Islam still retains its essential sense of cultural unity – it's a throwback to a world before our relativist, contemporary life, before anyone ever conceived of the need for cultural relativism, postmodernism, or critical theory. The Islamic world believes in something, the elite journalists of the Western world think – why rob them of it and drown them in our dreary modern world, where we're «condemned to be free»? In a certain sense, the postmodernists are right: we don't believe in anything. But one thing is clear: we have to start believing in something again, if we're going to recover what made Europe the towering force it once was.

The Roots of the Left's Love Affair With Islam

The Daily Caller | 08.31.10

When, as a teenager, I became an atheist, I assumed that I would find some kind of sympathy from the left. Whatever the left's flaws, I saw it had no patience for the Christian Right's nonsensical obsession with abortion, school prayer, and gays. An atheist's natural position on the social-issues spectrum, I figured, was the left.

Wrong. Totally, utterly, blindingly wrong. And I was wrong for this reason: I committed myself to consistent rationalism, not merely to a political crusade against conservative Christianity. A consistent rationalist has no home on the modern left, because the left has no particular problem with religion. Its problem is with Christian Republicans. The left doesn't love Darwin, for example; it just hates Palin. It doesn't love reason, it hates conservative Christianity. With the left, we are dealing with a political ideology that is completely defined by what it hates. And what it hates is anything at all that stands in support of traditional Western values — whether they are Judeo-Christian religious ones or Greco-Roman pagan ones. Anything that obstructs tradition is held as sacrosanct and untouchable.

Why?

Postmodern identity politics, which has infected the left to a degree greater than its exponents know, views all conflicts through the lens of power. The fundamental job of politics, in the eyes of the rank-and-file left-winger, is to lift up the oppressed, to empower the "wretched of the Earth." This is why it can't bring itself to oppose Islamic fanaticism. American leftists view Islam as under assault: Muslims, mostly non-white to begin with, are viewed with suspicion thanks to the acts of some of their co-religionists. Couple this so-called climate of fear with post-colonialist anguish nourished by 60's radicals, and Islam is granted a blank check. Fundamentally, Islam is weak and the West is strong. Leftist ideology views weakness as virtue.

When you're out of power, standards change. The entry-level qualification for "moderation" in Islam has thus shape-shifted into nothing more than a proclamation that 9/11 might not have been cause for celebration. Anyone who thinks that publicly executing homosexuals is a little archaic is now a "voice of reason" in Islam. That's really all it takes. Imagine, by way of comparison, a priest who refused to condemn abortion-clinic bombers, explaining meekly that he was not in the business of politics. "It's a complicated issue," he'd say, and leftists would screech at Sarah Palin to condemn him. The left can't bring itself to condemn the Muslim equivalent of this — the very imam leading the effort to build a mosque near Ground Zero — because good and evil on the left are determined by nothing more than who's got access to power. To paraphrase Ann Coulter: take away the terrorism, and the left would hate Muslims; they'd just be another raving band of anti-choice, homophobic extremists. But through the left's prism, they're opposed by

Christians and whites — the "power structure" — and are therefore victims.

It is imperative to understand that, for the left, the Christian Right exists in an air-tight compartment. Left-wing principles in dealing with Christian fanatics are insulated from all external concerns: the issues surrounding them have nothing whatsoever to do with anything else. Pat Robertson and Mike Huckabee exist in a little box that, if one is feeling angry, he can insert knives into to blow off some stress. But there's no way into the box and no way out of it, either. In the box, Mike Huckabee's refusal to accept the truth of evolution qualifies him as a fanatic; if I point out that most Muslims refuse to accept the same, I'm deemed a "racist." Muslims are outside of that little box, because nothing on the left actually has anything to do with anything else. All that matters are identity traits: race, class, sex, and so forth. Do you qualify as a victim? Congratulations, you've earned a blank check to spew venom.

There's an unholy alliance brewing between the Religious Right and the postmodern left to elevate religion above the realm of criticism. Anatomy, skin color, sexual orientation, height and weight — all of these traits are rightly considered irrelevant in imparting moral judgment. The crusade to add religion to this list has been, despite the cries of those like the Caller's own S.E. Cupp, pretty successful. The idea — something straight out of the pre-American era — is disturbing for its regressiveness. To declare oneself a believer in religious dogma is to invite profound philosophical and metaphysical beliefs into one's life. These beliefs have real moral import. They are not above criticism. If you declare fealty to the Qur'an (or the Bible, or any other ancient book of myths), you'd better be prepared to repudiate the parts that say that I deserve to burn in a lake of fire for all of eternity if I want to have sex with my boyfriend. It's not a mark of "bigotry" — narrow-mindedness — for me to ask this. To the contrary: it's bigoted to embrace the book that declares such a thing! Religion is the realm of bigotry, not the beliefs of Voltaire and Hume. When on Earth did the left forget this?

With Roy Moore, Anti-Muslim Bigots Tear Off Their Masks

Facebook | 12.12.17

By supporting Roy Moore, the anti-Muslim demagogues have torn off their own mask. It was always clear that when they waved the rainbow flag or expressed concern about Islamic treatment of women, it was not to support gay people's right to exist without fear of persecution, or to support gender equality — but simply to use groups favored by liberals as a fig-leaf to bash Muslims. Now we have proof.

Let's remember that, while ISIS and al-Qaeda and their ilk are evil, they are not clinically insane. They have internally coherent arguments and a holistic vision of society that makes sense to tens of millions of people. As with references to Hitler, people often think Islamists exist in this special realm of evil that nobody else could possibly reach; that it's categorically outrageous to accuse someone of having descended to those depths. But that's not true. And there is not much distance between Roy Moore and ISIS on a host of social issues, from secularism to homosexuality to education — hell, they're even on the same page when it comes to underage girls and on the question of whether America is an evil empire. When we have to start splitting such hairs that we arrive at the conclusion that the major difference between Moore and ISIS on homosexuality is that Moore won't literally throw gay people off of buildings, we know where the argument has brought us.

So the next time some right-winger tells us about how horrible it would be to invite more Muslim refugees to the United States because we can't trust that they won't hold extreme socially conservative views, just remember that when those same views are held by a white Christian man, they'll happily cheerlead to include them in the United States Senate.

Multicultural Europe On the Brink

Personal Website | 11.14.15

The window of opportunity for reasonable European leaders to address the cultural cancer of Islamism before there's a major right-wing backlash — is getting smaller and smaller. Islamist ideology isn't new, and it isn't going anywhere — once again, we're dealing with the same worldview that was behind the '93 WTC bombings, the embassy bombings of the 90s, the attack on the USS Cole, 9/11, the London and Madrid attacks, the execution of Theo van Gogh, the Fort Hood massacre, the attack in Benghazi, the Charlie Hebdo executions, the rise of ISIS, and on and on and on —

What's particularly frightening about the ongoing situation in Europe is how many of the attacks there have been home-brewed. And the problem is not limited to acts of terrorism: in Muslim ghettos in countries once thought to be bastions of tolerance, like Holland, sharia law has as much or more sway than the true laws of the government. Gay-bashings are happening again in cities that once thought they'd done away with them. Anti-Semitism is on the rise again. A recent poll showed 16% of Frenchmen call themselves supporters of ISIS, and you can bet they aren't named 'Francois.' Another poll showed 98% of British Muslims morally disapproving of homosexuality. Can there be any debate any longer that multiculturalism and cultural relativism have failed Europe?

The middle way is always to take in a moderate number of newcomers from foreign cultures and to insist on assimilation. There is no reason why Europe can't take in a number of Muslim immigrants and turn them into successful Europeans. As President Obama has pointed out, America's Muslim community is well-assimilated and should serve as an example to the world. But if the choice facing Europe boils down to voting in more high priests of multiculturalism and open-borders — and voting in right-wingers who want to totally seal national borders and keep them all of 'them' out — well, it's not going to take very many more attacks like this before the post-Cold War dream of a unified, open, multicultural Europe goes up in flames.

After the Pulse Nightclub Shooting

Facebook | 06.12.16

1. ISIS claimed responsibility for the attack — but so far all we have is their word for it. ISIS wants you to fear them. Let's wait for more evidence to come out before we judge the extent to which the attack was coordinated by ISIS. It's more than possible that this guy 'self-brainwashed' and swore allegiance to ISIS because he admired them and wanted his attack to have a larger-than-life dimension to it — terrorism is theatrical, after all. Yet, swearing allegiance isn't the same as actually coordinating with ISIS members to pull off an attack. We need to be more conscientious, not less, about how we absorb information during times when emotions run high. Do not fall for potential jihadist propaganda!

2. We are not Europe. Our Muslim population is very small. We do not take in many immigrants from the Middle East, Central Asia, or North Africa. Moreover, the shooter was born in America — the problem is already here. The idea that can we can 'fix' this problem with a neat and easy policy change is beyond disingenuous. However, this probably signals an end to any remaining political will to bring in refugees from Syria.

3. It's equally disingenuous to claim that piecemeal gun-control reforms like additional background checks would have done anything to stop this. Viewed through the lens of gun control, the only serious legislative solution to this sort of incident is mass confiscation. That is politically unacceptable, and for good reason. But the right should be self-aware: it expects people to tolerate the murder of elementary school children as the price of freedom, so I am not sure why they would expect progressives to assent to a blanket ban on migration by people of a particular nationality or religion, which is just as radical as any kind of gun confiscation.

4. When Islamists bother to single out identity groups, it's usually one of two demographics: gays and Jews.

5. The vast majority of Muslims are peaceful people, but to a certain extent, you have to ask: so what? The vast majority of Confederates in 1862 had never owned a slave or lynched a black man. The vast majority of Germans in 1942 had no voluntary involvement with the Nazi Party. Let's compare Islamism to a disease: The rest of the body can be fully functional when its parts are considered in isolation, but that cancer will just grow and grow unless peaceful Muslims work to eradicate it. There are over a billion Muslims in the world, Islam is not just going to go away — and we can't eliminate an decentralized fundamentalist ideology with brute strength alone.

6. This attack fits the pattern of children of Muslim immigrants being more likely to hate the West than their parents — and their being more likely to identify first of all with their ancestral homeland and religion than with liberal democracy than their parents — a trend which is well-documented in Europe.

7. It's not really surprising that this event would seem to confirm everyone's pre-existing biases — it's not as if there's something unique about this attack that would cause anyone to change their minds about how they view radical Islam, gun control, etc. So that criticism is kind of stale.

Instead of Mosque, Build Another Sex Shop

The Daily Caller | 08.27.10

Anti-sex left-wingers are caterwauling over the fact that conservatives' antipathy toward Islam outweighs their aversion toward sex. The Christian Science Monitor breathlessly reports that the lack of outrage over a sex store near Ground Zero reveals the hypocrisy of the right: the "eyesore" of the Pussycat Lounge is infecting the 'hollowed ground' more than any Islamic center would.

More sex and less religion? Personally, I find this to be a very promising development on the right! In the heyday of Irving Kristol and

Ed Meese and his self-parodying Commission on Pornography, one can bet that we would have heard about these "sleazy shops" long ago. But their presence is really not a defense of the proposed mosque.

In fact, I say: all the more reason to protest it. Instead, let's build more sex shops. First of all, I like sex. I don't like Islam and Islam doesn't like sex, so I figure I'm striking two blows against religious puritanism with such a proposal. America's refusal to censor pornography and sexual expression is glorious. Contrary to the overtones of the self-righteous neo-Victorians of the left, complaining about "sleaze," there's really nothing wrong with strip clubs or sex stores. Would Ayman al-Zawahiri frequent the Pussycat Lounge?

I'm not being facetious. I loathe this proposed mosque. The imam is clearly a "moderate" only insofar as he doesn't want to blow up buildings, and, as an atheist, I don't exactly oppose Islam on the grounds that Muslims need them some Jesus. Moreover, I'm a proponent of what pretentious academics call "low culture" — the fast-food joints, sex clubs, and novelty shops that are such "eyesores" to Nicolaus Mills of the *Christian Science Monitor*. Remember Britney Spears' recent #1 hit "3" — a song about a one-girl/two-guy threesome — with its immortal line "Livin' in sin is the new thing"? That's what Islam needs.

It's not just Mr. Mills of the Monitor who is engaging in this nonsense. Run a simple Google search and you'll find thousands of supporters of the mosque project complaining about the strip club. The right can take solace from this fact, I suppose: beyond allowing their teenage daughters to use birth control, the left is basically as sexually hung up as the right is. But the fact that there are strip clubs near Ground Zero is precisely why we *shouldn't* promote mosques nearby. What an ugly contrast: a shrine to an ancient book of myths juxtaposed with sexual freedom. What better way to demonstrate our differences with Islamic totalitarianism than to declare proudly that we, as a culture, are okay with sexual expression? Let's ditch this mosque and build another sex store.

Psychiatry and Mental Illness

A Brief General Critique of Psychiatry

Personal Website | 03.26.15

First, so as to prepare one's expectations accordingly: People often think, consciously or otherwise, that denying the validity of the theory of mental illness — that is: the dominant paradigm of psychiatry — is tantamount to denying the suffering of people who are called 'mentally ill.' Psychiatrists, of course, have both a personal and financial interest in ensuring that people respond to critiques of their discipline with this sort of emotional revulsion. I will attempt here to summarize the core of my problems with psychiatry, much of which is influenced by Thomas Szasz's excellent critiques. It is crucial to recognize at the beginning of any conversation like this that Szasz never denies that people labeled as mentally ill are suffering (and certainly I don't). He denies that they are ill. Illness causes suffering (or worse) — but not all suffering is a sign of illness, and if we are to effectively help people, it is imperative to know the difference, and to build our social systems according to our understanding of those differences.

I would ask anyone reading this to keep an open mind: It is easy to ridicule the dogmas of the past, but all of those past dogmas held themselves up as the pinnacle of human understanding, too — it is the dogmas of the present that deserve the most intense scrutiny. I am convinced that sometime in the not-so-distant future, people will view psychiatry much like they do alchemy: as a precursor; a stepping-stone to real science. Neurology will and should eventually take over all legitimate (but poorly-understood) brain disorders that so happen to have been clustered under the 'mental illness' umbrella — just like Parkinson's Disease and neurosyphilis in the past, real disorders like bipolar and schizophrenia(s) will eventually be treated by brain specialists, not psychiatrists.

What is distinctive about psychiatry, insofar as it claims to be a medical science rather than a humanistic endeavor? It is the only field of 'medicine' whose members vote in a central committee on whether or n ot a condition qualifies as a disorder. It is the only field of 'medicine' that purports to be able to 'cure' 'diseases' through the use of speech — 'psychotherapy.' (Can we heal the flu by learning to change our perspective?) It is the only field of 'medicine' in which the line between illness and health is a fundamentally political question: consider the status of sexual minorities in the history of psychiatry, including the status of transgendered people today — but, more broadly, consider that the 'mentally ill' person is frequently less disturbed by his own thoughts and behavior than by other people's reactions to his thoughts and behavior — that is: by society's unwillingness to understand his condition, and its unwillingness to accommodate his problems. We should absolutely help people fit in with society — including, possibly, through the use of humanistic counseling and mind-altering drugs — but that does not necessitate deeming them 'ill.' (A TV can be playing an unusual channel without being broken, after all.) Finally, psychiatry is the only field of 'medicine' whose professionals are legally permitted to forcibly commit someone who wants to be left alone. The standard here is that one must be 'harmful to oneself or others' to justify this kind of action. But a cancer victim who refuses chemotherapy is undoubtedly harming himself. Shall the police forcibly constrain himself and impose treatment on him?

Counseling ('psychotherapy') can be very helpful to people, as long as everyone involved respects each other's boundaries, dignity, and agency. Moreover, free adults ought to be allowed to use any drug they want to relieve their suffering. But the fact that a drug has a positive effect is not evidence that it has 'treated' anything. If you buy ketamine from someone on the street to induce euphoria, you are called a 'drug abuser' participating in a 'crime.' If a Yale professor gives you ketamine to induce euphoria and calls it a 'research study,' then ketamine is a 'medicine' that 'treats' 'depression.' This is not 'semantics': it is the difference, as Szasz points out, between typhoid fever and 'spring fever.' If someone with 'spring fever' is given some amphetamine, he will no longer be listless, apathetic, or disconnected from society. Is this proof that 'spring fever' is a real illness one can 'treat' with 'medicine' called 'Adderall'?

Let us consider 'depression' as an example. The arguments I am about to make are mine and not Szasz's, though he would likely have agreed. Few people doubt that 'depression' is an 'illness.' Let us first consider, however, that the world is not simply objectively 'there,' waiting for us to correctly perceive it. The world, in fact, discloses itself in different ways to different people. ("Our temperament sets a price on every gift bestowed by fortune" says La Rochefoucauld) Some people are actually born with tendencies toward 'hypomania' — eager, active, confident, sociable, driven. Others are born with tendencies toward 'depression' — reluctant, passive, self-critical, isolated, apathetic. Both tendencies are foreign to most people; their center of gravity is somewhere in between these extremes. Is either class of people described above perceiving the world inaccurately? Is there not injustice as well as opportunity in the world? Is there not cruelty and fear as well as love and hope? Is there not disappointment as well as excitement? Is it a sign of 'illness' to fixate on one rather than the other? If someone is melancholic by nature, perhaps it would behoove them to explore perspectives that can mitigate the negative sides of this temperament — and perhaps it would even be to their benefit to take drugs, as those diagnosed as mentally ill are usually advised to do, to help take the edge off of those darker moments. Maybe this is the burden of a melancholic temperament. But where is the tangible evidence of 'illness'? The empty theory of 'chemical imbalance' is finally losing favor among academics, but it is still heavily favored by advertisers (and the people). The notion of a 'chemical imbalance' implies that there is a 'balance' — which implies, as we have seen, that there is a particular 'correct' way of experiencing the world. What does a 'chemical balance' look like? How should we properly view the world? Szasz suggests that we will discover the 'cause' of 'mental illnesses' like this at the same time we discover the chemical 'cause' of being a Democrat, or being a Taoist. Psychiatry, in this sense, is part of a popular political trend toward homogenization and the blotting out of human differences that threaten to undermine the democratic-liberal-capitalist order.

No 'anti-stigma' campaign will work; psychiatrists' insistence that they care about mitigating stigma is either naive or a facade. I am sure most psychiatrists care deeply about making sure most of their 'patients' are treated well — but stigma is an unavoidable byproduct of being a patient, an 'ill' person. Someone who is sick and in treatment is not ordinarily considered a full and able participant in society. It is impossible to erase the stigma attached to incomplete participation in society — there is a stigma attached to being on welfare, being disabled, being in treatment for a bodily disease, and being very old (or very young) for identical reasons. Why should we anticipate that society would allow for an objection in the case of the 'mentally ill'? People, fortunately, are actually willing to accept and help others labeled 'mentally ill' — but we must state what their problems are in plain English, not in pseudo-medical jargon, in the hopes that the legitimacy usually accorded to real medicine will 'rub off' on psychiatry.

Ultimately, there is simply no coherent definition of 'mental illness.' There are bodily diseases, including diseases of the brain, and they are the concern of medical science — and there are humanistic concerns, problems in living. Psychiatry approaches problems in living (as well as a handful of real diseases) through the language of medical science. The results are about what we'd expect.

Step One to Combat the Heroin Epidemic: Stop Blaming the Heroin

Personal Website | 07.19.15

The national heroin epidemic has reached Maryland, where last year there were over 500 overdose-related deaths. Gov. Larry Hogan, who has already declared a state of emergency over this issue, recently announced the creation of a task force to combat the problem, according to a news report:

Heroin use has risen dramatically across the United States, according to a new report from the Centers for Disease Control and Prevention.

In Maryland, a task force is looking at ways to tackle the problem.

Governor Larry Hogan placed Lieutenant Governor Boyd Rutherford in charge of the state's Heroin and Opioid Emergency Task Force.

Last week, the group concluded a series of six meetings held all around the state.

"The next step is we have an interim report that is due in mid August, and then a final report and recommendations to the Governor in December," Rutherford tells WTOP.

He says the state wants to take a multifaceted approach: "You have to look at prevention as one of the elements, treatment for those who have become addicted, as well as recovery efforts."

After half a century of propaganda promoting the Drug War, Americans have been conditioned to fear pleasure-inducing drugs in a manner akin to how people used to fear demons. Drugs like heroin (and methamphetamine, cocaine, etc.) are viewed as quasi-magical substances that rob us of our self-control and sound judgment — and have the potential to transform us into addicts, in spite of ourselves. In short: heroin is said to rob people of their free will. It is of course imperative that Americans address the heroin epidemic before it worsens. But we cannot begin to overcome it until we break open the long-petrified conversation about drugs and addiction. What does it mean to be addicted? Why do some people become addicted where others don't? The first — and perhaps the most difficult step toward healing is to stop blaming the heroin. It is actually possible to use any drug recreationally without becoming an 'addict' — even powerful ones like opiates. Anyone who has ever gotten regularly drunk, yet still fulfilled their obligations, knows this — and so do the millions of people who have taken prescription opiates for pain and then successfully tapered off of them under the supervision of a doctor. If opiates were inherently addictive and robbed us of our self-control, it should not be possible to use them for an extended period of time for medical purposes without forcing the patient into addiction. But this isn't what happens.

The difficult truth that addicts and their loved ones often don't want to face is that it is not all that difficult to taper off of opiates: it takes weeks — not months, not years. The difference between long-standing addicts and those who taper off of them after using them for pain is that the latter group actually wants to be off of them — because they want to resume their daily lives. Contrary to what they will tell you, many long-time 'addicts' are not actually interested in getting clean. Once a person really wants to get clean, it doesn't take very long — and with the proliferation of methadone and suboxone treatment centers and professional rehab programs, it is easier and safer than ever to get off of opiates. But many, if not most, people who pursue this line of treatment are those who have been caught using by horrified friends and family — or the cops — and so they need to make it look like they are making an effort to get clean — even if, secretly, they really just want to get their tolerance down so they can get high again — or perhaps they just want to keep others from getting angry at them. This is an all-too-common scenario, and it is a recipe for relapse after relapse. I know more than one person who has been to rehab more than once — and in each case, the reason for their failure is obvious: they went to rehab for others, not for themselves.

The only way to truly convince someone to get clean and stay clean is to demonstrate to them that there is something waiting for them beyond opiate use that will be better than the high. This is far easier said than done: many addicts turn to constant opiate use because they feel trapped by their circumstances and see no viable way forward in their lives. The heroin epidemic, in this sense, is really an epidemic of meaninglessness and brokenness. We'll never begin to tackle the problem until we wake up to the fact that heroin itself is not the root of the problem — and resolve to do the difficult work of trying to mend lives that have wandered off-course.

It's Time to Stop Scapegoating the Mentally Ill for Gun Violence

Huffington Post | 04.09.13

While President Barack Obama and the National Rifle Association have very real philosophical differences regarding gun ownership, they agree on at least one policy goal: keeping guns out of the hands of the mentally ill. In the aftermath of the tragedy at Sandy Hook, the NRA called for a "national database" of the mentally ill, against which new gun sales can be checked. Similarly, President Obama has consistently advocated that Congress do something to prevent the mentally ill from possessing guns.

The general public's thought process seems to be something like this: Anyone who would use a gun to murder children must be crazy — and crazy people should not have access to guns in the first place. But it is impolitic to use the word 'crazy,' which sounds too loaded, too politically incorrect. The polite way of expressing such a sentiment is to declare that 'mentally ill' people should not own guns.

Contrary to the general public's ignorant abuse of the term, though, 'mentally ill' does not mean 'crazy.' The term covers an extremely broad spectrum of disorders whose symptoms and causes vary significantly. Paranoid schizophrenia is classified as a mental illness, but so are Attention-Deficit Hyperactivity Disorder, and anorexia nervosa. The real question, then, becomes: Which mental illnesses should disqualify a person from owning a gun, and by what grounds do we justify singling out the people who suffer from them?

And this is where the argument starts to fall apart. As is usually the case, crafting a specific, viable policy plan is a bit more difficult than making empty emotional pleas to do something. While people with severe mental illnesses — such as paranoid schizophrenia or major depression — are somewhat more likely than the average person to commit acts of aggression, they account for only 4 percent of all violent crimes. Virtually all people with severe mental illnesses are just everyday men and women, no likelier than you or I to commit an act of violence. Of course, the authorities should investigate any credible claims of violent tendencies, but this is true regardless of the status of the suspect's mental health. The logic of a blanket policy targeting the mentally ill is identical to the logic of racially profiling Arab Muslims at airports.

My own experience as the close friend of a young woman with severe mental health issues has taught me that politicians, insurance companies, and the general public are astonishingly unfamiliar with what such people's day-to-day lived experiences are like. One of the most debilitating issues that my friend confronts is simple ignorance: Misconceptions about mental health issues are frighteningly common, and they can cause problems in school, work, and family life. Most mentally ill people have the ability to live normal lives — but only with a network of support. This is why a national dialogue about mental health is so urgently needed: because these people deserve our compassion and understanding, but are too often met with indifference, ignorance, and fear.

The reader can determine for himself whether the past few months have produced any ideas to actually help the mentally ill in their day-today lives. Michael Fitzpatrick, the director of the National Alliance for the Mentally Ill, expressed hope that President Obama's call for dialogue would help combat the stigma against the mentally ill. It hasn't, and it won't — and it's easy to see why. The framing of this 'dialogue' is in the context of Sandy Hook; that is: in the context of violence and fear. What message does it send to the public that we only bother to talk about mental illness after an act of mass murder against children has taken place? The central question of the dialogue should be "How can society help those who suffer from mental illness?" But the dialogue as it has actually happened has centered around the question, "How can society protect itself against crazy people?" That's no way to craft good public health policy. It's time to stop scapegoating the mentally ill — and start looking for real ways to help them.

American Civic Life

Guns Don't Kill People, Political Rhetoric Kills People

361 Security | 06.21.17

A troubling number of Americans have apparently decided in recent years that guns don't kill people — political rhetoric kills people. Shootings in America inevitably turn into political feeding frenzies, and one of the frequent practical results of this is to drain and demoralize those who are not inclined to participate in these repetitive, nasty, fruitless exchanges. Over time, more and more of the discourse is ceded to ideologues and partisans who are incapable of seeing them as anything but new skirmishes in the ongoing battle of us-versus-them.

We saw this tendency creep into the left in 2011, when former Rep. Gabrielle Giffords was shot by an assailant during a routine public event. Through what can only be called a series of bizarre leaps of logic, more than a few prominent left-of-center pundits arrived at the conclusion that their *bête noire* of the moment, Sarah Palin, was partially morally culpable for this event, since in 2010 she distributed an electoral map showing 'targets' over vulnerable Democratic districts, including Giffords'. Besides the striking fact that there was no evidence demonstrating that the shooter (whose name I will not write) had ever even seen the hitherto-obscure map, the perpetuation of the idea that a symbolic or metaphorical 'target' on an electoral map could be construed as incitement to violence was a new and unsettling interpretation of the relationship between speech and actions.

It didn't take long on Wednesday to discover that the man who shot Majority Whip Steve Scalise was motivated by partisan concerns and had volunteered for Sen. Bernie Sanders' 2016 presidential campaign. Perhaps it was only a matter of time before many on the right adopted the same attitude so many on the left took toward Sarah Palin in 2011 – and, indeed, in 2017 — but, somewhat shockingly, similar accusations were leveled by the New York Times, which published an innuendo-laden piece that day about how the shooter's actions serve as a kind of 'test' for Sanders' movement. That one of the most important news outlets in America would unhesitatingly embrace this narrative is proof that it is no longer isolated to the fringes.

The language of competition and conflict often invokes metaphors about fighting, violence, and war. No reasonable person could mistake them for a call to literally employ lethal force. If we value free speech — if we give speech the benefit of the doubt, if we err on the side of protecting speech — then we must hold to the idea that rhetoric, no matter how distasteful, cannot be justly perceived as tantamount to incitement to violence. The right pointed Wednesday to an 'atmosphere of hate' against President Donald Trump and his supporters, just as the left pointed to one against President Barack Obama in 2011. But we are experiencing a not-minor political crisis — out-of-control polarization, an increasingly fragmented electorate, legislative paralysis, and lingering economic problems from the Great Recession — and it is hardly a surprise that passions are running high, nor that they occasionally even overheat in tragic ways. A just government can contain those passions and give ordinary citizens space to work through these challenges, and can deal with political criminals appropriately. America has endured major divisions before — most recently in the 1960s — and it can work through them again if we honor our shared Constitutional inheritance. Our commitment to free speech, and especially free political speech — not just in the law but in the culture that sustains that law — is singular among nations. If we adopt the standard that politicians must cater their rhetoric to the most unhinged among us, lest they become morally culpable for the potentially disturbing actions of those individuals, we will have taken a major step away from that commitment.

To be sure, this does not mean we cannot condemn some speech as irresponsible — one may legitimately question the wisdom of Kathy Griffin mock-beheading President Trump, or Trump himself suggesting on the campaign trail that "Second Amendment people" could figure out a way to stop a President Hillary Clinton from appointing judges. And this should not be construed as just another call to not 'politicize a tragedy': it is legitimate and appropriate to debate gun control and the state of our discourse in the light of Wednesday's actions. But we cross a line when we assign blame to individual politicians or to factions as a whole. We cannot water down the distinction between words and actions without suffering terrible consequences to our culture of free speech, and therefore to our ability to ultimately deal with the many problems we face.

The us-versus-them mentality compels us to take whatever opportunities are in front of us to take down our opponents — but some issues are fundamental, and must transcend it: everyone has something at stake in upholding these norms. If we abandon them, we will ultimately only become more like that which we say we are trying to resist.

'Alternative Facts' and the Media Crisis of Legitimacy

New American Perspective | 01.22.17

President Donald Trump and his legion of lackeys rolled the dice on the theory that left and right now live in totally different realities: that we no longer agree on what constitutes a legitimate source of information, that motives and intentions now count for more than diligence in 'getting the facts right,' and that a forceful Republican candidate can bypass the mainstream media altogether as long as he steadfastly refuses to cater to their standards. To a large extent, this is true, and is one of the major truths Trump accurately perceived that caught Washington by surprise. Rather than seeing polarization as a problem to be overcome, Trump sees it it as an opportunity to be embraced. There have been occasions in which Trump has been shown a tape of him saying something, after which he denies having said it. But rather than abandoning him over such a blatant act of charlatanism, his supporters love it: he is their liar, engaged in combat against the other liars — and his lies drive those other liars up the wall. He lies for them, and against Obama, the Clintons, and progressives — and that perceived loyalty means more than any factual account: motive trumps all.

Not surprisingly, a campaign based on this attitude became a magnet for grifters, media-whores, trolls, has-beens, and malcontents — an army of the alienated: everyone from Sarah Palin to Martin Shkreli to Milo Yiannopoulos — excuse me: MILO — to Richard Spencer to 4chan to Alex Jones eagerly hopped on the Trump Train, perceiving that this opportunity to help usher in a world where everyone has their own — liar-for-hire Kellyanne Conway's words, not mine — 'alternative facts' — would be a boon to them. An environment like this is something of a free-for-all, and every niche figure can be included and validated in it. There is no umpire, no referee — every man and woman can be their own final arbiter of what counts as true.

Obviously, none of this started with President Trump. In some ways it is merely the 'postmodern' condition at work. And it is certainly not an exclusively right-wing problem: the mainstream media deserves blame for its role in exacerbating the problem. At times — not always, but at times — reporters' widespread enthusiasm for the Obama personality cult led them in this direction themselves. In a perfectly just world, this might have increased the right's enthusiasm for an honest and balanced press, which they once pretended was their goal during the Clinton and Bush years. But instead they came to view it as an opening to break away from the mainstream press entirely: to drum up every example of bias, real or imagined, as proof-positive that the mainstream press as it exists is irredeemable and must be perceived as an enemy. The calling card of right-wing new-media sites like Breitbart, the Blaze, and the Daily Caller is that they are upfront about their bias, unlike the mainstream press, which pretends to be neutral but really tilts toward the left — the broader implication being that reporting which is basically neutral is neither possible nor desirable. Since there is no general consensus for or against any source of information that can't be painted as merely the nay-saying of another side, they have largely accomplished their mission: on the right, it is commonplace to perceive Breitbart as the heads to the New York Times' tails.

It is imperative to note that there has always been this tendency in politics, and always will be; there is no lost golden age in which truth and reason ruled and partisans cooperated and got along simply civilly. But it can be a minor problem — easily contained, widely recognized for its dangers — or it can be an alarming problem — spinning out of control, widely embraced. Traditionally, we have kept watch for demagogues who would try to exploit these tendencies for their own gain at the expense of the nation as a whole. We are not in a 'post-fact' or 'post-truth' era, as some pundits have rushed to declare. Most people want facts — but if they do not trust any source of information to report or interpret them neutrally or fairly, then they figure they might as well consume news from sources which speak to their values instead. What is most alarming of all is that nobody has a road map back to a place where we can agree on the fundamentals: the problem is not destined to resolve itself, and may simply grow worse and worse.

Ten Unpopular Opinions

Facebook | 12.18.16

Here is my very own vain list of ten unpopular non-political opinions:

People who claim to categorically loathe pop music are either lying or are pretentious snobs — and people who claim that music isn't as good as when they were young are either not looking for new music or are blinded by nostalgia.

Gays and lesbians were almost certainly not born that way — though most of them, especially gay men, were probably predisposed to homosexuality.

Psychiatry is a basically humanistic-political endeavor, with the scientific-medicinal aspect serving only as an auxiliary function.
Americans rich and poor, white and black, male and female — in a

word, the overwhelming majority of Americans of all types — have a grotesquely distorted view of the proper role of money, and transform everything they touch into handmaidens of acquisitiveness — including most people who claim to have a dim view of materialism.

The overwhelming majority of unhappy people are responsible for their own unhappiness — and most people are about as happy or unhappy as they deserve to be.

Empirical science will never solve the mystery of consciousness.

The idea that opiates are inherently more dangerous than alcohol is a superstition.

The health-and-wellness obsession among college-educated whites is a quasi-religious phenomenon that is more about morality and class-distinction than about actual maintenance of the body.

So is the obsession with traveling, which seems to me to be linked very closely with warding off ennui. I want to shove pinpricks in my eyes when some rich kid tells me how eye-opening their excursion through the EU was.

The only paths to anything resembling happiness are through philosophy or revealed religion, religion providing a second-best alternative that is rooted in life-giving images and myths that approximate essential truths — but for those for whom revealed religion is not plausible, there is no alternative to philosophy

'Tiger Moms': Training Kids to Be Submissive Drones

The Re-Examiner | 02.02.11

For whatever reason, I'm just now hearing about this deranged essay by Amy Chua in the Wall Street Journal, which could otherwise be titled "Raising Submissive, Obedient Automatons for Dummies."

The essay is not, in fact, a hymn to demanding parenting, but a serenade to government institutions, establishment mores, and passive obedience to authority. The one thing Amy Chua's children are never allowed to do is *think*.

In case you're not familiar with the 'Tiger Mother' style of parenting that Chua heralds, I would recommend at least skimming the essay. The gist of it is this: quality, demanding parenting is about restrictions and demands. No sleepovers, no grades worse than a solid A, no television or computer games, take away kids' Christmas presents if they don't learn their piano pieces (which they practice for two hours daily), etc.

The Religious Right has had its own version of this garbage for a while, and many conservatives might instinctively cheer the fact that Chua discards the mush and the self-esteem garbage of the past couple of decades. But the end result of such parenting is not success — not by any meaningful metric, anyway — but submission. Take Ms. Chua's emphasis on grades:

For example, if a child comes home with an A-minus on a test, a Western parent will most likely praise the child. The Chinese mother will gasp in horror and ask what went wrong. If the child comes home with a B on the test, some Western parents will still praise the child. Other Western parents will sit their child down and express disapproval, but they will be careful not to make their child feel inadequate or insecure, and they will not call their child "stupid," "worthless" or "a disgrace." Privately, the Western parents may worry that their child does not test well or have aptitude in the subject or that there is something wrong with the curriculum and possibly the whole school. If the child's grades do not improve, they may eventually schedule a meeting with the school principal to challenge the way the subject is being taught or to call into question the teacher's credentials. ...

Chinese parents demand perfect grades because they believe that their child can get them. If their child doesn't get them, the Chinese parent assumes it's because the child didn't work hard enough. That's why the solution to substandard performance is always to excoriate, punish and shame the child...

Ms. Chua is certainly correct that children frequently fail to meet their natural potential — and she is also right when she implies that Western parents often place more of an emphasis on preserving the child's fragile little ego than in demanding performance. But what sort of performance is Ms. Chua demanding? She balks in horror at the suggestion that the government may have gotten something wrong in shaping what children should be learning — let alone how children should be learning. She passively accepts both the curriculum and the methods of government schools as the gold standard of earthly success: master the list of items that the state tells you a schooled person ought to know, and Chua is a happy mother. From beginning to end, she is a passive servant to the whims of authority. She values *schooling*, not education.

Western mothers are equally oblivious to this truth, of course, and Chua is absolutely right that the majority of Westerners who call the school's curriculum into question do so out of ego-preservation, not independent thought. But Chua's medicine is worse than the disease: more obedience, more submission, less critical thinking. A quality parent should immerse her child in independent thought, critical thinking, and personal autonomy — and, vitally, all of the responsibilities that come with them — as soon as possible. The parent should seek to be a guide, not a master. She should seek to foster self-sufficient adults who aren't afraid to ask 'Why?' — not drones who passively accept whatever is bestowed upon them by authorities. We want a society of independent, inquisitive, thoughtful adults — not a society of automatons whose well-being begins and ends with kind words from authorities. This is a model of authoritarianism, not of constitutional republicanism. (Compare the governments of China and America.)

Chua cites Confucius in her Journal piece as a possible precursor to 'Tiger parenting.' Does she actually plan to educate her children about the philosophy of Confucius? It is something that every culturally literate person should have a passing familiarity with — and government schools certainly don't discuss his thought. Will Chua? Don't hold your breath. She won't discuss Confucius, Aristotle, Epictetus, or any other thinkers who had any independent thoughts whatsoever on the nature of the good life. She's too busy whipping her kids into shape for not being just like her: a passive servant of the whims of authority.

The Malaise of Liberalism

New American Perspective | 08.25.17

There are few things clearer in contemporary politics than the need for an alternative vision to *homo economicus,* in both its liberal and socialist manifestations — man with neither roots nor telos but content merely with animalized comfort — and the right's proposed flight back into the inadequate and unbelievable claims of the ancestral. It is also clear that there is no faction in American politics which can obviously serve as a vehicle for this alternative.

The right, even while holding political power, seems to understand itself today as the losers of recent history, and is resorting to tactics meant primarily to agitate, disorient, and inflame the winners; they are absolutely blinded by resentment, and no meaningful attempt at governing can be made until it is past this phase and reconciles itself to where we have arrived. So the way forward right now must come from the liberals, exhausted as they are — and despite that they are perhaps the least-inclined to recognize the gravity of the crisis. Why is liberalism once again susceptible to morphing in the direction of ideas it thought it had eliminated — socialism and nationalism? Victory in war, hot or cold, however dazzling, was clearly not sufficient to forever suppress the power of these ideas. Both promise a variety of security — economic and identity-based — against the rapid flux of things under liberal-democratic techno-capitalism, and the pace and intensity of that change has only grown faster in recent years. And a 'globalized' world of mass-communications is not just economically disorienting — it is spiritually disorienting, for young and old alike, the former of whom have not known a world unlike this, and the latter of whom have and are aghast at its disintegration. The greater the depths of disorientation, the greater the potential heights of reactive fanaticism. As we have said: people like Donald Trump simply do not come to power when people are not hurting, and badly.

Liberals need to be able to answer the question: Why liberalism today? What kind of life does liberalism help to enable, and why is it desirable? There is no doubt that liberalism benefits certain small groups in large ways — the bourgeois professional class continues to thrive materially, and writers and artists will always have a special appreciation for the liberties of free speech, religion, and association, for instance. But if we believe Aristotle that good government necessitates a balance between the needs of the few and the needs of the many, liberals have to be able to provide some account of what a good life under liberalism looks like for the ordinary citizen. With ideals of religion, race, education, property, family, marriage, and sex all unusually unstable, we are in dire need of a coherent blueprint for what life under liberalism ought to look like in the 21st century. A requirement of this project would be to acknowledge and adequately address the challenges posed by Nietzsche and Marx — it need not 'rebut' them, but it must address them — and would itself be tantamount to a long-needed contemporary defense of liberal democracy — a defense of the idea that it is capable of providing decent and substantive lives for the many.

Of course, liberalism has been in need of such a defense for quite some time, and little has been forthcoming. Perhaps liberal democratic capitalism has lurched through the generations out of sheer inertia and material might, the beneficiaries of a historical head-start. That variants of the zombie ideologies of socialism and nationalism are coming back to torment us again suggests that the need for a recuperation and rehabilitation of liberalism has reached a fever pitch.

The Malaise of Conservatism

New American Perspective | 10.09.17

I have argued elsewhere that liberalism — from its so-called 'classical' roots to its modern/progressive outgrowth — is the engine that moves America, and that the role of conservatism is largely to moderate or restrain liberal excesses. In this sense, the right is almost necessarily defined by what it opposes. The great conservative (or, right-liberal) triumph of the 20th century within liberalism was the rise of Ronald Reagan, who decisively repudiated the infinite growth of the welfare state and reinvigorated the power of our civic mythology. But it only took the center-left a couple of election cycles to accept and absorb that new consensus and integrate it into its economic platform.

Democrats in the 1990s embraced welfare reform, middle class tax cuts, budgetary prudence, and even American exceptionalism, thereby ensuring a bulwark against greater reaction. Obama has not overtly repudiated this approach, and has embraced a successor set to continue it. So what is the point of conservatism today? Quite simply, Reaganism's success domestically has left the American right without a unifying cause in the post-Soviet era. Once Trump is defeated, the Republican Party will have lost the popular vote in six of the last seven presidential elections — and the one they won was a terribly narrow victory during wartime, three years after the worst attack on the country in our history.

And why not? Who needs Republicans? The variety of conservatism offered by most of the Republican Party is fundamentally in agreement with the variety of liberalism offered by most of the Democratic Party. They both aim toward maximizing material luxury, coupled with expanded individual choice and social access (prosperity, liberty, equality). The most evocative international threat comes from a sprawling network of paramilitary operations, and Democrats have been at least as successful at confronting it as Republicans — so the idea of a new 'fusionism' is useless. (We should note here that 'fusionism' was about fusing against something, not for something!) Rates of crime, divorce, abortion, teen pregnancy, and other 'social indicators' are better than they have been in decades. The last Republican president has been judged to have been a supreme screw-up economically. Maybe John Kasich could have defeated Hillary Clinton this year, but the populists are right: aside from a few social issues primarily of interest to niche factions, Kasich is not actually terribly different than Clinton.

At most, there are some disagreements between party establishmentarians about how to reach the liberal goal of free and equal prosperity: how high we should aim in what period of time, which entities should oversee the administration and distribution of various goods and services, whose needs are to be prioritized first, etc. Even the nationalist/internationalist divide is something of a chimera, since everyone agrees on the overarching goal — in a vital sense, even the hardcore nationalists think liberalism is actually pretty great, but that too many Muslims and Mexicans will end up ruining it for everyone. If Democrats agreed to limit immigration and insist on assimilation, the right would be robbed of yet another argument.

But isn't this okay, or even good? Isn't this how it is supposed to work? The right's skepticism toward mass immigration and so-called 'globalism' is not without merit, after all, and democratic governments must satisfy (or at least pacify) their right-leaning factions. If liberalism is the engine and conservatives are the moderating forces (in a historical sense, not a temperamental one!), then isn't the theatrical bluster of election season little but noise? We must assume Trump, Brexit, and the German refugee crisis will be sufficient warning signs for 'elites' that something has to give. (If not, the impending right-wing reaction will be practically deserved.) But as the liberal project advances and more large-scale questions are decided, the differences in the visions between the two parties is bound to become even smaller, and the purpose of politics is bound to narrow further, and the stakes decrease. We are quite possibly rushing toward what amounts to a virtual consensus. Eventually, the need for high-stakes politics might be eliminated entirely.

What is the point of a center-right party in an era of global liberal hegemony, then, beyond opposition to excessive multiculturalism and social permissiveness? Are there possibilities for liberalism beyond the ideological consensus? Is it possible to forge a vision that goes beyond identity politics and class politics without dismissing the truths of either? The right is running out of things to oppose — it's time to start innovating. A clever conservative might be elected president if he (or she!) can provide a compelling answer to that question — one that looks beyond merely trying to agitate against the left — and toward a loftier vision of the possibilities afforded by liberal democracy. That might get sucked into the consensus, too — but it will at least serve the noble goal of elevating it beyond mere 'identity' and consumption.

Against Voting Third Party

Facebook | 10.25.17

I have felt doubt about almost all of my political convictions at some point in my life, but I have never for a second doubted that voting third party in an even remotely competitive race is a complete waste of time, and almost always driven by some combination of vanity and ignorance. We are a two-party system. Maybe we shouldn't be, but we are. If you give a damn about the outcome of a contest and it is even marginally competitive, you need to vote for a Democrat or a Republican.

Why do people vote third-party in competitive races? I think it is because they wrongly believe that voting is primarily or even entirely about registering the innermost contents of one's private conscience and conviction. I cannot express emphatically enough how little respect I have for this point of view. We are a two-party system, which demands that we form large, broad coalitions and rally behind candidates we will almost always find highly imperfect. Oftentimes we will even find both candidates repellant. That's too bad — we still have a responsibility to determine which candidate is better.

Smash the Nationalist Personality Cult

Facebook | 11.08.16

Tomorrow, we smash the nationalist personality cult. And when we do, we should not indulge the desire to issue phony, faux-gracious bromides about setting aside our differences after a difficult campaign season. This election cycle played out like a war, and I fully plan on savoring the victory and rubbing the loss in the faces of all those who thought it would be a good idea to put an American Caesar in power. We must consider the prudence of Lincoln and remember that there can be no compromise on the fundamentals. Threatening to disrupt the peaceful transition of power, threatening to imprison the opposition, promising to commit war crimes, using cruelty and humiliation as tools of debate, and scapegoating minorities and foreigners are never permissible in a liberal democracy. After this demoralizing, draining, long, ugly slog, we will be able to exhale. But we will not be able to just make nice and come together.

Apology

Facebook | 11.11.16

I do want to apologize for that post. I have to watch my words more carefully in high-stress situations. I let anxiety and exhaustion overwhelm my better instincts. All of what I listed is indeed unacceptable, but rubbing it in after a defeat is pointless at best. I will not delete it; I do not want to falsify the past. But this was a good example of me exacerbating the divide in a needless way, and I should not have done it. Some people take what I say into consideration when deciding how to interpret events — and besides, sore losers suck, but sore winners (prematurely or not) suck even more.

Don't Pity the White Working Class

Facebook | 09.21.16

Something that bothers me about all the upper-middle/aspiring-class pity-driven hand-wringing over the white working class and their economic woes is that we would-be sympathizers too frequently overlook the sense of economic entitlement among these people — as if the government is even just a little bit obligated to freeze the decaying status quo for these people *and just for these people* and not allow the rest of the country and the world to move on. These people seem to expect good jobs to be hand-delivered to their communities — rather than, for instance, moving to where the jobs are — as if anyone has an obligation to locate their companies in their towns in particular, because those people sure could use the business activity. Then, the people who choose to remain in decaying communities complain about how things aren't like they used to be. No, I'm sorry: *you* aren't like what Americans used to be like. You lack the adventurous spirit. Your ancestors were willing to live like paupers, take very real risks, uproot themselves again and again, and work like dogs in the pursuit of long-term economic gain. If you want to settle down, that's fine; I sympathize to some extent with that impulse. There are legitimate reasons for it. But if this is the choice you make, please don't complain when these habits don't make you or your community rich.

Whose 'Bubble'?

Facebook | 11.20.16

We must overturn the entire global economic order so that folks in Ohio can work the same factory jobs their dads and grandpas worked. And if you think it is unreasonable that we should put all economic, cultural, technological, and political movement on hold specifically for these people, you obviously are a privileged, selfish little shit who lives in a bubble.

On My Work History

Facebook | 02.19.17

In general, it does not bother me when people mistake me for something I am not; I try to respond playfully to dumb assumptions. But it truly annoys me when people — two in the last 24 hours — try to fling the obnoxious, already-dried-up "out-of-touch coastal bubble-dweller" crap at me — as if my loathing toward Dear Leader is indicative of, if not snobbish elitism, at least my insularity. I have been working part-time, working-class jobs from the time I was an underclassman in high school, whether that has been selling corn at a roadside produce stand, delivering pizzas, loading up trucks for FedEx or the USPS, cashiering at Sears, or punching in numbers at a data entry job. My mother is a special education teacher and my stepfather is a farmer, and they did not pay for any of my college tuition. I have grown up living on a farm. I am the only one in my family with a degree from a national university. And while I live in Maryland, I live in Hagerstown, not Silver Spring or Bethesda. West Virginia and Pennsylvania are each a ten-minute drive from me. I know many people who are struggling — and not just with money: I also know more than one person who knew someone who has died or gone to rehab over heroin.

Why do I rarely mention this sort of thing? Because I try to focus on where I am going and who I am trying to become: I have never believed that my origins determine who I am or what I can do with my life. While growing up, I was encouraged — in traditional American fashion! — to go as far as my talents could take me, and that has resulted in a quality liberal education, a solid network with lots of connections to DC and city culture, and many opportunities to have my voice heard over the years. I have seen my name in the *New York Times* or had an article receive hundreds of shares on the *Huffington Post* in the same week I was typing in data entry or delivering pizzas. I can be talking with professionals on social media who take me completely seriously — and then have to ask Mom for a few dollars to tie loose ends together. The world is not so neatly divided into haves and have-nots, successful and unsuccessful. Nobody ever told me that you are not allowed or able to pursue your ambitions at the same time you are making ends meet. But apparently being successfully driven and aspirational in any meaningful sense means you must have also become "out of touch."

And believe me, when I went to American University, when I go to my DC circles, I meet people who have not had these experiences: people with upper-middle class professional family backgrounds, people whose parents gave them all the money they wanted in school so they would not have to work, people who grew up traveling around the world. There are plenty of times when I have looked around at the people in a room and thought "I am the only one here who has ever loaded a package onto a truck or delivered a pizza to the back roads of West Virginia." And yes, you'd better believe it annoys me a little. But the bottom line here is this: there are tens of millions of voters who know what a "hard day's work" is like, who did not grow up in obvious privilege or luxury, who see firsthand how people struggle — and yet think Trump is only going to make the problem worse. To paraphrase Kevin Williamson: Trump speeches make struggling people feel good in the same way heroin does. And the final result of injecting Trumpium into the national vein will be be much the same.

Political Theory, Philosophy, and Religion

Nature and Artifice In Hobbes' Leviathan

St. John's College, Politics Seminar | 04.07.14

Thomas Hobbes' *Leviathan* is a systematic attempt to construct an objective foundation for the study of politics through the application of the methodologies of empirical science. His highest aim is to dethrone the prevailing Aristotelian paradigm: according to Hobbes, ancient philosophy, and especially the philosophy of Aristotle, has not provided us with an intelligible account of the origin of the state. Indeed, Aristotle implies that the question does not even demand an answer. The existence of the state – the city – may be considered as a given, because we observe that men everywhere organize into political societies; hence, we may deduce that "man is, by nature, a political animal." But humanity did not emerge from the primordial swamp under the aegis of the state. Before there were political societies, there must have been only individuals. Aristotle's investigation into politics presumes that men as individuals can only be fully understood in light of the existence of the state – any attempt to examine solitary man, isolated from civil society, is senseless, much like inquiring into the nature of the heart without reference to the body. Hobbes takes the radical step of detaching the individual from civil society to examine his nature in isolation. If the state is not natural to man, we cannot refer to it in our attempts to understand human nature. Because we can only intelligibly account for the existence of the state if we understand human nature, we therefore must proceed from solitary man outward. The Aristotelian paradigm has been turned on its head.

Hobbes arrives at such a radical mode of thought by treating the state like a machine, disassembling its parts with the aim of figuring out how to put it back together: "For seeing life is but a motion of limbs, the beginning whereof is in some principal part within; why may we not say, that all Automata...have an artificial life? For what is the heart, but a spring; and the nerves, but so many strings; and the joints, but so many wheels, giving motion to the whole body, such as was intended by the Arificer? Art goes yet further, imitating that rational and most excellent work of nature, man. For by art is created that great Leviathan called a commonwealth, or state...which is but an Artificial Man...". (Introduction) Philosophy, for Hobbes, must not be an *a priori* investigation into abstract first principles, but is rather "the knowledge acquired by reasoning, from the manner of the generation of any thing, to the properties, or from the properties, to some possible way of generation of the same; to the end to be able to produce, as far as matter, and human force permit, such effects, as human life requireth. So the geometrician, from the construction of figures, findeth out many properties thereof; and from the properties, new ways of their construction, by reasoning...". (Ch. XLVI) True philosophy is an outgrowth of science, "the knowledge of consequences, and dependence of one fact upon another." (Ch. V)

True philosophy must therefore only attempt to describe what is observable and measurable. Abstract concepts like "...Good, Evil, and Contemptible, are ever used with relation to the person that useth them: There being nothing simply and absolutely so, nor any common rule of good and evil, to be taken from the nature of the objects themselves, but from the Person..." and hence are of no use to the scientific-minded philosopher. (Ch. VI) Previous philosophers' attempts at discovering a universal morality have amounted to little more than a convoluted series of word-games, the inevitable consequence of faulty methodology: "... [I]t is most true that Cicero sayth of [philosophers] somewhere; that there can be nothing so absurd, but may be found in the books of philosophers. And the reason is manifest. For there is not one of them that begins his ratiocination from the definitions, or explication of the names they are to use; which is a method that hath been used only in geometry, whose conclusions have thereby been made indisputable." (Ch. V) The possibility of a state founded on abstract first principles –

virtue, 'the good,' etc. – must be ruled out.

Hobbes' empiricism is the keystone of his political philosophy, and so the *Leviathan* begins with a dissection of man. In an attempt to dispense with the possibility of a rationalistic study of man – and therefore of politics – Hobbes identifies sense-data as the origin of all thought: objects impress upon the body, and we proceed to name and categorize those objects in accordance with the variety of those impressions. Once accounted for by the intellect, we can manipulate the myriad memories of those sense-impressions to form more complex, goal-oriented thoughts. The complexity of such thoughts leads many men to mistakenly assign a primary epistemological role to pure thought – but all thought, in the final analysis, can be accounted for solely by reference to sensory impressions. The memory of pleasant sense-impressions leads to a desire to repeat the experience, directing one's passions toward the pleasure-inducing object, such as food. Men claim to 'love' certain objects, which they deem 'good,' but such names are actually just metaphors for desire.

Having accounted for man's underlying drives, Hobbes turns his attention to man in nature. Strikingly, he does not attempt a definition of pure nature – a glaring omission rendered all the more curious for his insistence on strict precision in operational definitions. Hobbes explicitly defines dozens of controversial concepts – from reason, memory, and madness, to science, faith, and sense – but the most radical innovation of the *Leviathan* – the state of nature – is left without a specific definition. 'Nature' appears to be synonymous with 'anarchy,' but this is only implied; what is philosophically vital to Hobbes is what characterizes men in nature: their natural equality, in both body and mind. Although some men are physically stronger than others, "when all is reckoned together, the difference between man, and man, is not so considerable." (Ch. XIII) Although a physically strong man may be able to kill a weak one in direct melee, the weak man can subdue the stronger "by secret machination, or by confederacy with others," and hence "the weakest has strength enough to kill the strongest." Hobbes concedes that his assertion of the *mental* equality of all men may strike the reader as "incredible," but insists that only a "vain concept of one's own wisdom" could lead one to think otherwise; the product of seeing one's "own wit at hand, and other men's at a distance." The natural mental equality of all men is evident in our opinions about ourselves: "For there is not ordinarily a greater sign of the equal distribution of any thing, than that every man is contended with his share." This argument is in tension with Hobbes' strict empiricism: he mocks and dismisses men's opinions of their own intellects, but points to those very same utterly subjective, unverifiable opinions as the theoretical basis of their natural equality.

The equality of man, coupled with his natural desire, inevitably leads to violent conflict. "From this equality of ability, ariseth equality of hope in the attaining of our ends. And if therefore any two men desire the same thing, which nevertheless they cannot both enjoy, they become enemies, and in the way to their end...endeavor to destroy, or subdue one another." (Ch. XIII) Because no man can trust that his life and possessions are enduringly secure against the desires of other men, from the state of nature always emerges a state of war "of every man, against every man," rendering society, industry, and culture impossible, plunging man into a state of "continual fear, and danger of violent death." The state of war is not a literal competition of arms between equals, but a universal state of fear instilled by the awareness that no man's security can be guaranteed against the desires of another. Absent such a guarantee, life in the state of nature – of war – is "solitary, poor, nasty, brutish, and short."

Men in nature all possess the right of nature, "the liberty each man hath, to use his own power, as he will himself, for the preservation of his own nature; that is to say, of his own life...". (Ch. XIV) All values presuppose life, the most fundamental value. This inalienable right to self-preservation may thus be enforced with violence or the threat of violence, a prerogative to be exercised at the sole discretion of the individual. For in nature, "all men [have a] right to all things." Abstract concepts like 'justice' and 'property' are merely names; unintelligible without recourse to a common power to give them meaning. 'Justice' in the state of nature is meaningless; 'property' is simply whatever one can hold onto. But the right of nature is accompanied by its corollaries, the eternal laws of nature – including that every man ought to seek peace, and that he ought to lay down his right to all things when other men are willing to do so in return. When men mutually renounce their right to all things, they enter into contract with one another, to be fulfilled by a covenant, or promise, sworn to by an oath. Men enter into convenants out of fear – the only stable foundation for lasting peace between men. The common recognition among men that the renouncement of natural right is the only way to truly guarantee security implies that the 'golden rule' is a law of nature, and hence we are bound by duty – by reason – to fulfill our oaths and uphold our convenants. (Ch. XVII). This is the origin of true justice.

But covenants between solitary individuals are insufficient to guarantee peace; some men may violate the dictates of reason, and, in the absence of a "common power to keep them all in awe," we are liable to be thrust right back into the state of war. This necessitates the creation of a commonwealth – the state, our 'leviathan' – an artificial political body in which men "confer all their power and strength upon one man, or upon one assembly of men, that may reduce their wills, by plurality of voices, unto one will...and every one to own, and acknowledge himself to be author of whatever he that so beareth their person shall act...in those things which concern the common peace and safety; and therein to submit their wills...to his judgment." (Ch. XVII) The "one man, or assembly of men" is the sovereign, in whom all power to resolve disputes between men is invested, and from whose judgment there can be no appeal. The sovereign may be chosen by methodically debating the individual merits of each man to rule, or he may be chosen by drawing straws – it really does not matter; anyone's rule is an improvement upon anarchy. Our single goal is to escape the state of nature and ensure lasting peace. The state, thus created, is an *artificial man*; a political body imposed upon nature by universal consent for the common good of all.

But why is this 'artificial man' artificial? Hobbes' thought experiment – a rigorous account of man's nature and the basic political mandates of his reason – always results in the creation of a state. If the creation of a state is both in accordance with our nature *and inevitable*, then it would appear that the distinction between nature and artifice is a strained one; the two seem to threaten to conceptually collapse back into one another – perhaps, even, back into Aristotelian premises. Why, we may ask, can we not conceive of the creation of the state as being akin to using a ladder to elevate ourselves from lower to higher ground – after which the ladder can be left behind, so that we may pursue nobler aims than flight from the threat of death? But Hobbes denies that we can leave the ladder behind – and he denies that men create the commonwealth to pursue noble aims: the universal fear of violent death is always lurking just beneath the artifice of the state, and cannot simply be forgotten, since it is the one common benefit all men derive from the existence of the state.

While Hobbes largely succeeds in providing a rational, enduring foundation for government, then, his success may be Pyrrhic: in his relentless pursuit of scientific objectivity, he has unapologetically discarded all of man's higher aims, finding only the will to self-preservation as a political goal strong enough to perpetually unite us. Although he briefly laments the absence of industry and culture in the state of nature, they are presented as peripheral benefits of government; ones that may be of interest to individual men in society, but which cannot provide an objective basis for government – what would be "worst of all" to *all* men is not the absence of the arts and letters, but the prospect of a bloody, violent death. With solitary man – complete in his nature in isolation – as his muse, Hobbes coherently provides us with an objective basis for government, but he has sacrificed much to arrive there.

Jefferson and Madison, Hobbesians

Comments Compiled By Jon Rowe, American Creation | 01.09.16

It is commonly argued that our Founders, though devoted Lockeans, were not especially influenced by Thomas Hobbes. This is false — for Lockeanism is a variant of Hobbesianism: Thucydides teaches us in the Melian Dialogue that legalistic justice originates between competitors of approximately equal strength; that when there is inequality between competing forces, there is only domination by the strong and submission on the part of the weak. Greco-Roman politics was defined by a relatively rigid — though not ironclad — social hierarchy, held in place by an understanding that certain types of people are by nature fit to rule over others. Democracy came into being in Greece when the myth of the 'great chain of being' became unbelievable — the ancient parallel to the 'death of God' — which untethered 'eros' and eventually led to the dissolution of antiquity.

Modern philosophers, starting with Machiavelli, sought to conceive of a new, more stable vision of justice — one to replace the chain-of-being/hierarchy myth — based on that which is common to all men. If we can conceive of a new vision and spin a 'rational mythology,' then we can reboot Western civilization, 'liberate it from the barbarians [Christians],' and avoid a repeat of the collapse of antiquity and the tragic thousand-year-reign of Christendom, which 'turned Europe into another appendage of Asia.' Hobbes knew his Thucydides — as Nietzsche says: to be untimely is to know the Greeks — and recognized that In order for there to be enduring justice among all people, they must be convinced of their essential equality. Anything else will result in another unstable hierarchy. In Hobbes we find the rational mythology called for (to those who had ears to hear) by Machiavelli — the roots of materialism, egalitarianism, secularism, and natural rights doctrines, based on what Hobbes insisted was a purely technical account sufficient to cover the sweep of human experience. These planks of the liberal doctrine are designed to neutralize that which makes men distinct from one another — especially religious belief, but also physical (and yes, even mental) strength, and ancestry. But most of all, what unites us is our common fear of death and our craving for security and safety. If we are all equal, then none of us stands any better chance than anyone else of surviving against the other — so let's agree to pursue justice together rather than attempt to dominate one another. Hobbes was much-persecuted in his native Britain, though, and had to cloak his brutal attack against Christendom as a defense of monarchy.

When a little more time had passed and attitudes toward the Church continued to soften, Locke came along: Lockeanism is practical, humane Hobbesianism — democratic Hobbesianism. But Hobbes himself knew his face-value doctrine was inhumane — he simply had no choice but to cater to those in power if he wanted to avoid persecution. Hobbes would have undoubtedly approved of Locke — and would have fully recognized himself in the Constitution and the Declaration of Independence.

The difference between European liberalism and American liberalism can, with only a bit of exaggeration, be explained by reference to the fact that the American Founders just barely missed the emergence of Rousseau on the scene. They built a regime fundamentally grounded and fixed in the thought of John Locke and various contemporaries (eg, Montesquieu), which has since then absorbed only a refracted view of everything which has dialectically proceeded from Rousseau. Hence, for instance, the otherwise near-inexplicable fact that the thought of Herbert Spencer resonated with Americans more than that of his contemporary Marx. Certainly much so-called 'continental' philosophy and political theory remains totally elusive to Americans.

This is not to say that Rousseau would necessarily be more pleased with Europe in 2018 than with America: Rousseau was not above playing with the fire of populism, the popular denigration of the arts and sciences, or the glorification of militarism; there is no necessary support for a larger welfare state in Rousseau, no necessary support for liberal internationalism, no necessary support for multiculturalism — the list goes on (though we can be sure that he considered himself part of a spiritual 'elite' exempt from ordinary laws and customs) — but merely that, as a regime built on fixed ideas, America receives the insights of Rousseau and everything proceeding from his thought, or at any rate what it represents, through a refracted lens and hence will never see eye-to-eye with 'the continent.'

Rights, Radicalism, and Revolution:

The Conservative Vision of Edmund Burke

East Coast Graduate Liberal Studies Conference | 04.25.13

Georgetown University

Few terms in contemporary American political discourse are as riddled with ambiguity as *conservatism*. The word at once evokes notions of atomistic individualism and uncritical nationalism, country-club elitism and blue-collar populism, free-market capitalism and religious traditionalism. Conservatism often appears to be at odds with itself, uncommitted to any timeless first principles, yet ferocious in its defense of its objects of affection. What mode of thought, then, can be properly characterized as authentically conservative?

The philosophical roots of modern conservatism date back over two centuries, to the speeches and writings of Edmund Burke, an Irishman who rose to prominence in the late 18th century as a parliamentarian in the British House of Commons. Despite his unassuming temperament, his subtle and powerful defense of tradition and order against sociopolitical fads and militant ideologies has come to provide an enduring groundwork for philosophical conservatism. Burke's conservatism is fundamentally a *disposition*, not an agenda, and is animated most by its skepticism toward ideology. Ideology, in the Burkean worldview, is a false promise of understanding; a fixed set of abstract assumptions through which all incoming information is filtered and instantly explained away. In short, it promises simple, elegant solutions to complex human problems. The ideologue views the world as an *idea* to be manipulated at-will by the power of his intellect, rather than as it truly is – an infinitely complex, interconnected nexus of individuals and their many institutions, great and small, which have reached this point in history through an organic process of social evolution – not through rationalistic manipulation from on-high by political theorists and their fellow-travelers.

A politics whose foundation rests upon abstract metaphysical absolutes utterly lacks the capacity to prudently assess the specific situational needs inherent in all sociopolitical problems. The statesman, ever wary of the possibility of the unintended consequences of imprudent political action, must look not to speculative philosophy, but to the *lived experiences* of the individuals whom a newly-proposed policy would affect. Metaphysical notions of man's rights, for instance, so favored by political radicals, arbitrarily detach particular elements of a political culture from their full and necessary context, rendering them all but meaningless in practice. For Burke, the isolated concept of a "right to food or medicine" is as absurd as a discussion of the heart or lungs without reference to a fully-functioning body. It may very well be that circumstance allows the statesman to intervene on behalf of the hungry. High-sounding moral abstractions, however, will be of no use in making that decision: "What is the use of discussing a man's abstract right to food or medicine? The question is upon the method of procuring and administering them. In that deliberation I shall always advise to call in the aid of the farmer and the physician rather than the professor of metaphysics." (*Reflections* 151-152)

Political radicals, intoxicated by the intellectual rush of abstract ideology, care nothing for circumstance, process, or compromise. In his most famous work, *Reflections On the Revolution In France,* published at the midpoint of the dawn of the revolution and the advent of the

Reign of Terror, Burke inveighs against the designs of the French revolutionaries: "They have the 'rights of men.' Against these there can be no prescription; against these no argument is binding: these admit no temperament, and no compromise: anything withheld from their full demand is so much fraud and injustice." (*Reflections* 148) What they possess, in a word, is "armed doctrine," to which all else must be subordinated. "The pretended rights of these theorists are all extremes...the rights of men in government are their advantages; and these are often in balances between differences of good; in compromises sometimes between good and evil, and sometimes between evil and evil." (*Reflections* 153) The absolutism of "political metaphysics" must inevitably clash with the complexities and ambiguities of the lived experiences of individuals and their societies. The prudent statesman must tend to society as he finds it, not as he would imagine it in his speculative philosophical fantasies.

Such flights of fancy characterized the ideological core of the French Revolution. Like God on the Day of Creation, the revolutionaries sought to restyle the nation in their own image, as articulated in the works of contemporary political philosophers like Jean-Jacques Rousseau. The abstract beliefs to which they swore allegiance had no basis in lived experience and so by no legitimate measure could be said to have stood the test of time. For the radical, however, this objection is irrelevant: it is enough simply to haul one's beliefs before the grand tribunal of his own individual reason – a trial in which he acts as defendant, plaintiff, judge, and jury. But "the science of constructing a commonwealth," says Burke, "is...not to be taught *a priori*. Nor is it a short experience...the real effects of moral causes are not always immediate; but that which is prejudicial may be excellent in its remoter operation; and its excellence may arise even from the ill effects which it produces in the beginning. The reverse also happens, and very plausible schemes, with very pleasing commencements, have often shameful and lamentable conclusions." (*Reflections* 152) The evolution of a nation is slow, careful, and organic. Social progress is attained through "wisdom without reflection," the collective benefit of prudence. (*Reflections* 119) "The multitude is foolish; but the species is wise." The French revolutionaries, animated by fanatical hubris, considered themselves fit to draw up a new constitution for all of mankind out of the stock of their own individual reason.

Burke identifies the abuse of reason as the catalyst for such unbridled radicalism. The French radicals held reason to be the godhead of human epistemology; an illuminating, liberating force with the power to sweep away the cobwebs of oppression, irrationality, and injustice from human life. If a tradition could not be justified before reason, it was to be cast away, like a prisoner throwing off his chains. For Burke, however, a prosperous society is characterized not by strict obedience to rationally articulated abstract absolutes, but is "furnished from the wardrobe of a moral imagination," which "harmonize[s] the different shades of life." (*Reflections* 171) Reason is in fact a rather limited instrument: "We are afraid to put men to live and trade each on his own private stock of reason; because we suspect that this stock in each man is small, and that the individuals would be better to avail themselves of the general bank and capital of nations, and of ages." (*Reflections* 183) The uncritical worship of individual reason is the vice of "sophisters, economists, and calculators," who in France had "torn off" the "decent drapery of life" and the "pleasing illusions" that sustain civil society. (*Reflections* 171) The moral imagination of a culture is what gives individual lives meaning and purpose, granting a measure of existential comfort to each person, regardless of his rank or title.

Burke does not oppose reason *per se*. His objection, rather, is to its dogmatic representation of itself as the only valid method of human discovery. Reason is an essential tool of the intellect, but unaccompanied by the temperance that only practical wisdom can provide, it is simply incomplete. "I flatter myself that I love a manly, moral, regulated liberty as well as any gentleman of that society...," (*Reflections* 89) yet "[W]hat is liberty without wisdom, and without virtue? It is the greatest of all possible evils; for it is folly, vice, and madness, without tuition or restraint. Those who know what virtuous liberty is, cannot bear to see it disgraced by incapable heads, on account of their having high-sounding words in their mouths." (*Reflections* 373) The "real rights of men" are not discovered by a philosopher in his study, nor do they permeate nature like an invisible force. Rather, they are are prescribed by tradition as the inheritance of a culture. Their definitions are imprecise, yet their principles echo throughout society with unmistakeable clarity. Among the rights of Englishmen cited by Burke are those "to the fruits of their industry," "to the nourishment and improvement of their offspring," and "to instruction in life." The

Englishman can reasonably expect "a right to a fair portion of all which society, with all its combination of skill and force, can do in his favor." (*Reflections* 149) In other words: the free citizen can expect the government to serve the common good, prudently balancing individual prerogatives with the needs of society. These rights are authentic for the simple reason that they are honored in everyday life by the nation which they govern. They are specifically *British*, a natural reflection of the nation's unique history and culture. Government and culture are in harmony, united by the rule of law. The wisdom of one's ancestors – those who built and sustained the nation – is contained within those rights, and we surrender them to faddish intellectual innovators at our peril. Society, in essence, is a contract between past, present, and future generations. Each generation preserves and improves upon what is judged to work on behalf of the common good and passes it onto their descendants.

Such improvement is vital to the health of a culture. "The people of England well know that the idea of inheritance furnishes a sure principle of conservation, and a sure principle of transmission; without at all excluding a principle of improvement." (*Reflections* 119) Burke's respect for tradition does not degenerate into slavish loyalty to the *status quo*: "A nation without the means of some change is without the means of its preservation." Refusal to bow to circumstance may "even risk the loss of that part of the constitution which it wished the most religiously to preserve." (*Reflections* 106) Rights may manifest themselves in different ways across generations without abdicating the core of the national inheritance. Burke approvingly cites the English Bill of Rights of 1689, the culmination of the Glorious Revolution of 1688, noting that "the two houses [of Parliament] utter not a syllable of 'a right to frame government for themselves.' You will see, that their whole care was to secure the religion, laws, and and liberties, that had been long possessed, and had been lately endangered." The ordering of the Bill of Rights is precise: "in the first place," before any offer of the throne to William and Mary, there is listed an enumeration of traditional British political liberties. This unequivocal defense of the inherited rights of man is such "as their ancestors in like case have usually done": it is "for the vindicating and asserting [of] their ancient rights and liberties." (*Reflections* 118-119) Those rights, which we revere precisely *because* they are ancient, must be constantly renewed and reasserted in the face of turbulent change. Burke, then, was no reactionary. His conservatism does not reject outright the right of revolution, but simply insists that its justification cannot stand on mere policy disagreements. The French revolutionaries claimed "'a right of cashiering their governors for misconduct'...No government could stand a moment if it could be blown down with anything so loose and indefinite as an opinion of 'misconduct.' They who led at the Revolution grounded the virtual abdication of King James upon no such light and uncertain principle. They charged him...with having broken the original contract between king and people. This was more than misconduct. A grave and overruling necessity obliged them to take the step they took, and took with infinite reluctance, as under that most rigorous of all laws." (*Reflections* 112) It is striking that Burke sympathized with the American colonists in their opposition to King George's abuses of power. The French revolutionaries insisted upon nothing less than a total upheaval of the *ancien régime*. But the colonists sought nothing more from the monarchy than full respect for their traditional rights as Englishmen. In his 1775 Speech on Conciliation With the Colonies, Burke warns of the danger of King George's refusal to compromise with the colonists: "For, in order to prove that the Americans have no right to their liberties, we are every day endeavouring to subvert the maxims which preserve the whole spirit of our own...we never seem to gain a paltry advantage over them in debate, without attacking some of those principles, or deriding some of those feelings, for which our ancestors have shed their blood." (Burke, *Speech On Conciliation*) These words, spoken a year before the signing of the Declaration of Independence, proved prophetic. Indeed, the American Constitution, the political culmination of the American Revolution, is in great measure a reassertion of the ancient, inherited rights of Englishmen. Its ancestry can be traced to the Magna Carta, through the Bill of Rights of 1689. In this sense, the American Revolution was, in fact, a conservative one.

Burke's brand of philosophical conservatism often sounds foreign, even reactionary, to contemporary American audiences, who have been baptized into a culture that teaches that rights come from God, not from cultural tradition. But the themes that color his thought are familiar: skepticism, prudence, and deference to circumstance. Conservatism proper is *not* an ideology. It is fundamentally a *disposition*, not an agenda. Conservatives may cordially disagree amongst themselves about contemporary political issues without raising the specter of loyalty oaths, purity tests, or purges – the surest signs of radicalism, and the hallmark of the Reign of Terror of the French Revolution. But what conservatives have in common cannot be doubted: a healthy respect for tradition, reverence for the wisdom of our ancestors, and skepticism toward abstract doctrines that promise simple solutions to complex problems. In this sense, the political philosophy of Edmund Burke as relevant today as it was two centuries ago, offering lessons that apply not only to history, but also, for their endurance and timelessness, to contemporary human affairs.

Bibliography

Burke, Edmund. *Reflections On the Revolution In France.* Ed. Conor Cruise O'Brien. Harmondsworth, Middlesex, Great Britain: Pelican Classics, 1978. Print.

Burke, Edmund. *Speech On Conciliation With the Colonies.* 1775. Project Gutenburg E-Books. Ed. Charles Franks. 2004. Web. Apr. 25, 2013.

Can American Conservatism Address Income Inequality?

East Coast Graduate Liberal Studies Conference | 04.25.14

St. John's College - Annapolis

It is no longer a question that income inequality has emerged as one of the defining socioeconomic issues of our time. Polling conducted this year by the Gallup Organization shows that 67% of American adults, including 54% of self-identified Republicans, describe themselves as either 'somewhat' or 'very' dissatisfied with the current national distribution of wealth, and data from CNN/ORC International indicates that 66% of American adults agree with the statement that "the government should work to substantially reduce the income gap between the rich and the poor."

Economic data lends credence to the public's concerns. Since the year 2000, the median income in the United States has risen by only 0.3%, compared to a robust 19.7% in both Britain and Canada ·and although the American economy has been steadily recovering since the financial crisis of 2008, the wealthy have disproportionately felt its effects: a 2013 study by the Economic Policy Institute finds that "following a 15.6 percent decline from 2007 to 2009, real annual wages of the top 1.0 percent of earners grew 8.2 percent from 2009 to 2011," while "the real annual wages of the bottom 90 percent have continued to decline in the recovery, eroding by 1.2 percent between 2009 and 2011." Additionally, in 2011, total student loan debt held by Americans passed $1 trillion for the first time — a burden, according to Dr. Jason Houle of Dartmouth College, carried disproportionately by children from middle-class families.

Political progressives in government and academia have taken notice. In a high-profile March meeting with Pope Francis, President Barack Obama declared that reducing the gap between rich and poor "isn't just an economic issue, it's a moral issue," and concurred with the pope that there is a "danger that over time we grow accustomed to this kind of inequality and accept it as normal. But we can't." April saw the arrival of the English translation of French economist Thomas Piketty's *Capital In the Twenty-First Century*, which meticulously argues that the sharpening disparity between the incomes of rich and poor is rooted in the structure of capitalism — and will only grow larger in the future. As a policy corrective, Piketty proposes a global tax on wealth and a more strongly progressive tax system. The book was greeted with widespread acclaim: in his *New York Times* column, progressive Nobel Prize-winning economist Paul Krugman hailed the book as a "bona fide blockbuster, ·arguing in the same column that American conservatives have demonstrated an unwillingness to provide a compelling competing vision to that of men like Piketty and himself ·and so it is therefore clear that they have "run out of ideas" and are incapable of offering an alternative account of the origin of income inequality, or any means to combat its growth.

It is difficult to avoid the conclusion that American conservatives have all but ignored the issue. The Republican-controlled House of

Representatives has not produced a single bill explicitly aimed at reducing income inequality, which Speaker John Boehner (R-OH) blames on President Obama: "Incomes are lower under his watch. As a matter of fact, I would argue that his policies are driving a lot of the income inequalities that we see today." It should not surprise anyone that the leader of the national opposition party is in the business of opposing the president, but the economic trends in question predate President Obama's tenure in office — and President George W. Bush's, for that matter— by many years. American conservatism has not, as of yet, produced a policy vision aimed at reversing or containing those trends. This is troubling not because it speaks to conservative malfeasance, but because it is not in the public interest for conservatives to voluntarily exclude themselves from one of the most pressing socioeconomic debates of the moment. A two-party system, at its best, performs as weight and counterweight. Progressive Democrats and conservative Republicans each speak to concerns that have some hold over the American public, and policy solutions to major public concerns ought to be informed by both perspectives. The essentially conservative pursuit of stability and order is not served when only one party is offering policy proposals in response to public opinion.

But if conservatives ultimately opt to abdicate the task of addressing income inequality, they will have done so only by neglecting the lessons of their intellectual heritage. To disregard the issue would not only be to fundamentally misunderstand the character of the American people, but would also be counterproductive to conservatives' own economic goals, since inaction risks the prospect of the passage of more-stringent federal economic regulation than had they chosen to act and provide input.

This is the conclusion one may derive, at least, from a contemporary application of the teachings of Alexis de Tocqueville and Edmund Burke, who together provide a stable theoretical justification for a conservative policy response to income inequality.

Tocqueville's seminal work, *Democracy In America,* completed in 1840, is a thorough dissection of American culture and character. Among its most enduringly relevant insights is its identification of the "equality of social conditions" as the defining characteristic of American society. Equality is both an attitude and an aspiration, for Americans: in their daily lives, they attempt to interact with each other on equal terms as individuals, but always with an eye toward social and economic improvement, perpetually striving toward a more perfect actualization of their ideal. According to Tocqueville, one cannot understate the "extraordinary influence this fundamental fact exerts upon the progress of society...it forms opinion, creates feelings, proposes ways of acting, and transforms anything it does not directly instigate itself."

This claim is purely descriptive. "Reading through the pages of our history, we shall scarcely find any great events which did not promote the cause of equality over the last seven hundred years." Tocqueville traces a line through the decline of feudalism, the rise of Protestantism, and the triumph of classical liberalism in the founding of the United States. Since the time of his writing, America has abolished slavery and racial segregation, expanded the legal rights and social opportunities available to women, racial minorities, and sexual minorities, and has instituted federal programs which seek to ensure universal access to education, health care, and a monthly pension. "The gradual unfurling of equality in social conditions is, therefore, a providential fact," he writes. And despite the eminently practical nature of the American people, they love equality for its own sake, not simply for its utility: "The first and liveliest of the passions inspired by equality of status, I need not say, is the love of equality itself." To underestimate the taste for equality in Americans' hearts would be to misunderstand their character.

Equality in social conditions is inextricably linked to the pursuit of shared material prosperity, and the promise of comfort it provides. "In America, the taste for material prosperity is not always exclusive but it is general; if everyone's experience of it is different, nevertheless it is felt by all." The chief aim of material prosperity is comfort: "The love of comfort has become the dominant taste of the nation. The main current of human passions runs in that channel and sweeps all before it in its course." Americans wed their passion for material prosperity to a general belief in the perfectibility of man: "Some changes improve his lot and he comes to the conclusion that, in general, man is endowed with the faculty of indefinite improvement." Indefinite improvement in the service of material prosperity can be seen at the heart of several classic American aspirations, including the social goal of individual upward mobility and the political goal of ensuring that each successive generation is more prosperous than the last. This anticipation of progress leads to a dread of loss.

Naturally, these passions may lead to excesses: Americans' love of equality, says Tocqueville, can foster "very dangerous instincts." Their taste for comfort is "overly fervent" and "exclusive." Equality "exposes their souls to an excessive love of material enjoyment." It also cultivates a desire for instant gratification: "One of the distinctive features of democratic ages is the taste shared by every man for easy success and immediate enjoyment." But Tocqueville's temperamentally conservative skepticism toward egalitarianism does not blind him to political realities: when the majority has arrived at a conclusion about a contentious public concern, he reasons, it is only a matter of time until that thought is translated into political action. The majority, in his view, is "omnipotent." "The majority in the United States possesses immense actual power and a power of opinion almost as great; and when it has once made up its mind over a question, there are, so to speak, no obstacles which might, I shall not say halt, but even retard its onward course long enough to allow it time to heed the complaints of those it crushes as it goes by."

If Tocqueville is right, then Americans' concern with income inequality is likely not a passing political fad, but an outgrowth of their basic social character. As we have seen, public polling concerning income inequality indicates that strong majorities of Americans, driven by their love of equality and material prosperity, now support federal intervention intended to shrink the gap between rich and poor. If the majority is truly the seat of power in the United States, then the issue will inevitably be met with legislation ·and conservatives must confront the notion that it may no longer be a question of *whether* Congress will pass substantial legislation aimed at reducing inequality, but rather, *what* that legislation will look like.

Therefore, it is incumbent on conservatives to actively involve themselves in this debate. In his *Reflections On the Revolution In France,* the conservative statesman Edmund Burke cautions that refusal by a political actor to bow to circumstance may "risk the loss of that part of [the object] which it wished the most religiously to preserve." Burkean political theory, long considered the fountainhead of modern conservative thought, is characterized by a skepticism toward abstract ideology, deference to the tried and tested, and a belief in the primacy of the virtue of prudence in politics. Prudence, or, applied wisdom, insists on addressing political problems as they arise based on the conditions at hand, informed by the accumulated experience of the ages. It may be that there is no way to address income inequality without expanding the federal government's power over business and finance ·but politicians in a democracy cannot indefinitely resist the will of a resolute majority, and if conservatives do not act, the immediate practical consequence will be the abandonment of the issue to progressives, who may eventually craft the law solely in accord with their own beliefs. For conservatives who especially value property rights or libertarian notions of personal autonomy, addressing income inequality via legislation might be a particularly bitter pill to swallow. But according to Burke, "the rights of men in government are their advantages; and these are often in balances between differences of good; in compromises sometimes between good and evil, and sometimes between evil and evil." There is no prudent justification for inaction when the culture has made up its mind.

Conservatives must instead look to the lessons of history to discern how best to constructively contribute to an orderly, balanced execution of the public will. Burke and Tocqueville agree that the love of equality, if imprudently applied, can lead to potentially destabilizing excesses, and both are troubled by the tendency of egalitarianism to degenerate into homogeneity and economic leveling. The conservative temperament, cautious and empirical, can serve as a counterbalance to progressive overreach, and sees what its foil is prone to overlook: "Very plausible schemes, with very pleasing commencements, have often shameful and lamentable conclusions," Burke writes. Change is inevitable in public affairs, however, and the statesman cannot mindlessly cling to the status quo: "A nation without the means of some change is without the means of its preservation."

Conservatism, we may conclude, might not be naturally enamored with the pursuit of ever-increasing socioeconomic equality, but it must grant the national mood its due if it is to serve its noblest public purpose. The spirit of equality is perpetually on the forward march in American society, which will only tolerate a limited disparity in relative material prosperity, and which will unapologetically employ Congressional power to correct for unequal conditions that have grown intolerable. Although often at odds with this egalitarian impulse, conservatism cannot afford to ignore it or deny its enduring relevance as the keystone of American public life. The presence of authentic conservatism ·

skeptical, empirical, cognizant of circumstance ·in the public discourse is vital to crafting balanced law. Conservatism's intellectual heritage demonstrates that it not only *can* address income inequality ·but that, in the name of good governance, it *must.*

On a Common Political Error

Facebook | 05.19.18

There is an almost universal tendency among the politically active to overreact to individual events; to read too much into them. The cause of this is less stupidity, corruption, personal gain, or even ideology, or vanity, but something more like having acquired a hammer and, little by little, seeing nails everywhere. You read too much into the motives of individual voters, you start overestimating how much others read and think about politics, you build a little bubble of people who give a damn about politics, you add a little partisan flavor to your news (and then a little bit more, and more...) and you get used to the adrenaline rush and stimulation. The key danger of living a political life seems to be, then, a danger of developing an exaggerated and amplified political lens over your eyesight, so that everything passes through a political filter as it is processed. For the good party man, this becomes second nature. In practical terms, this leads to a forgetfulness that one's 'enemies' are also one's fellow citizens and patriots who happen to think differently than you and whose ideas aren't all terrible.

On 'Legislating Morality'

Facebook | 02.17.14

I wish people would stop saying they're opposed to "legislating morality." All laws are premised on some sort of moral assumption. What they usually mean is that they're opposed to legislating particular religious sensibilities about homosexuality or abortion. But we all want to see morality encoded in the law. The argument is simply about what is moral in a legal context, not about whether we ought to encode morality in the law at all.

God As Artist

Facebook | 03.24.18

I envision God as a kind of artist. In His Infinite Love and Goodness, God extended Himself across the void and filled it with beings, corresponding across many realms. He did this because it pleases Him to create, just as it might be pleasant for a human being to sing, or paint, or write.

When any potentiality is brought into actuality, though, it leaves the realm of pure thought and enters the process of becoming, which is marked by a dualistic transformative process. Heat cannot exist without the potential for cold also existing; though they are governed by the same principle, there must be presence and absence if a being or principle enters existence. In other words: God cannot make a burrito so hot even he cannot eat it. The creation process takes time and is limited by it, which is to say, many mutations of substance — in man's realm, matter — must occur, many of which are very strange and unpleasant, before the Work can be complete.

The ultimate aim of God's plan is to establish a universal earthly regime for those who love Him and His creation. This process seems very bizarre and unfair to our limited perception, but all will be redeemed and reconciled in due time. Since we as humans have a spark of the divine within us, we have a fraction of freedom to choose what we do with ourselves, though this freedom takes place within very many confines and limitations. We have some freedom, but freedom doesn't mean 'anything goes.' We can use our freedom to pursue more pleasure than is necessary, since such potentials exist in this material realm, but the negating process of becoming insists that something in your orbit in creation is going to have to 'balance the account'; your 'sin' will catch up with you or your loved ones; 'karma' is for real, the soul and the spirit are not silent about these things, and we are unified in our thought through the Holy Spirit.

We cannot reason our way to God through our own devices; we have to be receptive to the Mystery before the Holy Spirit can fill up that part of us which was empty. We are not gods or demi-gods, but very limited beings — though we have a spark of the divine, we also have much in common with the animals of the earth. A happy life entails letting that which is divine in us govern that which is bestial in us — not hating it or denying it, but treating it well. There is not a one-size-fits-all prescription for this sort of thing; God is often hard at work among those who are strangest or most blamed or most peculiar or most foreign to us. But union with God in joyful contemplation of creation grants us a self-evidently good and happy life. God wants us all to recognize that this is so, and uses the Holy Spirit as his intermediary, his brush, his melody, to remind people of His presence. If we cooperate, we can be part of that and be perpetually happy here and after death.

God Does Not Need Protected From Our Mockery

Facebook | 01.09.15

As someone who takes the divine rather seriously in my private life, I think free inquiry without boundaries is essential to a free society. God does not fear mockery, and men and women who really know God do not react to offenses against their beliefs with anger, rage, or resentment. The sacred is far more powerful than the damage that any cartoon can do to it. But it is important that we be able to mock even our most cherished beliefs and symbols — it is the only way to avoid sliding into dogmatism in our earthly, political lives. I think we have made genuine progress in allowing religion to be publicly satirized, just like politics — because religion has social and political implications. As long as religion still greatly affects society at-large, it should never be considered obscene by society for it to be satirized, mocked, and criticized.

Christianity: The East Within the West

New American Perspective | 04.03.18

Today it is often impossible to discuss Christianity with non-believers: the words in which its core mission are expressed are simply too loaded with the baggage of politics, history, and the residue of probing philosophical investigations. Hence it has become all but impossible to represent the perspective from the inside of a genuine belief in God, the Monad, the All-In-All, in a way that will electrify the mind, or rouse the soul from its slumber.

I have recently flummoxed many of my readers by re-embracing my lapsed Christianity. I do not like the word 'conversion' and do not see myself as a 'convert'. What I am experiencing feels more like a fulfillment or reconciliation of various disconnected fragments of thought that had been bouncing around in my mind — or we could say, perhaps: I feel I have finally obtained an instrument with which I can whack away the thorns and weeds which have been covering my eyesight for some time now. I do not claim to have anything original to say on these matters, although I hope I can help point the way toward the path of illumination, for those who have eyes to see. On the other hand, since I can offer only my personal testimony and study as evidence for what I claim, the reader ought to take anything I say with the appropriate grain of salt.

I do not believe that anyone can reason his way to belief in God through his own devices. Rather, he must prepare the ground for the experience by which the essence of God can be revealed to him. Catholic intellectuals — like John Paul II — pushing the likes of Thomas Aquinas, with his 'proofs' of God's existence, and the high-minded likes of C.S. Lewis, with his gimmicky 'trilemma', or those still pushing Pascal's Wager — are all wasting their time. Our knowledge of the material world has become too vast and too deep; reconciliation of belief in the existence of God to what we know about the world requires something truly out of the ordinary. As mankind digests more and more of the Apple of the Tree of Knowledge, we grow more distant from the Holy Spirit and from God. We require something more like what Socrates evokes in the Meno: like the rainbow fish, he stuns his interlocutors — into a state of perplexity. Only a direct encounter with the reality of Beyond-Being, of transcendence, can prove its reality, and its relevance. No abstract argument will do: it is something which must be revealed to someone. Reason can tell us the conditions under which revelation is most likely to take place, and it can speculate about what revelation might mean, but only a direct encounter can ultimately supply the evidence demanded by today's skeptics.

I would wager that most people already have, without knowing it, some direct realization of the Holy Spirit, and of the soul, which participates in the 'overmind' of the Holy Spirit and whose nature is oriented toward beauty and harmony; it corresponds to what Sigmund Freud deemed the 'oceanic consciousness,' which he called the origin of all religious sentiment, while acknowledging that has never personally experienced that state. The 'oceanic' nature of this consciousness is the esoteric significance of the sacrament of baptism in water, although the 'higher' baptism is that which takes place in the soul, as one's eyesight into this mode of 'seeing' life 'breaks in' and recognizes the Holy Spirit for what it is: an intermediary between God and Man. Many people report that music 'takes them places.' They are more right than they know: overwhelmingly, they are experiencing a withdrawal into the perception of the soul, as their attention fixates on the beautiful arrangement of the music and temporarily reconciles emotional tensions that ordinarily remain at odds in everyday life. This way of perceiving can go deeper and deeper — into a euphoric and alien mode of experience. The Orthodox call the process of training these faculties *theosis*: a seeking of unity with God; they say this is the meaning of life.

Soul is not all there is to our inner faculties, although it is the most accessible; Spirit is distinct from Soul, although only a beautifully harmonized soul can serve as a vehicle of ascension toward Spirit. The 'realm' of Spirit is also the realm of the Monad, or, God; philosopher-mystics like Plotinus and Proclus claimed to have perceived it directly. The esoteric vision of Christianity seeks to emulate the incarnation of God in the man of Jesus so that we may become more like God ourselves. As Clement of Alexandria writes: "For if one knows himself, he will know God; and knowing God, he will be made like God."

Christianity, in this sense, is the East within the West; it resembles Hinduism and Daoism as much as it resembles Judaism or Islam; it is the mystical counterweight to the metaphysically and epistemologically individualistic rationalism and empiricism that is so characteristic of the West: that which takes the realities of the Self and Being for granted. Modern science and philosophy is approaching a point of maxing out on these assumptions; it is, through postmodernism and quantum physics, unveiling the indeterminacy of the subject, the intertwining of perceiver and perceived, and the instability and interdependence of concepts — and the most reliable defenders of Enlightenment thought are unable to rebut these theories and have resorted to attempts at laughing them out of contention. It will not work.

What will work is an integration of Eastern thought into modernity. By Eastern thought I mean that which recognizes the reality of Beyond-Being and the indeterminacy and interconnectedness of any sense of our individual 'selves.' In the past, Christianity has not recognized itself as the East within the West; in this vision, therefore, we as Westerners in philosophic crisis must rediscover and rehabilitate the tools already in front of us. The West is not done with Christianity, and Christianity is not done with the West. If rationalism and empiricism, and their fruit, technology, build up the I, or the Ego, or the Self, Christianity helps to tear it down; reconciliation of our consciousness to divine consciousness, Man to God, requires an emptying of self, a recognition of our limitations, our dependencies — it requires an education in the highest kind of humility. The West is in dire need of it right now — and so am I, which is why I wish to submerge myself into Christianity. I wish to learn more fully how to empty myself into God.

Of course, in a very important sense, Christianity stands or falls on the incarnation and resurrection. When I contemplate the incarnation, I can believe that the Monad manifested in the person of Jesus — with the important qualifier that through Jesus, God has called us all to become 'sons of God'. The mystery of the resurrection eludes me, but I have arrived at a place at which the faith makes enough sense to me as a whole that I imagine my understanding is lacking rather than the faith, and so I choose to be open to the Mystery; I choose to embrace the teaching handed down across the ages in the faith that more will be illuminated to me in time. The incarnation and crucifixion are vital patterns guiding our lives in God, regardless. All new orders, whether in a polity or an individual, require a destructive or deconstructive phase, only after which the renewal or redemption can take place. When we have awakened to the reality of God, we must put our personalities through a crucifixion-in-miniature, to empty ourselves of attachments to worldly things and sublimate them into the love of God, which renews, redeems, and makes beautiful again all that was first given up. Only then can one be 'born again' as a 'child of the kingdom.' Christianity echoes both Heraclitus and Nietzsche here, the former of whom declared that 'the kingdom is a child's; eternity is a child at play,' and the latter of whom said that maturity consists in once again discovering the mentality of a child at play.

This vision of Christianity must strike many as radical. This is as it should be, for God is at all times and places mysterious and elusive. Any authentic openness to the Mystery must therefore require a giving over of oneself, a transformation of perspective. Christianity must not be permitted to be a blank check to engage in an endless cycle of sinning and repenting; neither is it a fossilized list of rules to obey in order to score points with God. Religion must be about reconciling man to the divine; life requires an answer to the religious questions. Although I have at times fled into the arms of the Eastern traditions, I ultimately had to conclude that the West already has a spiritual order: Christianity — and it is perfectly capable of serving as the vehicle of spiritual renewal for the West in 2018 — and for me as an individual.

How Ought We to Live?:

Philosophy and Its Challengers In Book I of Plato's *Republic*

Mr. Alexander Knepper

02/27/2015

Submitted in Partial Fulfillment of the Requirements for the Master of Arts Degree

"...The discussion is not about some random thing, but about the way one ought to live."

•— Socrates, 352D

•

The first thing to notice about the *Republic* is that Socrates is the only speaker in the dialogue. We are asked as readers not only to imagine a conversation as it unfolds, but also to remember that it is one man's account of it. We are in turn prompted to ponder what could have spurred Socrates to recount such a lengthy story, as well as to whom he would want to recount it at all. It is no small undertaking to deliver someone such a long and detailed account, and one must imagine that Socrates would not tell it casually.

But we are not listening to Socrates' account: we are reading it. The *Republic* is presented to us as a transcript of Socrates' spoken recollection of a conversation between him and several other people. The careful reader is therefore asked to imagine this conversation through at least three layers of communication: Plato's writing, Socrates' verbal storytelling, and Socrates' words emerging spontaneously in the original conversation — four layers, if the reader is considering another speaker's words, or even five, if the many assumptions brought to the table by the reader are also considered. Much of the original context in which the conversation took place is obscured; perhaps much is inevitably lost. Reading a book is profoundly different from listening to a conversation. Speech lacks the permanence of writing, but it progresses according to the wishes of the speaker for as long as he is speaking. Reading, on the other hand, does not necessarily progress according to the wishes of the author. The reader may easily skim, creating the danger that parts of the whole might be considered out of context. Writing, however, is planned and refined, while speech in a conversation is spontaneous and freewheeling — although a verbal storyteller combines elements of both writing and conversational speech. Writing beautifully is therefore a different sort of undertaking than speaking beautifully ·although a careful writer, addressing careful readers, may be able to close the gap between speech and writing.

No one can accurately recall all of the details of an all-night conversation about frivolous concerns, let alone about weighty ones like justice. The *Republic*, considered as a whole, is therefore an image, a sort of philosophical poetry: no real-life discussion actually occurs in the manner in which Socrates recounts his tale. We see throughout the course of the dialogue, too, that Socrates is as masterful a storyteller as the poets he banishes from the just city. His intent in telling stories can be discerned from the context in which he tells them. The Allegory of the Cave and the Myth of Er, the two most powerful images of the dialogue, are both addressed to Glaucon — although not only to Glaucon. These stories, while of particular interest to Glaucon, are told freely in the presence of the rest of the group that has been assembled at Polemarchus' house, including men like Cleitophon and Lysias, who remain silent or all-but-silent during the course of the conversation. All of them hear every word Glaucon hears. It is likely that they do not derive the same lessons from these myths as a young man like him, in whom there is a powerful inclination toward philosophy as a way of life, but they can only benefit from considering the meaning and purpose of such stories. Perhaps the *Republic*, as a written work, could be said to operate in much the same manner. Its intended primary audience seems to be young men (and women) like Glaucon, but its words are available for anyone to examine, and almost anyone who considers them in even a cursory manner will benefit.

Young men like Glaucon, brimming with potential, could resolve to channel their talents into a number of different ways of life. The *Republic* presents a compelling vision of philosophy as the truly just way of life, while undermining the claims made by representatives of other, non-philosophic ways of life. Book I is a microcosm of the whole, sketching a series of character portraits of various political men — including the philosopher himself, who necessarily relies on the presence of some degree of justice in the regime under which he lives for his way of life to remain possible. The philosopher, as a political man, has no choice but to attend to the city and contend with those whose way of life is in tension or conflict with philosophy and its aims: "the wages of the best men," after all, are to avoid being ruled by someone less worthy (347 B-C).

Yet, while Cephalus, Polemarchus, and Thrasymachus are not philosophers, none of them are bad or stupid people, nor are their arguments simply *wrong*. Indeed, there is much that is admirable about what each of them represents. To use the language of the metaphor of the tripartite soul: each of them, like Socrates, has fostered a distinctive and recognizable balance of appetite, spiritedness, and reason — and each man's opinion about justice is a reflection of the state of his soul. If Socrates is to justify philosophy as the best way of life, for both the man and the city, he must first contend with the most compelling alternatives on their own terms.

Socrates' story begins with a descent to the Piraeus with Glaucon. The two of them have gone there to pray to the goddess Bendis (354A), and "at the same time also" to witness the manner in which the festival, conducted jointly on her behalf by local residents and the Thracians, will take place. Socrates' careful language, coupled with the fact that he and Glaucon attempt to return to the city before the procession at nightfall, suggests that their primary intention was to pray; that witnessing the festival was a secondary concern motivated by a love of novelty. Socrates explicitly states that he is interested in the festival "since they were now conducting it for the first time." But he and Glaucon are not so interested that they care to stay to witness the evening's events. As the two of them start walking back up to the city, Socrates is stopped by Polemarchus' slave and ordered to wait. Glaucon (not Socrates) says that they will wait. Socrates recounts this incident thus: "Spotting us from a distance then as we headed home, Polemarchus, Cephalus' son, ordered his slave to run and order us to wait for him. And grabbing me from behind by my cloak, the slave said 'Polemarchus orders you to wait.'" Already, the significance of the narrative structure of the book is evident. As these events were actually taking place, Socrates first would have felt the tug on his cloak, and only then would have known that Polemarchus had spotted them from a distance – but while telling the story, Socrates is able to weave in and out of involved first-person commentary and detached third-person narration. This dynamic would not be possible if Plato chose to narrate the story himself, or if the story were not being told in hindsight.

"A little later," Polemarchus arrives alongside some others, including Adeimantus, Glaucon's brother. Polemarchus playfully but sternly asserts dominance over Socrates by pointing out that they outnumber him, and that he needs to "get stronger than they are" or else assent to their demand to stay where he is. Socrates wonders whether he might be able to persuade him to let them go, but Polemarchus says bluntly he will not listen. Adeimantus addresses Socrates on his own terms and tries to persuade him. Could it be that he does not know about the horseback torch race to take place tonight? Socrates is intrigued by this; perhaps he was not aware this event was to take place (in which case we are given more evidence that he came to the Piraeus primarily to pray, which none of the other men present were doing). He asks Adeimantus to confirm his understanding of how the race will be conducted, but Polemarchus interrupts before he can reply. Polemarchus informs Socrates that his understanding is right, and adds that, afterward, there will also be an all-night party, during which they will "rouse themselves up" and talk with some other young men. Socrates and Glaucon decide that they ought to stay, and all the men present make their way to Polemarchus' house, where several other young men are already gathered.

Here, we have seen the founding of a sort of city-in-miniature. Without the protections afforded by the city, strength always overpowers persuasion; force overpowers reason. Only compulsion can forge a political consensus in the face of irreconcilable differences. Polemarchus, the ringleader in cornering Socrates, is somewhat presumptuous and has a high opinion of his capabilities; perhaps he resembles most politicians in this way. He interrupts people. He speaks down to them. Yet, something about Socrates intrigues him, and he cannot resist compelling him to spend time with him. Polemarchus, the founder of this city-in-miniature, we see, is the catalyst for the conversation that is to unfold.

As the men enter Polemarchus' house, his father Cephalus greets

Socrates right away. Immediately Socrates notices two things about Cephalus: he is very visibly aged, and his piety is displayed outwardly and perhaps ostentatiously. This display of piety is strikingly different from the private prayers offered by Socrates at the Piraeus.

Socrates has not seen Cephalus for quite some time, so he is struck by just how old he looks. As he begins to speak, he reveals that this first impression is telling; he is in fact preoccupied by his age and cannot help but refer to it, right away and repeatedly. He insists to Socrates that he ought to come visit him more often: for, although in old age he has come to love good conversation, he is now old and weak and cannot make the journey to the city. The fact that Cephalus asks Socrates to visit him more often, and that he implores him to make room for him in between his time with the youngsters ·like his son, tells us that they are old friends.

Socrates recognizes that Cephalus is fixated on his old age and politely states that he enjoys "talking with those who are very old very much," since he too, after all, will be very old one day. Socrates then asks Cephalus, in so many words, what old age is like, "especially" since he does not have much longer to live — a somewhat peculiar way to greet an old friend: "And from you especially I would be glad to learn how this looks to you, since you are just now at that point in life which the poets say is 'on the doorstep out of old age,' whether it is a hard part of life or how you report it.'" This question, although phrased in a somewhat blunt manner, demonstrates a trust between the two, and grants Cephalus an opening to talk about that which is preoccupying him while also giving Socrates the opportunity to learn about one of the things philosophy cannot teach him. The conversation is repicropal and friendly.

Cephalus reports that when he gathers with friends of the same age, they indeed often find much to complain about. Many bemoan especially the fact that their bodies can no longer handle the erotic pleasures of their youth: drinking binges, sexual indulgences, feasts, and other excesses. He believes they are misguided to complain, though, and explains his disagreement by way of an entertaining anecdote: once, when he was near the renowned poet Sophocles, he heard a man ask him whether he could "still be with a woman" — to which Sophocles replied that, in fact, he was glad to be free of the "insane masters" of his youth, like sexual desire. Cephalus concurs, and says that old age can be very tolerable indeed — as long as one has a well-ordered disposition.

Socrates sees much that is admirable in Cephalus' answer, and "nudges him on" to reflect further by, essentially, reminding him that his wealth makes much of the order in his life possible — although Socrates politely chooses to put his reminder in the mouths of "most people." Cephalus concedes that this point has some merit — but not as much as some would like to imagine. He suggests instead that old men with poorly-ordered souls would be miserable whether they are rich or poor. Implied is that, therefore, his being at peace must be due largely to his good character.

Socrates, wondering how someone more concerned with his soul than with money could have come to be so wealthy, then asks Cephalus whether most of his money came from what he earned, or whether it came from his inheritance. Cephalus replies that the amount of money he has now is roughly the amount his grandfather inherited. His grandfather turned it into a real fortune, but his father squandered it, making it "even less" than it is now. He does not aim to pass on a fortune to his children, but just wants them to be a bit better off than he was.

This is not a direct answer to Socrates' question, but Cephalus has revealed that he pursued moneymaking out of a sense of duty rather than out of a love of the art. Perhaps it is not surprising, then, that when Socrates asks him what the greatest benefit of his wealth has been, he answers that it is the ability to easily repay his debts. Cephalus does not delight in his money for the material goods or status it allows him to possess, but because it allows him to easily fulfill his obligations. This, he hopes, will please the gods, should they exist; he cannot help but wonder whether "the stories that are told" about the afterlife are true, and "wakes up often from sleep in terror, the way children do" when he imagines that unjust men might really be punished there. Nonetheless, he asserts that, for a man who lives justly — a man such as he, who lives his life in a "holy way" and fulfills his obligations — "good hope is always present to nourish," and invokes the poet Pindar as an authority. Cephalus concludes that his money is of good use to him because he is not a liar or a thief, and that in the hands of such a person, it would be useless.

Much has come to light about Cephalus. From his stories, we know that he was a pleasure-seeker in his youth · and also that he lived an active and varied enough life to be the sort of old man who is full of interesting anecdotes. Few men have brushed shoulders with poets such as Sophocles. As a moneymaker, Cephalus describes himself as a "mean" between his father and grandfather; perhaps one could say that the way he has lived his life is an attempt to split the difference between his grandfather's discipline and his father's indulgence. Now in old age, his appetites have burnt out, and, having been unable to control them in his younger years, he has learned to revile them, throwing in his lot with Sophocles by bidding them good riddance. Now that material conditions have at last freed him from temptation, he can finally do what "decent," "holy," and "just" men — that is: all men who are not liars or thieves — do: fulfill without hindrance their obligations to man and the gods. Yet, despite his insistence that he has a well-ordered soul, he is utterly restless, anxious about the fate of his soul after death.

Socrates, too, is concerned with the fate of the soul after death, and he too believes that the just man, with a well-ordered soul, will be happier and sleep more soundly than an unjust man with a disordered soul. In many ways, Cephalus' notions of justice align with those that will emerge as Socrates' own, later in the *Republic*. But while he acknowledges that Cephalus' words are "beautiful," it is not difficult for him to conceive of a scenario in which this legalistic definition of justice does not apply. If justice is simply "truth and giving back anything one takes" — that is: not being a liar and not being a thief — then are we therefore obligated to return a borrowed weapon to a friend who happens to not be of sound mind at the moment? And are we moreover obligated to tell him the truth about the situation? Cephalus concedes the point, and Socrates declares that his definition of justice cannot be right. Cephalus seems somewhat indifferent to this conclusion; he does not seem to think it implies anything important. Perhaps on a certain level it does not: exceptional cases such as this are unlikely to occur in daily life — and as even Socrates acknowledges, the general principle at hand is still beautiful. To a man like Cephalus, Socrates' objection must seem downright pedantic. Moreover, as his friend, Socrates must surely know that Cephalus is not really interested in this sort of philosophical questioning in the first place.

In many ways, Cephalus is a highly respectable everyman. His is a common-sense definition of justice, derived from everyday experiences; it is legalistic, reciprocal, and simple. But it is also simplistic, and cannot account for exceptional situations. Cephalus' definition of justice forgets the conditions that make it possible to practice — much like Cephalus the man prefers to forget about the fact that money makes living well in old age easier. Most men are like Cephalus, led here and there by the 'mad masters' of the appetites, unable to impose moral order from within. Most men therefore are in need of a set of external rules to obey — whether they are formal, such as the legal requirement to pay back money owed to another person, or informal, such as the social pressure to restore his family's financial status. It only truly occurs to a man like Cephalus to reflect on the whole of his life in old age, but, although he superficially believes that it is necessary to pursue justice, he has always chosen to let others do his thinking about the topic for him, and so in old age falls back upon custom. His instincts are admirable, but he did not receive the sort of education that could have drawn out his potential. He is an old friend of Socrates' and really does want to talk with him · but not about justice; he would rather tell entertaining anecdotes about his life and let Pindar and Sophocles tell him what to think about the gods and the human condition. Cephalus is a lively and gregarious entertainer and a good-hearted man, but he has no drive in him for philosophic reflection.

Yet, Cephalus' notion of justice, while conceptually unsophisticated, is not so different than Socrates'. It is not difficult to outwit a man like Cephalus in an abstract discussion about justice, but society depends on men like him: law-abiding, pious, and fundamentally decent. Men like Socrates, in fact, who are not skilled in any conventional craft, especially depend on men like Cephalus. And what good, after all, would it do a man like him to begin to philosophize at the 'doorstep of death'? All of the vexing and rigorous questions that have entranced Socrates since youth would only cause an old man like Cephalus needless pain. If the purpose of philosophy is to enable human flourishing — to enable us to live justly — then perhaps he is right to leave the conversation. Cephalus has spent his life doing what was required of him by his family, his city, and his gods, and he has done it gracefully and cheerfully. What more can be asked of most men? Not everyone, after all, can be a Socrates.

Socrates knows that not everyone can be like him, however, and he also knows that radical questioning cannot take place in the presence of a respected — and respectable — elder figure. Cephalus respects what

Socrates does with the youngsters and chooses to leave the conversation. For his own sake, though, he intuitively senses the dangers of philosophy, and does not care to take part in it. The philosopher is one who does not necessarily trust the law, tradition, or common sense regarding what is right and wrong. He is someone who makes everything questionable. When Socrates declares that Cephalus' definition of justice cannot be right, Polemarchus interrupts again, claiming that it certainly is — at least, that is, if the poet Simonides is to be believed. Cephalus reaffirms his belief in his definition and at this point excuses himself from the conversation to attend to his sacrifice.

Upon Cephalus' exit, Socrates assumes a more prominent role in the conversation. He immediately asks Polemarchus what he thinks is right about Simonides' notion of justice, and Polemarchus echoes but subtly revises the language of his father, claiming that justice is "to give what's owed to each person." The one-size-fits-all language favored by Cephalus has been replaced with a definition that varies by individual. Polemarchus is an "heir to a share ·of what belongs to his father — but only a share: he elects not to defend the notion that justice entails truth-telling.

It is far from obvious that this new definition does away with the problem that undermined Cephalus', however, and when Socrates points this out, Polemarchus quickly revises his definition to state that friends owe it to friends to do good to each other — and that, conversely, enemies owe it to enemies to be bad to each other. Since returning a weapon to a friend who is not of sound mind would be harmful to him, it cannot be an obligation, and therefore it cannot be just. Treating justice as a relative concern rather than an absolute one is Polemarchus' way out of the trap that ensnares his father's definition. But perhaps one should return a borrowed weapon to someone of unsound mind who has become an enemy — for, Polemarchus says, "what's owed from an enemy to an enemy is the very thing that's fitting: something bad."

Socrates ignores Polemarchus' discarding of the truth, but notices that the language of obligation has been subtly revised to the language of fitness, and suggests that "Simonides was being cryptic" for using the former when he meant to imply the latter. Socrates here is gently nudging Polemarchus to reflect more deeply without taking a sledgehammer to the notions he holds right now — which, though somewhat crude, and in need of qualifications, still demonstrate that he has given the question of justice a bit more consideration than has his father. Approaching the question of justice through a shared reference in Simonides allows Socrates and Polemarchus to speak a common language. For the sake of discussion, Simonides' opinions are presumed to be true, so the movement of the conversation is toward the gradual clarifying of what the truth about justice is: if a notion is found to be lacking, Simonides is simply said not to really hold it. Whether the beliefs being discussed are truly held by Simonides or not is ultimately irrelevant, since they *are* what seem to Polemarchus to be true.

Polemarchus does not see why Socrates perceives such an important distinction between obligation and fitness. Socrates tries to clarify Polemarchus' intent by means of two images, and asks him what Simonides would say if someone were to ask him what is 'owed and fitting' to the medical and culinary arts. Polemarchus replies, respectively, that drugs to bodies and seasonings to delicacies are fitting. But what is the analogous answer concerning justice? "If it needs to follow along with the things said before, Socrates," says Polemarchus, then justice is "giving benefits and damage to friends and enemies."

What has been brought to light here is that to speak of justice in terms of 'fitness' is to speak of it as an art, or skill: the just man, in this perspective, is a man of action, and his work therefore must be informed by a specialized sort of understanding, much like a doctor understands sickness and health, or a helmsman understands how to steer a ship at sea. But at what sort of skill does the just man excel? Polemarchus contends that the just man has the most power to benefit friends and harm enemies when at war and taking sides in a battle. The young man who earlier revealed himself to prefer compulsion to persuasion unsurprisingly offers an opinion fit for a warrior. He has also adopted, perhaps unknowingly, a definition that is peculiar to each man. Friendship and animosity is relative to each person · and to each city. But the just man, by this definition, seems necessary only in the presence of conflict, or competition. If doctors and helmsmen are useless when men are not sick or at sea, then the just man must be useless when men are not at war. This strikes Polemarchus as incorrect, and he revises his definition again to assert that justice is, in fact, also useful in peacetime: for securing contracts, or partnerships. But all partnerships aim at some goal, whether it is winning a game of checkers or building a house, and in any of these cases, the man most skilled at the particular art corresponding to the goal toward which which the partnership aims — in these examples, a checker-player or a housebuilder — would seem to be more useful than a just man in fulfilling that goal. Perhaps this argument is not entirely fair: politicians, for instance, could be said to secure the possibility of all of these pursuits, and governing cities is a necessary and noble art. But Polemarchus is not thinking in these terms; he is simply throwing out definitions to see if anything will stick. So he revises his definition again, this time claiming that the just man is needed to guard money. This does not do away with the broader problem Socrates has introduced, however: if this is the case, then justice in peacetime is only required when money is useless. If the money were to ever be put to use — say, for buying a horse — then some other kind of artisan — in this case, a horse-breeder — will surely be more useful than the just man.

Socrates then shifts the terms of the conversation and raises a curious question about the nature of artisanship: is it not so that those who are most adept at a skill are also most adept at its inverse? That is: the man who is most skilled at guarding against disease is surely also the most skilled at causing it, and the most skilled fighter will also be the most skilled in the art of self-defense. Mastery of an art can be used for good or ill, for private or public purposes, in any combination. So if the just man's skills are only required for guardianship, it is likely that he, as the most skilled guardian of money, is surely also its most skilled thief. Polemarchus is unconcerned with the fact that Socrates has altered the line of inquiry and is now following his lead. He assents to this line of reasoning, prompting Socrates to lightly scold him, attributing his sentiments to lessons he derived from Homer, who praised Odysseus' maternal grandfather for excelling at stealing and swearing false oaths. Socrates concludes that Simonides' just man has emerged as a sort of thief — albeit one who helps his friends and harms his enemies. (Are politicians 'sorts of thieves'?) Polemarchus insists that this is not what he meant ·but he has run out of ammunition, and finally concedes that he really does not know what he meant in the first place. Yet, like Cephalus at the end of his own exchange with Socrates, Polemarchus still clings to his original definition of justice — that it entails benefiting one's friends and harming one's enemies.

Socrates then breaks his original line of inquiry again, leaving aside the question of whether the most just man also is capable of the worst injustice. He now asks a question he could have asked Polemarchus in the first place: What do we mean by 'friends' and 'enemies'? Polemarchus declares that men love those they regard as trustworthy and hate those they regard as worthless. But any man who appoints himself fit to dole out help and harm to others must consider himself to be an exceptional judge of others' character. If justice revolves around our private judgments' of men's character, then the just man is tasked with a very heavy burden. Is it not the case that we often mistake friends for enemies, and vice versa? Polemarchus must admit that this is so — yet, this necessarily means that many men, in their attempts to be just, will inadvertently harm their friends. This conclusion spurs him to revise his definition yet again to state that it is just to benefit one's friends only if they both *appear to be and truly are* friends, and similarly for harming enemies — though it is still not clear what it is exactly that the just man *does* for these friends and to these enemies, or how we will know if they truly are as they appear.

Socrates then wonders whether the just man is really in the business of inflicting harm upon others at all. We observe that when horses or dogs are harmed, their behavior does not improve, but becomes worse, he points out, and suggests that humans are no different with respect to their own virtues, like justice. If justice is good, and the just man is good, then, as a musician cannot make men less musical by means of music, it cannot be the work of the just man to harm others, but rather the work of the unjust man. Polemarchus says that Socrates seems "to be speaking the truth absolutely."

"Then if someone claims it's just to give what's owed to each person," says Socrates, "and this carries the meaning for him that harm is owed from the just man to his enemies, but benefit to his friends, the one saying these things was not wise, since he wasn't telling the truth." Polemarchus agrees with this assessment, which revives the question of truth and links it to wisdom. Echoing various parts of the conversation, Polemarchus agrees with Socrates to "go into battle...in partnership, if anyone claims Simonides...or any of the other blessed and wise men has said that." Socrates here refers to Simonides as wise and not wise in the same breath, but Polemarchus does not notice.

Finally, Socrates asks Polemarchus if he knows whose way of speaking it seems to him to be "to claim that it's a just thing to benefit friends and harm enemies." "Whose?" asks Polemarchus, who has revised his definition so many times that he has forgotten that this was the very definition he attributed to Simonides and sought to defend. Socrates wryly remarks that it must be "the statement of Periander or Perdiccas or Xerxes or Ismenias the Theban, or some other rich man who imagines he has great power — the power to compel a philosopher to come to his house, perhaps.

Polemarchus views life as a competition: for him, justice is about loyalty and disloyalty, and actions helping and harming others are to be taken on this basis. This necessarily means justice is relative to each man, and that each of us is required to divide the rest of humanity into friends and enemies. The spirited man is a force of nature, seeking the thrill of victory. In politics, men like Polemarchus devote themselves to ascending through the ranks of power — necessarily at someone else's expense, since only one man at a time can be king. Friendships are less like companionships and more like alliances, or, as we have heard, partnerships. Trustworthiness, not truthfulness, is the hallmark of a good friend. So far, a casual observer, like Charmantides or Euthydemus, could be forgiven for wondering what all of the fuss is about this Socrates fellow. His questioning does not lead Polemarchus any closer to a coherent definition of justice than he was when he entered the conversation, and at times, his objections must seem frivolous. What, precisely, is Socrates implying when he points out that men make mistakes about their friends and enemies? That we should not distinguish between the two and treat them differently? To a competitive man — and to the city, which is exclusive and therefore competitive — this would be paralyzing. It would not only make lasting partnerships impossible, but, if taken seriously, would paralyze the city's ability to wage war and conduct politics. But perhaps political and military action by its nature is partially, or even largely unjust. Perhaps for a man like Polemarchus, the man most skilled in performing just deeds must indeed be the most skilled in performing unjust deeds. Perhaps this is even necessary for all of us to live together.

Polemarchus, however, does not treat his own arguments with the seriousness they merit. His raw spiritedness drives him to treat the conversation like just another competition; he tries to overpower Socrates just like he did after the parade. He shoots first and asks questions later, and seems to be making up his definition of justice as he goes along. Although he is more clever than Cephalus, and is able to revise his definition of justice more than five times before he runs out of ideas, he comes no closer than his father to articulating a definition that stands up to Socrates' relentless questioning, despite raising important questions. If justice is an art that revolves around private judgments, and the most just man is also capable of the gravest injustices, then he will have to make many profoundly consequential decisions when he applies his skills, especially if he attains political power.

Socrates is not necessarily privately committed to the notion that justice is an art, but he wants to explore the consequences of that belief — including the consequences of living a way of life that conforms to it. Polemarchus recognizes that taking justice seriously involves more than one-size-fits-all rule-following, but his perspective has introduced an array of new problems. Socrates ultimately makes it questionable whether the truly just man is even a man of action at all: a man who adheres to this view of justice will inevitably commit unjust acts. Socrates convinces Polemarchus to acknowledge this in the abstract, yet he cannot recognize that this insight has serious implications for his way of life.

At this point, Thrasymachus, who had been anxiously awaiting an opportunity to thrust himself into the conversation, springs forward "like a wild animal" and launches an acidic stream of invective toward Socrates. According to Thrasymachus, Socrates is nothing but a posturer, a kowtowing idiot who gratifies his love of honor by burdening other people with the task of rigorously demonstrating the truth of their opinions, while never offering any coherent beliefs of his own. Thrasymachus insists that Socrates put forward his own definition of justice: one that is "clear and precise," without any airy notions of "the needful or the beneficial or the profitable or the gainful or the advantageous."

Thrasymachus already is engaging in quite a theatrical display, and Socrates the storyteller is quick to spice up the narrative, playfully informing his audience that he was "quaking in fear" at Thrasymachus' bluster, "trembling" as he replied. It is unlikely that a man who faced combat in the Peloponnesian War would quake in fear at the sight a ranting professional teacher — but Socrates, as a poet, wants to put on a good show, too. Instead of putting forward a definition of justice, however, Socrates replies to Thrasymachus' attacks on his character. He insists on his earnestness in pursuing the truth, and playfully remarks that ignorant men such as himself ought to be pitied by wise men like Thrasymachus, anyway. Thrasymachus reacts to Socrates' light teasing loudly and with scorn, congratulating himself for informing the other men in advance about this sort of "routine irony."

Socrates then, in so many words, suggests that Thrasymachus is playing a little game: he has prohibited a variety of possible definitions in advance, but since we have not yet determined what justice is, he might be unknowingly prohibiting an accurate definition— as if we were barred from proclaiming that twelve is two times six. Thrasymachus dismisses the idea that the situation is like that, but Socrates insists that, either way, it will still *appear* that way to many people — and there is no good justification for preventing someone from suggesting such an answer and exploring its consequences. Justice, after all, is "more valuable than much gold," and we ought to have some skin in the game when discussing such matters. Cephalus and Polemarchus both have defended definitions of justice that seem to them to be not simply theoretically sound, but a basis for their respective ways of life. Our understanding of justice is not merely an abstract concern — like something we read about in textbooks — but one that informs a great many critical decisions in life. Ruling out certain possibitilies in advance presumes knowledge we do not yet have. Thrasymachus does not appear concerned with the implications of what he has done, however: he simply wants to know whether Socrates wants to use one of the banned definitions. Socrates again defers his answer, though, and says simply that he would not be surprised if one of them is correct.

Thrasymachus continues with his display and says that he has a definition of justice that is not any of the answers he prohibited — but before telling the group what it is, he revives the question of that which is 'owed and fitting'; particularly, he wants to know what penalty Socrates will suffer upon having his ignorance exposed.

Socrates matter-of-factly claims the suffering that is fitting for an ignorant man is simply to learn from one who knows. Thrasymachus feigns amusement, but states bluntly that what he really wants is a physical token representing his intellectual superiority: money. Socrates nonchalantly promises to pay him when he gets any, but Glaucon, ready for the conversation to move past Thrasymachus' theatrics, tells him that he and Socrates' other friends will pay on his behalf.

Socrates' linking learning and suffering might first be taken to be ironic, but the image of education presented in the *Republic* reflects a grueling, often tortuous process. Philosophic education demands that we radically and unsparingly examine and re-examine our most cherished beliefs — even, perhaps especially, those ones we have learned to love most, and which constitute the most fundamental principles that guide our daily lives. In the Allegory of the Cave, those who leave the shadows behind do not do so with joy; they are "dragged there by force." (516A) The man confronted with his ignorance "suffers pain" from being freed from his former captivity. (515D) Education requires us to recognize that we cannot necessarily trust tradition, the law, our parents, the poets, or even our own common sense to discern the truth about the most important questions. It is doubtful that anyone could recognize this without suffering.

Before offering his definition of justice, Thrasymachus cannot resist further insulting Socrates, and claims that, rather than showing gratitude by paying him, Socrates will instead "go on with his usual routine" and insist on "cross-examining" him. Socrates reiterates once again that he does not know and does not claim to know what justice is, and asks Thrasymachus politely not to be grudging if there is something he can teach him.

Glaucon and the others are now increasingly eager to hear Thrasymachus' definition. Socrates tells his audience (though not his partners in conversation), that Thrasymachus is clearly grandstanding: he believes he has a beautiful answer, and he wants to make a big show of it. And he simply cannot resist continuing to escalate his insults: "This is the wisdom of Socrates; he himself is not willing to teach, but he goes around learning from others and doesn't even pay them any gratitude." Socrates is irritated by the suggestion that he is ungrateful, and for the first time in the dialogue admits to directly insulting someone: he accuses Thrasymachus of lying. He will be nothing but appreciative if he is told the truth about justice, he insists.

At last, perhaps because he has finally provoked Socrates into insulting him, Thrasymachus offers his definition: "Then listen...I assert that what's just is nothing other than what's advantageous to the stronger." This is an incredible answer: it not only makes use of one of the very definitions he prohibited Socrates from using — that justice considers that which is advantageous — but it is neither clear nor precise. He has laid down one set of rules for Socrates and another for himself.

Socrates immediately recognizes this, and replies with a bit of biting humor — always anathema to cocky, vain men: since bull's meat is advantageous to Polydamas, the "no-holds-barred" wrestler, who is clearly stronger than anyone in the room, would it therefore be just for everyone else to eat it, too? Thrasymachus is so caught up in his act that he cannot recognize this as a joke. Exasperated, he accuses Socrates of twisting his argument. Socrates suggests, more than fairly, and surely while chuckling to himself, that Thrasymachus should simply be more clear about what he means — his own standard, after all.

Thrasymachus elaborates, positing that, while there is a diversity of regime types among cities, some are aristocratic, some are democratic, some are tyrannical, and so forth — all have laws that are arranged to benefit the rulers at the expense of the many. Ultimately, strength is the deciding factor in what variety of rule is established; 'might makes right.' At this point Socrates decides to mention to Thrasymachus that he has violated his own rule, and defined justice as that which is advantageous after explicitly prohibiting such an answer. Socrates, as it turns out, happens to agree that justice, whatever it is, must be something advantageous — the first clue we receive toward Socrates' own opinions, and perhaps a concession that justice may indeed be a sort of art — but he insists that whether the stronger are those for whom it is advantageous is still an open question.

Socrates then slyly takes advantage of Thrasymachus' status as both a professional teacher and a Chalcedonian, asking him whether it is not true that he claims that it is just to obey the rulers. As a professional teacher, he cannot expect to earn money or honor by legitimizing lawlessness — and as a foreigner, it would be especially inappropriate for him to advocate this view in this setting. He thus assents to Socrates' presentation of his beliefs — but also to the notion that rulers are fallible. If rulers are fallible, however, they must sometimes arrange laws that are disadvantageous to their rule — laws that we have already said are just to obey. By Thrasymachus' logic, it appears to sometimes be the advantage of the rulers for the people to behave in ways that undermine their rule.

The motion of this exchange parallels the conversation Socrates had with Polemarchus, who, perhaps recognizing this, feels compelled to interrupt. Polemarchus has stopped trying to overpower Socrates and now speaks up on his behalf: "By Zeus, yes, Socrates," he proclaims, annoying the hitherto-silent Cleitophon, who accuses Polemarchus of acting as a "witness" for Socrates. Cleitophon in turn acts as a sort of witness for Thrasymachus, insisting that what he truly meant was that the advantage of the stronger is that which the stronger *believes* is advantageous to himself. It is no great objection to point out that the rulers are fallible. Of course they are — but, as the strongest among men, they retain the power to institute laws according to their will.

Cleitophon's interjection suggests that Thrasymachus' presentation is compelling to at least one young man in the room. This is the first time since Cephalus left that anyone besides Polemarchus or Thrasymachus has spoken, and serves a pertinent reminder that this is not a private conversation, and that not all of the men present are necessarily sympathetic to Socrates. His argument is furthermore well-considered: whether or not a regime is consistently prudent, law-abiding citizens are still compelled to obey its commands. It is doubtful that any man seeking power would be persuaded to abandon his pursuit simply by having his fallibility pointed out to him — for ultimately, there is no higher appeal in the city than the rulers, and therefore no higher standard of justice.

This is the second time Thrasymachus' definition has been challenged and revised. Polemarchus rightly points out that he did not state his initial definition this way, but Socrates resolves to accept it this way if this is how it now appears to him. Thrasymachus, the man who stormed into the conversation demanding clarity and precision from Socrates, is insulted that Socrates now seemingly cannot perceive the intent behind his argument. Thrasymachus asks him incredulously whether he truly believed that he meant to posit the stronger man as the strongest while he is making mistakes. Socrates says that he did, in fact, believe this, but Thrasymachus bitterly calls him a liar. What is curious about this harsh exchange is that Cleitophon, moments earlier, asserted quite confidently that Thrasymachus indeed believed that the stronger man could make mistake — but Cleitophon, who rose in Thrasymachus' defense, does not find himself on the receiving end of accusations of lying. Thrasymachus, we see, is also in the business of helping his friends and harming his enemies.

Rather than making use of the common-sense argument suggested by Cleitophon, Thrasymachus elects to defend his theory by bringing the argument to a higher level of abstraction. He posits that, since it is resolved that we must speak precisely, we cannot consider an artisan a true practitioner of his craft at the time he is making a mistake. We must only truly consider a doctor a doctor insofar as he heals the sick, and not when he misdiagnoses a patient. Similarly, we must only truly consider a ruler a ruler insofar as he correctly institutes laws for the sake of his advantage and not when he makes mistakes about this. Thrasymachus reiterates his definition of the stronger man, but adds that he is referring to the one who is a ruler in 'precise speech'; that it is he whose rule is just and for whose advantage the weaker man must act. He then dares Socrates to misrepresent his argument with lies. Thrasymachus has his guard up, and thinks Socrates is trying to set up traps for his arguments. Socrates balks, and wonders how Thrasymachus could think he is "crazy enough to try to shave a lion" or "misrepresent [him] by lies."

Since justice is once again being considered as an art, Socrates presses forward by reviving images used in his exchange with Polemarchus. He and Thrasymachus agree that a doctor in the precise sense is a healer of the sick, and that a helmsman in the precise sense is a ruler of sailors. A helmsman is incidentally a sailor himself, we see, but his distinguishing quality as a helmsman is his status as a ruler — and it is in an art's distinguishing quality that we must discern its natural advantage.

Thrasymachus successfully avoids the objection that compromised Polemarchus' definition of justice. But in considering justice as a purely abstract question, we cease to treat it as a recognizably human concern. We somehow are able to speak of human things while forgetting human affairs. With this in mind, Socrates asks Thrasymachus whether it is not the case that each art seeks its advantage in attempting to be "as complete as possible." Sensing another trap, Thrasymachus asks what he means by this. Socrates points out that medicine exists because bodies are insufficient on their own to provide for their well-being; they need the medical art fully flourish. But the medical art must consider itself in much the same way; there are no abstract doctors in abstract worlds, and to fulfill its purpose, it too must turn to something outside of itself, namely: a body to treat — and it is the advantage of that body which a doctor must consider, rather than the advantage of 'medicine' itself, in the abstract. Thrasymachus concedes that this indeed appears to be the case. Socrates then suggests that artisans are 'rulers' over the art which they practice, and Thrasymachus agrees to this, too, grudgingly. But if this is the case, then a ruler, insofar as he is a ruler, rather than a moneymaker or an honor-seeker, will not consider his private interest, but the interest of the ruled.

Thrasymachus finds this argument naive and utterly contemptuous, and launches into a lengthy speech revealing the full implication of his thesis —which turns out to be not so much a theory of justice but a rejection of its possibility. 'Justice,' it turns out, is nothing but an empty word, a metaphor for simple-minded weaker men's private desire to constrain the stronger man in his pursuit of happiness. The advantage at which the ruling art aims is indeed that which its art considers. But rulers do not rule out of consideration for the good of the ruled, but for their own sake —just as a shepherd does not raise sheep for the good of the sheep, but for the good of the shepherd. Men who attempt to live a 'just' life are only digging their own graves, shutting themselves out of power, riches, and prestige, and needlessly antagonizing those close to them by refusing to perform deeds that will secure those benefits.

In fact, we see, it is not the just man, but the unjust man, who is happier, and the most unjust man — the tyrant — is surely the happiest of all. The tyrant performs acts of injustice on such a grand scale that weaker men are powerless to hold him down with their petty insults, abstract theories, and ancient traditions — and those weaker men thereby become nothing to him. The tyrant is liberated from all external restraints. "This is the way, Socrates, that injustice, when it comes on the scene with sufficient strength, is stronger, more free, and more overpowering than justice, and the way that what's just is exactly what I was saying from the beginning, what's advantageous to the stronger..."

Having 'sloshed a lot of speech into their ears,' Thrasymachus starts to walk away from the group. But Socrates is not prepared to let him go, and asks him pointedly whether he really thinks the question of justice — the question of the best way of life — is such a small matter that he, as a teacher, should stomp away like that. Socrates states plainly that he is not persuaded that the tyrant is a happy man.

Thrasymachus is incensed at Socrates' refusal to budge, and wonders how on Earth he can possibly persuade him at this point, short of spoon-feeding the argument to his soul. "By Zeus...not that ·not you," says Socrates, and asks Thrasymachus whether he is not playing fast-

and-loose with the concept of 'precise speech.' The goal of his shepherd in precise speech — one who fattens up his sheep to eat them — on further examination seems more like the goal of a banquet-goer in precise speech. And if the tyrant rules in order to acquire money, then he is surely considering his interests as a moneymaker in precise speech, rather than as a ruler. This is an easy mistake to make — but it is why, Socrates reminds Thrasymachus, they arrived at an agreement that the ruler considers the advantage of that which he rules. In fact Socrates the one playing somewhat fast-and-loose with the concept of 'precise speech,' given that he previously declared that rulers are concerned with the good of that over which they rule — and surely the wage-earner is not concerned with his own good and not the good of his money. But Socrates appears not to be so concerned with speaking properly in this convoluted language as he is with clarifying the stakes of the discussion.

Socrates then raises a curious question. He asks Thrasymachus whether he imagines that rulers of cities — rulers in the 'precise sense' — rule willingly, to which Thrasymachus answers that he does not simply imagine it, but that he knows it. Socrates rejects this answer outright and asserts confidently that "no one willingly desires to rule." There would be no incentive for an artisan to practice a skill from which he personally derives no benefit, and so he demands wages in return for practicing his art. This being considered, Socrates asks Thrasymachus whether the various arts each have a different sort of power — and then impugns his sincerity by demanding that he not "answer contrary to his opinion."

Thrasymachus agrees with this, and with the assertion that each of the arts benefits people in a different way: as stated before, the doctor is concerned with health; the helmsman, with safety at sea, and so forth. Each of them demands some kind of wage, but their wage-earning is incidental to their art, precisely considered. Otherwise, we would have to consider medicine and helmsmanship to be the same sort of art, insofar as they are both concerned with wage-earning. It is true that all artisans do aim at wage-earning, but the wage-earning art is not one that they apply in their capacity as artisans.

Having assented to this line of reasoning, Thrasymachus can no longer deny that the artisan will not derive any private benefit from applying his skills except insofar as he operates in a secondary capacity as a wage-earner — and that, if an artisan works for free, someone or something other than the artisan himself must benefit. Socrates reminds Thrasymachus that they have already been saying this "for so long," and that it is for this reason he claimed that the ruler, being an artisan, does not rule willingly, but, "as is fitting," demands some kind of wage: "either money, or honor, or a penalty if one does not rule."

This last contention intrigues and puzzles Glaucon, who declares that he does not understand what Socrates means when he refers to a "penalty" for refusing to rule. Socrates tells Glaucon that he "does not understand the wages of the best people," who crave neither money nor honor, and who would therefore make the most decent rulers. Since these people do not respond to traditional incentives and are not, like other kinds of rulers, trying to profit privately at the expense of the city, they would need to incur a penalty for refusing to rule. "And the greatest sort of penalty is to be ruled by someone less worthy, if one is not oneself willing to rule." These decent men rule, then, out of fear, and treat their rule as a necessity to be shouldered, rather than a prize to pursue willingly. "Because, if a city of good men were to come into being, they'd be liable to have a fight over not ruling just as people do now over ruling...". "Everyone with any discernment" — apparently not men like Thrasymachus — would "choose to be benefited by someone else rather than to have the trouble of benefiting someone else."

Socrates decides, however, to put this question to the side, and asks Glaucon whether Thrasymachus has convinced him that the unjust man lives a better, "more powerful" life. Glaucon affirms his belief that the just life is superior, and states that he is not persuaded by Thrasymachus' arguments. Socrates then wonders how it is that men are able to persuade each other of anything at all — and how they might persuade Thrasymachus to change his mind. He sees two ways of approaching the matter: he and Thrasymachus could engage in a debate by exchanging speeches, and let a jury decide who got the better of the argument ·or they could meet one another on mutual terms and be "jurors and advocates at the same time."

Through his deeds, Thrasymachus has made it known that his preference is for delivering speeches; in this style of argument, there must ultimately be a clear winner and a clear loser. But the latter method — dialectic, the so-called 'Socratic method' — appeals to a gentler side of reason, and assumes that, as reasoning beings, people really ought to agree with one another. Dialectic does not presume to know what the truth is, but it trusts that there is a discernible truth that *can* be uncovered, if we are willing to devote our passion and energy into the mission of uncovering it. Friends in truth-seeking therefore should meet on mutual terms, starting from where they agree and working outward to see where their premises are in tension, with the aim of resolving them and inching a little closer toward the truth.

Socrates and Glaucon resolve that the latter way is preferable, and Socrates asks Thrasymachus to reaffirm his belief that complete injustice is more profitable than complete justice. He does so, and elaborates by declaring that justice is "well-bred simple-mindedness" while injustice is simply "good judgment." Thrasymachus adds that he is not referring here primarily to the likes of petty thieves — although they too profit if they are able to remain undetected — but to the most truly unjust, the ideal of a happy human being: tyrants who conquer cities and bring men under their control. Injustice, in *this* sense, can be ranked in the same category that includes even wisdom and virtue.

Socrates is taken aback somewhat by Thrasymachus' candor, and tells him that he now seems to be speaking the truth as it truly appears to him, rather than posturing for his audience. Thrasymachus fails to see any significance in this: "What difference does it make to you..? Aren't you just cross-examining the argument?" "No difference," says Socrates — but of course there is a profound difference: Thrasymachus is no longer simply trying to score points in a debate, but is advocating a distinct way of life, and talking about human affairs as they really appear to him.

Socrates asks next whether the just man wants anything more than any other just man. Is there some benefit derived from justice that a particular just man desires, but that he demands other just men go without? This cannot be the case, Thrasymachus says, or else he would not be such a simpleton. Similarly, the just man would not try to "go beyond a just action." However, the just man still "considers it appropriate and even wants" to gain more than the unjust man, who in turn considers it appropriate to gain more than the just man. Socrates' wording is striking: 'considering something appropriate,' it seems, is not necessarily the same as actively 'wanting' it. We see that, according to Socrates, the just man believes he deserves something greater than the unjust man — but this is not necessarily synonymous with 'wanting' more than the unjust man. This echoes the discussion concerning the 'wages of the best men,' who do not crave money or honor, even though, as the best men, they are those most likely to make the best use of these things. The best men, it seems, are unlikely to be honored for minding to their business, even if, considered in some cosmic sense, they might deserve such honors. By pursuing justice, the best men demonstrate that, in a very real sense, they do not really 'want' the things acquired by so many unjust men —money, power, prestige — even if, when considered in the abstract, it would be more appropriate for them to have such things. The best men do not want to rule and even try to avoid ruling, even though what is most 'fitting' for them is, in fact, to rule.

When considered by himself and not in relation to the unjust man, the just man wants something whose acquisition does not involve denying it to someone else. If one man is king, another man cannot also be king. The quest for power is a zero-sum game. But the just man is concerned with something else — something that does not require him to embroil himself in pereptual conflict with other men of his kind. The unjust man's satisfaction depends upon his degree of control over external conditions, which he must try to command against the ambitions of countless men who would like to move beyond him in their own quests to maximize their pleasure. But the just man's life is not made worse by improving someone else's. The just man loses nothing when he shares his profits with others.

Thrasymachus affirms that his argument demands that the unjust man be called intelligent and good, and the just man neither of these. Socrates again revives imagery from his exchange with Polemarchus: there are men who are musical and men who are not, and men who are medical and men who are not, and surely we would call the former intelligent in those respects and the latter unintelligent. But, again speaking precisely, we see that musical and medical men do not try to go beyond others of their kind: the best harpist is not trying to compete with other harpists, but is trying to make the best use of his own instrument. Similarly, medicine is not a zero-sum undertaking that pits doctor against doctor. Doctors, insofar as they are doctors, are all working toward the same goal: healing the sick. We can reasonably conclude from this that a man who is knowledgeable in some way is not trying to "take or do or say more" than any other man like him. Thrasymachus admits that this seems to be a necessary conclusion.

Conversely, Socrates points out, people who lack knowledge *will* try to go beyond those who are like them and those who are not. Thrasymachus says that it "maybe" is possible that this is the case — but he agrees, too, that a knowledgeable man is wise and that a wise man is good. Therefore it seems that the just man — he who does not try to go beyond others like him — has come to light as knowledgeable and good, and the unjust man stupid and bad.

Thrasymachus is now sweating profusely, and, in a pivotal moment of the drama, he blushes. He is ashamed, and has good reason to be ashamed. His animalistic behavior throughout the conversation has reflected his brutal theory of justice: like his happy tyrant-in-precise-speech, Thrasymachus has attempted to control the conversation through domination and intimidation. Socrates first appeared to him to be a manipulative lawyer, "cross-examining" others' opinions to "gratify his love of honor." As a professional teacher, Thrasymachus could not pass up the opportunity to humiliate the vaunted Socrates in front of a number of ambitious and intelligent young men. But he has fundamentally misread Socrates, whose so-called 'cross-examinations' are never simply an attempt to achieve victory over an opponent, but rather are an effort to bring to light the knowledge we hide from ourselves. Thrasymachus, at last compelled to speak frankly about his opinions rather than making use of weasel arguments premised on 'precise speech,' reveals to himself and to his audience that, despite his grandstanding, his own opinions are actually in conflict with one another. Socrates the storyteller informs his audience that Thrasymachus did not reach this point eagerly, but had to be "dragged" here, foreshadowing the language of the Allegory of the Cave (516A), in which trapped prisoners do not seek the light of their own initiative, but are also "dragged" by someone or something "into the light of the sun," and feel "pain and anger from being dragged." As Socrates has already suggested, education can be a highly distressing experience. The punishment Socrates proposed for the ignorant (337D) has been dramatically inflicted on Thrasymachus.

Socrates is not done with Thrasymachus, though, and asks him whether it was not the case that he also claimed that injustice is strong. Rather than answering, he lashes out one last time in a fit of impotent frustration, demanding to make yet another speech, and warning that any additional questions will only be met with a patronizing response, such nodding or shaking his head, as if he were speaking to an old woman. But it is abundantly clear now that the lion has been tamed: the mighty Thrasymachus is reduced to whining at Socrates, even petulantly accusing him of not letting him speak — patent nonsense, given that Socrates just patiently sat through his long-winded speech about the glories of the life of the tyrant-in-precise-speech.

Socrates ignores Thrasymachus' complaining and returns to the question at hand: Now that we have resolved that injustice is stupidity, it seems that it cannot possibly be more powerful than justice. But Socrates wants to consider the question in another light: would an unjust city unjustly enslave other cities? Thrasymachus, standing by his opinion, affirms that this is the case, and moreover that the best city would enslave as many people as possible. This being so, is it not also the case that the most powerful city will have acquired its power unjustly?

Deliberately or not, Thrasymachus begins to imitate Socrates in speech, and answers by exploring possibilities rather than by jumping to a conclusion: "If, as you were saying just now, justice is wisdom, with justice. But if it's the way I was saying, with injustice." Socrates is delighted with this answer, and praises him for not merely nodding or shaking his head, but answering beautifully instead. Thrasymachus, still stinging from having the tables turned against him, insists that he is only doing so to "humor" Socrates.

Socrates ignores this petty remark and permits Thrasymachus to lick his wounds. He asks next whether any association pursuing a common goal will be able to achieve it if the members of that group behave unjustly toward one another. Thrasymachus agrees that people must be just toward one another to achieve their shared goals. Socrates suggests that injustice is what breeds factionalism, and that justice produces harmony. Thrasymachus tells Socrates he agrees with this too, but adds that he is only agreeing so that their opinions will not be at odds — a nod, perhaps unknowingly, to the beauty of this notion of justice. The two of them resolve that factionalism also undermines relations between two people and also the unity of mind in individuals — and that anything ridden by faction is an enemy to itself, to just men, and to the gods, who are also just.

As Thrasymachus had wanted to do to him, Socrates is humiliating Thrasymachus a bit here, showing the spectators that it is indeed possible to tame a lion — and Thrasymachus knows it. He feels that Socrates is twisting the knife in deeply simply to punish an enemy, and bitterly tells him that he may continue to "gorge himself" on the argument without opposition. But what looks like 'gorging' to Thrasymachus is also a further clarification of the stakes of the argument — and according to his own premises, no less. Socrates is not being hateful toward Thrasymachus: he suggests, in a thinly-veiled account of Thrasymachus' character, that while the just man has come to light as the wisest and best of men, a fully unjust man would be paralyzed to act at all. Thrasymachus was *not* paralyzed. It seems, then, that he was only a 'semi-vicious' man — one who turns out after all to be capable of philosophic discussion, under the right circumstances. Socrates, who would not dare try to "shave a lion," has instead tamed him and thereby made him "gentle." What is just in a man, we see, can oppose that which is unjust, so that what is good in him may rule — but not tyrannize — what is not.

However, the question of whether the just man is truly happier than the unjust man has not yet been considered with the degree of seriousness the question demands. And it certainly needs to be examined, for "the discussion is not about some random thing, but about the way one ought to live."

Now Socrates begins his discussion of 'work' by asking Thrasymachus whether there is a particular work that belongs to a horse. He says there is, and Socrates asks if whether he means by the 'work' of a thing that which "one could do only, or best, with it." For instance: only eyes can see, only ears can hear, and, although there are many tools with which we could cut a branch from a vine, there will be none better than a pruning knife designed specifically for that purpose. This, Socrates says, and Thrasymachus agrees, must be the 'work' of a thing.

For the work of each thing, there is also a corresponding virtue, as well as a vice which undermines it. Thrasymachus approves of this account and suggests that it is the work of the eyes to see, that the faculty of sight is its virtue, and that blindness is its vice — but Socrates refuses to affirm this directly, and states that for the moment he is simply concerned with whether virtue is that with which a thing performs its work well, and vice is that with which a thing performs its work badly. Thrasymachus says that, on this matter, Socrates is telling the truth.

The argument now comes full circle, returning to Cephalus' initial concern: the proper ordering of the soul. What is the 'work' of the soul? There is nothing but a soul, we see, that can attend to the business of "managing and ruling and deliberating and everything like that — including, and, according to Thrasymachus, "especially" life itself. Since there is work belonging distinctly to souls, there must also be a corresponding virtue ·and whatever it is, it cannot perform its work well if it is corrupted by vice. Since Thrasymachus was forced to concede that justice is virtue of the soul, we must therefore conclude that "the just soul and the just man will live well and the unjust badly." And since the man who lives well is happy, and happiness rather than misery is what is called profitable, we must also conclude that it can never be profitable to be unjust.

Thrasymachus has been soundly defeated in speech. "Let these things be your feast in the festivities for Bendis," he says.

But if Socrates has been feasting, then, by his own account, he has behaved like a "greedy eater," taking little bites of whatever appears before him before he has fully enjoyed the previous dish. Although Socrates could not resist rising to the defense of justice upon hearing it spoken of so poorly, he concedes that he does not even know what he was defending. Justice has somehow been vindicated in speech, yet we still do not have a coherent account of what it is. "And so it has come to pass that now I know nothing from the conversation, because when I don't know what the just thing is, I'm hardly going to know whether it happens to be a virtue or not, or whether someone who has it is happy or unhappy."

Thrasymachus is in many ways the most important and complex of Socrates' many interlocuters. Although he initially behaves in a way that Socrates deems "savage" (354B), his theory of justice turns out to be not only highly credible, but a seemingly inescapable conclusion of any empirical investigation of politics. Socrates' behavior in this respect is more revealing than even his most incisive questions, having consented to the will of the pushy Polemarchus after the festival. Whatever Socrates may claim in speech about justice, his deeds demonstrate a certain resignation toward strength as the foundation of all political associations. And whatever reason may desire — that politics be conducted according to persuasion rather than strength — politics, which is factional by nature, *must* ultimately proceed according to the will of the stronger.

Cleitophon instinctively recognizes this as the essence of Thrasymachus' theory, and makes the common-sense argument on his behalf that, while rulers are fallible, their will is ultimately the basis for the law, and therefore, in our daily lives, the foundation of justice. In this view, there is no 'justice' beyond the law, whose origin is in the desires of the rulers, and hence there is little sense in seeking any universal, abstract definition of the term. Justice is simply what *appears* to the stronger to be advantageous.

When Socrates offers to work with this definition, Thrasymachus dismisses it as a willful misrepresentation of his argument ·although he accuses only Socrates, and not Cleitophon, of lying. Instead of considering rulers as they are, he makes the peculiar decision to treat the argument as an abstract concern, insisting that a ruler in 'precise speech,' the ideal ruler, cannot err. 'Precise speech' is the basis by which every proceeding argument will stand or fall. Although this strategy exposes his theory to a host of vulnerabilities, not the least of which is that the argument is not applicable to anyone in particular, it serves the vital purpose of allowing him to avoid having to praise lawlessness. If justice is the advantage of the stronger — that is: the rulers — then it cannot be just to obey laws that are not to the actual advantage of the stronger. But even if the rulers are not really rulers at all at the time they are making mistakes, just citizens still must always obey one who *is* truly a ruler. And of course, all rulers claim to be legitimate — so this argument poses no serious threat to their interests. In an important way, Thrasymachus is simply praising his benefactor and advocating a view that supports his private interests as one who owes his livelihood to the city.

Socrates' own defense of justice, however, proceeds from Thrasymachus' premises, including the need to consider it in 'precise speech.' Yet, Thrasymachus himself serves as an example of the ineradicable tension between the 'precise' aims of artisanship and the context in which one's art is performed. Ultimately it makes little sense to totally detach the aims of the artisan from the aims of his art, just as it makes little sense to examine *any* of a person's behaviors in total isolation. If Thrasymachus had more self-awareness and admitted as much, rather than agreeing to Socrates' demand to consider wage-earning apart from artisanship, he could have easily denied that the ruler must consider the advantage of the ruled — as he attempts in vain to do by raising the example of the shepherd, who is clearly not concerned with the good of his sheep. Socrates is unable to rebut Thrasymachus directly, but Thrasymachus' insistence on employing such technical, abstract language has so obscured what is at stake that the discussion often plays out as a battle of wits rather than a serious attempt to bring to light the nature of justice.

Thrasymachus blushes only after he is compelled to lay something of consequence on the line and propose that injustice, and not justice, is conducive to human happiness, and can therefore be categorized alongside wisdom and virtue. The terms of the discussion have been brought back down to earth, and he must defend not just a theoretical definition, but a way of life. But he is already drowning in convoluted abstractions, and cannot provide an adequate account of the benefits of injustice without discarding most of what he has claimed up to that point. Backed into a corner by his own opinions, Thrasymachus is forced, for a moment, to stare into the face of his ignorance.

Yet, after this technical and often labryinthine exchange, we are no closer to a coherent definition of justice than at the outset of the conversation. Socrates has spoken beautifully of justice, and has compelled one of its critics to speak beautifully of it, too, but it is still not clear what is being spoken of so beautifully in the first place. Even false or deficient opinions can be made to appear beautiful, as we have already seen in the discussions with Cephalus (331C) and Polemarchus (331E), and so, when seeking truth, we must be wary of relying on the charms of beautiful speeches and images.

As the conversation with Thrasymachus concludes, Socrates reminds him that what is at stake when discussing the relationship between happiness and justice is not some random thing, but the question of the best way of life. It is from this concern that Socrates introduces the question of 'work,' or, the distinctive art that corresponds to each thing. Everything that exists — whether horses, knives, ears, or anything else — has at least one quality that distinguishes it from other things. Each human being has a soul, whose virtue is required to properly perform that work which is best suited to it. If the just man is to live well and be happy, he must discern what work is suited to him by nature, and what conditions are required for him to carry it out.

It seems most fitting to inquire, then, what it is that constitutes the work of the philosopher. Of course we cannot answer a question like this without first asking what is philosophy. But it is by no means clear by the end of Book I that the pursuit of a precise definition is likely to lead us to one. All definitions rest on our understanding of other words which themselves need to be defined ·and those definitions in turn rest on our understanding of *other* words, *ad infinitum*. When Thrasymachus defines justice as the advantage of the stronger, Socrates does not accept this definition but asks what it means to be the 'stronger'; he could also have easily asked what it means for something to be 'advantageous.' When Polemarchus defines justice as helping friends and harming enemies, Socrates wants to know what it means to be a 'friend' and what it means to be an 'enemy.' Perhaps, just as there is a gap between writing and speech, there is also one between language and thought. All of our definitions seem to threaten to collapse back into one another.

We can discover more about a man's way of life by considering his character as a whole than by simply listening to what he happens to say about it. Plato presents Socrates to the reader as a character portrait of a 'philosopher in the true sense.' Like the other men in the conversation, Socrates' thought, speech, and behavior all reflect his way of life, and must be considered as a whole. It is not only foolish but impossible to consider a man's opinions apart from his general character, and we cannot truly speak of philosophy apart from philosophers. None of the men in the conversation, Socrates included, is a mere stand-in for a theoretical argument; what we read are not speeches put into random people's mouths. With the character of Socrates in mind, a careful reading of Book I provides us with a powerful image of who the philosopher is and what constitutes his work.

We must be careful, however, not to ascribe this-or-that opinion to Socrates too hastily, or divorce his words or deeds from their full and necessary context. Book I concludes with Socrates' declaration that he still does not know what justice is, and that he has therefore learned nothing from the conversation with Thrasymachus (354C). He professes his ignorance both at the end of the conversation and at the beginning (337E). Therefore everything Socrates says about justice, and hence his way of life, especially to Thrasymachus, must be considered with heightened skepticism.

It is questionable whether Socrates really believes we can define justice at all. Perhaps it is the case that Socrates does not even mean to actually speak of justice to his interlocutors as this-thing or that-thing, but is being fully playful and ironic ·he is, after all, speaking beautifully of a word that, according to his own account, as yet has no content. If he is doing this, it is likely in the hopes that what is admirable in others might drive them to recognize the inadequacy of their own respective accounts of justice. Certainly Socrates cannot simply state outright to a man like Thrasymachus "the truth, that he has no sense in him and needed some, and that it's not obtainable unless one slaves over the acquisition of it..." (494D). This is not how men come to be persuaded. Socrates meets him on his own terms. Thrasymachus, in many ways a prototypical 'public intellectual,' turns out to be less skilled than Socrates at playing games with words —but there is also enough in him that is receptive to the pursuit of truth that, under these circumstances, Socrates is able to make him gentle where he once was savage, and therefore a friend in that pursuit (498D). Socrates more than once refuses to debate him. Ultimately he wants to leave men better than he found them, and this demands a certain method. Like the other men in the conversation, Socrates is convinced that his own way of life is best, and wants others to be more like him. He is a man who tries to see things as they really are. But he knows that before anyone can attempt to evaluate things as they really are, he must first come to terms with the utter inadequacy of his previous opinions.

Although the process of purging one's prior opinions is painful, the fruit of coming to grips with one's ignorance is the unique joy of living life in a constant state of wonder. Life appears to the philosopher as mysterious rather than meaningless, exciting rather than enervating. The world is full of novelties and curiosities, from beautiful processions for goddesses to thought-provoking conversations about justice with noble young men, and the philosopher is intrigued by all of them. The most powerful and fundamental erotic drive in him is the desire to know: he hates above all else the 'true lie' — the lie we know is a lie and yet continue to honor — and refuses to live by it. (382A) Hence he passionately desires to replace it with the truth. This drive is *erotic* because he craves the truth before he has even glanced at what it is — and therefore before he has any knowledge of whether it is even good for him. Our desire for truth seems to be driven by non-rational urges.

The knowledge the philosopher pursues is that kind which connects and makes sense of *all* human experience, in the trust that the pursuit of this knowledge constitutes the best way of life —or at least is its prerequisite. It is no "small matter to try to determine the course of a lifetime," after all (344E), and non-philosophic ways of life all seem to be premised on essentially arbitrary decisions, justified only after the fact. Although the non-philosophic man may live a decent and admirable life, he does not seek to examine *why* he believes or behaves as he does. Therefore he lives his life half-consciously, automatically. Socrates does not profess to be in possession of the truth, but he is constantly striving toward acquiring it.

The distinctive work of the philosopher, then, seems to be his relentless *seeking*. He knows that he does not know the truth, but something powerful in him believes in its possibility, and craves it. In the language of the tripartite soul, the philosopher's appetites, spiritedness, and reason are in harmony, in pursuit of a single goal: the quest for knowledge. He does not seek knowledge 'for its own sake,' but because it is what he needs most to live the good life. The philosopher communicates his findings first of all through his character, rather than simply giving beautiful speeches about his opinions. All men — Cephalus, Polemarchus, and Thrasymachus included — naturally desire what is good and pursue a way of life in accordance with what seems to them to be most aligned with it. ("If it seems good...that's what one ought to do" [328B].) But only philosophy can uncover whether our seeming is backed by truth —and hence only it can make sense of the competing urges of the soul and bring them into order.

Yet, our mission to understand the philosopher and his work is complicated by Socrates' ambiguous attitude toward the political role of truth. Socrates is not an ascetic monk holed up in his study, privately contemplating eternity — he is a citizen as well as a philosopher. Hence he is concerned not only with truth but with its political import. Socrates and Polemarchus agree that wisdom entails knowledge of the truth (335D) ·but Socrates has also told Cephalus bluntly that justice does not necessarily entail telling the truth (331D). The simple case of whether to return a borrowed weapon to a man who has gone mad demonstrates that there are truths that are worth possessing but not disclosing. In this case, it is advantageous to *know* that the man is mad, but not to *tell* him. What is questionable is therefore not *whether* we always ought to tell the whole truth —we clearly should not always do this —but *which* parts of the truth ought to be suppressed, and when, and why. The need to be prudent often trumps the need to be completely honest. In the case of the man who has gone mad, telling the truth would undermine the greater good: the physical safety of all involved. If the practical effect of communicating the truth is to harm human beings, it cannot be good to do so. The just man, after all, does not seem to be in the business of causing harm (335E).

It may be prudent for the philosopher to remain silent or speak ambiguously at times, since his goals are frequently in uncomfortable tension with the goals of the city. Money ‧or, more precisely, what money represents ‧fuels the lives of most men in a way it does not for the philosopher. Cephalus is motivated by love for his family and duty toward his city and gods ‧but ultimately he thinks the greatest gift he can give to his children is one that makes their lives even more luxurious than they already are: money. He cannot teach his children anything about what to do with that money beyond fulfilling their obligations, because that is all his experiences have taught him about the good life. When a man like Cephalus' duties are fulfilled and his work is over, he finds himself anxious and disturbed, and no longer knows how to make use of himself. His son Polemarchus seeks to overcome this limitation, and looks beyond his father's way of life, toward the pleasures that accompany honor and victory. But ultimately all victories are fleeting, and when a warlike man like Polemarchus must live in peaceful conditions, he finds that his skills are useful mostly for securing the fulfillment of others' obligations, including taking care of their money. He does not seem terribly concerned with what it is that men seek to gain and secure through their partnerships, or why they want to gain those things in the first place. Polemarchus' just man turns out to be one who creates and maintains the conditions necessary for men to live luxuriously. But this man also unwittingly paves the road for the arrival of the tyrant by rejecting his father's universally binding definition of justice — universal, at least, among citizens — and replacing it with a definition whose application is relative to each man and therefore is not subordinate to any higher standard. Polemarchus craves victory, but he has not given much thought to the consequences of its attainment. Thrasymachus is most transparent of all about his love for money, demanding it as a payment from Socrates in exchange for his teachings: as an 'intellectual,' he delights in what his cleverness can help him gain. Socrates, of course, cannot state outright that he does not value what most men value — but neither does he need to. He needs only to work to ensure that they are not working to deny the possibility of philosophy as a way of life. Socrates begins with the friendship of Cephalus and gradually earns the friendship of both Polemarchus and Thrasymachus. He does not need them to join him in his seeking — although any of them would be welcomed, should they choose to do this — but he *does* need them to tolerate it. The creation and maintenance of these conditions is the political work of the philosopher.

It is important to remember here that the philosopher must not behave like Cephalus does and allow himself to forget the role of money in his own life. The philosopher, like everyone else, needs shelter, clothing, food and drink, access to medicine, and so forth ·and these goods are not obtained by embarking on a quest for knowledge. For one man to attend to philosophy, there must be dozens of other men attending to shoemaking, farming, doctoring, etc. Similarly, the philosopher receives the same physical protection from the city as every other man ·and the moneymaker and the philosopher alike are targeted by foreign enemies during wartime. The philosopher cannot begin to philosophize if obstacles to its possibility are not subdued. Socrates, in the final analysis, needs men like Cephalus and Polemarchus, and he knows it.

This concern becomes most salient in Socrates' encounter with Thrasymachus, whose theory of justice turns out to be not simply divergent from the philosophic way of life but actively hostile toward it. The philosopher, for Thrasymachus, is a fool who leads men away from everything that could make them strong, free, and powerful. Philosophy is not just foolish but destructive of life. If the best life is the life of overpowering action — conquest, domination, and uninhibited indulgence — then the philosopher must look like the worst kind of man. We have already seen, in Socrates' initial encounter with Polemarchus after the festival, that the philosopher really is powerless to resist the will of the stronger through persuasion. But in front of philosophy's challengers, Socrates can disguise its vulnerabilities, at least in speech, by simply remaining silent about this question. To make Thrasymachus' argument for him would be to accept the conversation on his terms, and therefore to lend credence to these political considerations as fundamental to the best way of life. Instead of attempting to debate Thrasymachus, Socrates adroitly poses a series of questions to him designed to expose what sort of man adheres to such opinions: petty, slick, grandstanding. A teacher who claims to have discovered the right route to happiness but who behaves like an angry child is not one who makes his case very persuasively.

As it stands, Socrates himself has only begun to persuade his audience of his own case. Book II begins with Glaucon asking: Socrates, do you want to seem to have persuaded us or truly persuade us that in every way it's better to be just than unjust?(357B) Socrates has skillfully undermined the claims of various non-philosophic sources of justice — including the law, family and friends, popular sources of wisdom such as the poets, and the individual will. But the vision of justice he wants to take their place is strikingly radical, and maybe dangerous: the philosopher, in his relentless seeking, rejects the claims to truth made by *all* variants of authority — which, as Thrasymachus rightly points out, is an easy way to make a lot of enemies, very quickly, and perhaps needlessly. The philosopher, in coming to grips with his ignorance and resolving to seek knowledge, must leave behind virtually everything he thought he knew. It is little wonder that, in the Allegory of the Cave, the prisoners are dragged to the light, and initially feel angry, confused, and unable to consider anything in the way they once did (515D-516A). Over time, Socrates tells Glaucon, one who has ascended to the light adjusts to it and becomes happy there, pitying those who are still trapped in the shadows (516C). But this is a promise one must take on trust ˙we cannot know for ourselves whether this is really the case until we have glanced at the light for ourselves. We owe our livelihoods to the city, and the prospect of living a way of life that does not conform to its beliefs is unsettling. The city, in vital respects, is our home — but it is not our first home (516C), and the philosopher who strives to be a *whole* man and not simply a 'product of his time,' must look beyond the city if he is to live a life that is truly just.

After reading such an absorbing account, it is easy to forget that the conversation that transpires between Socrates and the others in the *Republic* takes the place of a torch race on horseback and the all-night party that was to follow. Polemarchus formed the city-in-miniature for the purpose of attending these events. But rather than attending the all-night party, these men took part in an all-night conversation about justice. From this fact alone, we have learned something about all of the characters of the dialogue, and, perhaps, about anyone willing to engage with the incomparable writings of Plato. At a time when they could have been witnessing a fantastic spectacle, or indulging in the finest pleasures, they chose instead to consider how they ought to live. And if everyone present considered that question with just a little more clarity, a little more insight, and a little more depth than they otherwise would have — then, perhaps, there was some element of justice there.